DREAMS
AS REVELATION

DREAMS
AS REVELATION

MARY JANE WOODGER
KENNETH L. ALFORD
CRAIG K. MANSCILL

SALT LAKE CITY, UTAH

All interior images © Brigham Young University, Division of Continuing Education. Used by permission.

© 2019 Mary Jane Woodger, Kenneth L. Alford, and Craig K. Manscill

All rights reserved. No part of this book may be reproduced in any form or by any means without permission in writing from the publisher, Deseret Book Company, at permissions@deseretbook.com or PO Box 30178, Salt Lake City, Utah 84130. This work is not an official publication of The Church of Jesus Christ of Latter-day Saints. The views expressed herein are the responsibility of the authors and do not necessarily represent the position of the Church or of Deseret Book Company.

DESERET BOOK is a registered trademark of Deseret Book Company.

Visit us at deseretbook.com

Library of Congress Cataloging-in-Publication Data

Names: Woodger, Mary Jane, author. | Alford, Kenneth L., 1955– author. | Manscill, Craig K., author.
Title: Dreams as revelation / Mary Jane Woodger, Kenneth L. Alford, and Craig K. Manscill.
Description: Salt Lake City, Utah : Deseret Book, [2019] | Includes bibliographical references.
Identifiers: LCCN 2019005947 | ISBN 9781629725727 (hardbound : alk. paper)
Subjects: LCSH: Dreams—Religious aspects—The Church of Jesus Christ of Latter-day Saints. | Dreams—Religious aspects—Mormon Church. | Revelation—The Church of Jesus Christ of Latter-day Saints. | Revelation—Mormon Church. | Dream interpretation. | The Church of Jesus Christ of Latter-day Saints—Doctrines. | Mormon Church—Doctrines.
Classification: LCC BX8643.R4 W66 2019 | DDC 248.2/9—dc23
LC record available at https://lccn.loc.gov/2019005947

Printed in the United States of America
Lake Book Manufacturing, Inc., Melrose Park, IL

10 9 8 7 6 5 4 3 2 1

Contents

Foreword vii

Acknowledgments xiii

Introduction xvii

  1. Revelation in the Form of Dreams 1

  2. Inspiration, Indigestion, or Imagination:
     Determining When Dreams Are Revelation 15

  3. Scriptural Dreams 36

  4. Dreams in Joseph Smith's Family 45

  5. Dreams of the Savior 60

  6. Dreams of Missionary Work and Conversion 77

  7. Dreams of Family History and Temple Work 106

  8. Dreams of Warning 120

  9. Dreams of Instruction 142

 10. Dreams of Callings 174

 11. Dreams of Comfort 195

CONTENTS

12. Dreams of Death 231

13. Dreams of Opposition 246

14. Dreams of Prophecy 253

Notes 269

Works Cited 275

Appendix: Dreams Listed by Dreamer 281

Foreword

ROBERT L. MILLET

One of the passages of scripture quoted by the angel Moroni to young Joseph Smith in September 1823 was from the Old Testament: "And it shall come to pass . . . that I will pour out my spirit upon all flesh; and your sons and your daughters shall prophesy, your old men shall dream dreams, your young men shall see visions: and also upon the servants and upon the housemaids in those days will I pour out my spirit" (Joel 2:27–28). You will recall that one fulfillment of this ancient prophecy came on the day of Pentecost, when the Holy Spirit fell upon the meridian Saints with power and great glory. The gift of tongues was dispensed as a fulfillment of John the Baptist's prediction that the Messiah would baptize the people with fire and with the Holy Ghost (Matthew 3:11; JST John 4:3). But Moroni's message concerned an additional fulfillment of Joel's prophecy that would take place in the latter days, but that in 1823 "was not yet fulfilled, but was soon to be" (Joseph Smith–History 1:41).

The length and depth and breadth of the love of Almighty God for his children is surely manifest in the myriad ways in which he chooses to communicate with us. Some are taken into visions, while others enjoy quiet promptings. Some hear a still, small voice, while others hear and feel the word of a loving Father in heaven to them through the inspired messages of his anointed prophets and apostles. Many of the Father's children recognize an answer to earnest prayer through a quiet peace in their souls, while others, like the Prophet Joseph Smith, find that certain subjects or matters of import seem to occupy their minds and even press themselves upon their feelings (Doctrine and Covenants 128:1).

In one of the very first treatises on the doctrine of The Church of Jesus Christ of Latter-day Saints, Elder Parley P. Pratt explained that "In all dispensations God has revealed many important instructions and warnings to men by means of dreams." He went on to explain that "When the outward organs of thought and perception are released from their activity, the nerves unstrung, and the whole of mortal humanity lies hushed in quiet slumbers in order to renew its strength and vigor," men and women may "recall some faint outlines, some confused and half-defined recollections, of that heavenly world and those endearing scenes of their former estate from which they have descended in order to obtain and mature a tabernacle of flesh."

Their loved ones "then hover about them with the fondest affection, the most anxious solicitude. Spirit communes with spirit, thought meets thought, soul blends with soul, in all the rapture of mutual, pure, and eternal love. . . . In that situation, we frequently hold communication with our departed father, mother, brother, sister, son, or daughter; or with the former husband or wife of our bosom." Brother Pratt later added that blessed "are they who forfeit not their claims to the watchful care and protection of, and communion with, the heavenly powers and pure and lovely spirits."[1]

One of the reasons that this particular gospel topic is extremely important to me is because dreams have played such a significant role in the divine direction, growth, and happiness of members of my family. I had the privilege of serving in the Eastern States

FOREWORD

Mission from 1967–69. Because the mission headquarters was at 973 Fifth Avenue in New York City, it was not uncommon for General Authorities to stop in, spend time with our mission president, and then move on to their next destination. One of those who was in the City quite often was President Harold B. Lee, then a senior member of the Quorum of the Twelve Apostles. Because he attended regular board meetings of a prominent corporation that had its offices in New York, we were privileged to see and hear from him more than once.

President Lee spoke to the missionaries as much as he could. On one occasion, our missionaries were fascinated to hear this mighty apostle's counsel to "Never disregard any dream, especially those that seem to stay with you, dreams about which you find yourselves reflecting often." That poignant bit of advice stayed with me, and when I returned home following my mission I discussed it with my Dad. He nodded and assured me that what President Lee had spoken was very true and that he (my father) had experienced several dreams that were revelatory in nature, dreams that had been foundational and formative to his faith and conviction of the restored gospel. He also encouraged me to take notice of those dreams that seemed to be teaching or impressing upon me something significant. I tried to do so over the years, and, like my father, I have from time to time been directed from the other side of the veil.

If I may, allow me to share one dream that proved to be especially meaningful to our family. One of our children chose to leave the fold and separate, not only from Church activity but also from family association. He became heavily involved with addictive drugs and managed to bury himself in a hellish world that held out little hope for normal living in the future. My wife Shauna and I had prayed and wrestled and yearned for his recovery and return, but instead we heard nothing and were left to wonder whether our child was dead, imprisoned, or lost. No word had come in many months, and the burden of pain and awful anticipation of a notification of incarceration or drug overdose grew heavier each day. One night as Shauna and I knelt in prayer, broken and torn emotionally and physically weak from worry, we wept through our prayers and pleaded long and hard, once again, for the Good Shepherd to lead his wandering sheep home. We went to bed and slept from exhaustion.

During that night I found myself dreaming. My father, who had passed away in March of 1988, came to me in the dream, embraced me, and then looked me in the eye and said quite firmly: "Son, I want you to pull yourself together. I am going to help you with those children of yours. Be patient." I awoke and immediately sat up in bed. My sudden movement awoke Shauna, and she replied: "What's wrong? What happened?" I explained that I had seen Dad in a dream and that he told me he planned to help with our wanderers from the other side of the veil. Through our tears, deep feelings of gratitude and reassurance flowed into our souls.

Only days later the phone rang during the middle of the night. Then came these words: "I just can't live like this anymore. Can I please come home?" We were so thrilled to hear something, so grateful to know that our loved one was still alive, that we felt no need to set the terms or specify under what conditions a return would be permitted. We simply welcomed him home with tender affection.

A short time later my son and I sat together on the sofa in the living room. He turned to me and said hesitantly, "Dad I need to share something with you." I nodded and encouraged him to proceed. He said: "I know this sounds strange, but one night some time back I was on the verge of doing something terrible that would definitely have cost me my life. Before I could do it, I heard Grandpa Millet's voice say, 'Don't do that! You have been taught better. Now get up and go home.'" He then asked, "Dad, is that too weird to be true?" With some emotion I said that it was not and added, "Now I have a story to tell you." I then related to him my dream. We felt the Spirit of the Lord resting upon us, sensed that the entire experience was true and from God, and embraced.

My father was a wonderful man who loved his children and his grandchildren. He did all he could to assist us while he was alive, although in the closing decade of his life he wrestled with one physical ailment after another. Without question, his greatest impact on my family—which, of course, is his family, too—has come since he has passed through the veil of death and been allowed to minister on occasion to loved ones. That dream changed my life.

I express my gratitude to BYU Professors Woodger, Alford, and Manscill for pursuing this topic, a vitally important one to be sure, nevertheless a subject about which Latter-day Saints can find very little in bookstores throughout the world. One need only peruse the table of contents of this volume to recognize just how much effort has been expended in bringing this project to publication. The compilers have searched the canon of scripture, as well as attended to numerous historical moments of the past; such moments demonstrate just how often inspired or revelatory dreams have played a meaningful role in the lives of both great and small. I extend to readers the invitation to read this book and become acquainted or reacquainted with this singular means by which the will of God in heaven is communicated to and carried out by the Father's children.

ROBERT L. MILLET
Professor Emeritus of Ancient Scripture
Brigham Young University

Acknowledgments

Our main objective in creating this volume was to look at dreams within the context of the gospel. This systematic collection studies dreams as recorded in the scriptures and in the lives of General Authorities as well as some individual Church members. By examining dreams as a source of revelation, we address questions such as: "Why are dreams manifest as revelation?"; "How can we better understand and interpret dreams?"; and "Who is entitled to dreams and their interpretation?"

It is our hope that many will benefit from the contribution of those who added to this volume. The power of these inspiring dreams has been re-created in this work and our hope is that these dreams will have an impact on readers. We, as the authors, own any mistakes that might be found; however, we do wish to acknowledge that we have felt the accompaniment of spiritual assistance in the process of our research. This book, which was a work in progress over the better part of a decade, is written so that others may carefully observe revelatory dreams and draw inspiration in seeking divine direction in identifying their own spiritual dreams.

Any book is a collaboration and an unconscious recipient of indebtedness to others. Our appreciation goes to Brigham Young

ACKNOWLEDGMENTS

University for the support we have received throughout this project. Most especially we wish to express our gratitude to the Church History and Doctrine's Department Chairs Paul H. Peterson, Arnold K. Garr, Richard E. Bennett, and Alexander L. Baugh and Religious Education Deans Terry B. Ball and Brent L. Top who not only provided the necessary secretarial and research staff, but also infused confidence in this scholarly pursuit. We appreciate the Religious Studies Center who supplied funding of our research. Specifically we are indebted to Religious Studies Center Directors Robert L. Millet, Richard Neitzel Holzapfel, Dana M. Pike, and Thomas A. Wayment for their support. We also appreciated the support and suggestions received from Lisa Roper and her excellent support staff at Deseret Book.

The authors wish to express our deepest appreciation to our researching and writing team consisting of Jessica Biancardi, Kinsey Davis, Megan Perkins, and Kurt Laird made possible through a mentoring grant from Brigham Young University's Office of Research and Creative Activities. In producing this book, we are also thankful to several student employees who were surely some of the most cheerful, dependable, and intelligent of research assistants who have been involved in varying degrees in the large task of selecting, typing, sourcing, and editing the material in this manuscript, including Jami L. Jackson, Kalli K Searle, Kathryn Lemon, Kiana Kekauoha, Kiersten Robertson, Landon Hamren, Natalie Packard, Rebecca Russavage, Sarabeth Campbell, Sean Worsley, Tiffany Alexander, Miranda Lape, and Zachary Lambert. To the Harold B. Lee Library and staff goes our sincere gratitude for the Interlibrary Loan Office and Faculty Delivery Service.

We appreciate the support of Brigham Young University's Division of Continuing Education and the BYU Copyright Office in making available the images that illustrate the opening page of each chapter in this book. We are especially indebted to the talented artists and supervisors who created those excellent images:

ACKNOWLEDGMENTS

Glenn Anderson, Joseph Buenning, Kelsey Christiansen, Rebekah Concidine, Robin Conover, Scott Gutke, Dakota Sheperd, Alicia Scott, Elizabeth Smith, and Ryann Bailey Wawro.

Finally, we wish to thank the dreamers themselves for their willingness to share their revelatory experiences, which ultimately testify of our Father in Heaven's love for us and of his involvement in the details of our lives. Ultimately, this volume is a fulfillment of Joel's prophecy that "It shall come to pass afterward, that I will pour out my spirit upon all flesh; and your sons and your daughters shall prophesy, [and] your old men shall dream dreams" (Joel 2:28).

Introduction

Some revelations come by dreams. Most of our dreams are flighty and have no meaning, but the Lord does use dreams for enlightening his people.
—Spencer W. Kimball[1]

Dreams have played an important role throughout the scriptures and world history. From Lehi's pronouncement that "I have dreamed a dream" about the tree of life to Abraham Lincoln dreaming about his own death, there is truly something fascinating and other-worldly about dreams.[2] The purpose of this book is to illustrate the important role that dreams can play as a method of revelation and inspiration from our Heavenly Father.

Following this Introduction are two chapters that explore "Revelation in the Form of Dreams" (chapter 1) and provide an examination of the sometimes-revelatory nature of dreams (chapter 2: "Inspiration, Indigestion, or Imagination: Determining when Dreams Are Revelation").

The Lord has often used dreams to communicate important truths and guidance to his prophets and other beloved children. Chapter 3, "Scriptural Dreams," includes scriptural examples of

INTRODUCTION

influential dreams from the Old Testament, New Testament, and Book of Mormon. Revelatory dreams were also received in the earliest days surrounding the restoration of the gospel. In "Dreams in Joseph Smith's Family" (chapter 4), we have assembled many of the dreams received by member of Joseph Smith's family to prepare them to assist in the Lord's unfolding work.

Just as not all dreams have been recorded, not all recorded dreams are revelatory. So how did the editors decide whether or not to include a particular dream? A majority of the dreams included in chapters 5–14 were either received or shared by General Authorities of The Church of Jesus Christ of Latter-day Saints. Many of the remaining dreams were previously printed in a Church publication, such as *The Improvement Era,* the *Church News,* the *Journal of Discourses,* the *Ensign,* or *The Friend.* Journals kept by early members of the Church and respected publications by Latter-day Saint authors also contributed some of the dreams published here. Most dreams have a clear connection to the topic of the chapter in which they appear. There are several dreams, admittedly, that could have been comfortably placed within two or more chapters within this book. For those dreams, the editors tried to place them where they were a best fit.

The dreams included in chapters 5 through 14 are generally listed in alphabetical order by name of the dreamer or the person who related the dream. A majority of the dreams have a direct connection to one or more Church General Authorities. Each dream includes a short title assigned by the authors, the name of the person who received the dream (or, in several instances, the person who related the dream), the text of the dream (as it appeared in the original publication), and a source citation following the text of the dream.

Chapter 5 ("Dreams of the Savior") shares several beautiful experiences when prophets, apostles, General Authorities, and other members have seen the Savior in a dream. Beginning with chapter 5, each chapter shares a common organization—a short explanatory introduction followed by numerous dreams that have been excerpted from a wide variety of sources and organized from previous publications, such as Church magazines, general conference talks, biographies, books, and other sources.

Chapter 6, "Dreams of Missionary Work and Conversion," shares dreams that advanced the work of sharing the gospel and often led to the conversion of the recipient. Examples of dreams that have facilitated temple and family history work have been gathered in chapter 7, "Dreams of Family History and Temple Work." Some dreams can provide timely warning of pending events. Chapter 8, "Dreams of Warning," includes several of them. Chapter 9, "Dreams of Instruction," shares numerous examples of dreams that provided counseling, instruction, and helpful preparation to the dreamer. Chapter 10, "Dreams of Callings," is a collection of dreams in which dreamers were notified and prepared to receive upcoming Church callings and assignments.

In chapter 11, "Dreams of Comfort," the editors have assembled examples of dreams that have provided much needed comfort to individuals in various kinds of need. As illustrated in chapter 12 ("Dreams of Death"), dreams can also be connected, in numerous ways, to death and dying. Dreams that teach how to remain faithful and triumph over Satan's temptations are found in chapter 13, "Dreams of Opposition." The final chapter—chapter 14, "Dreams of Prophecy"—provides numerous examples when the subject matter of dreams has proved prophetic. It is important to note that the dreams listed in this book are not comprehensive or exhaustive, but they do represent a good sample of the many revelatory dreams that have been received.

After the notes and works cited sections is an appendix that lists the person associated with each dream (either the dreamer

INTRODUCTION

themselves and/or the person who related the dream), the title of the dream, and the page where it is located in this book.

We hope that this book will teach, inspire, cause you to ponder, and serve as a reference for talks, lessons, and future research.

CHAPTER 1

Revelation in the Form of Dreams

It was the fall equinox on Sunday, September 21, 1823, when the angel Moroni appeared to the Prophet Joseph Smith (see Joseph Smith–History 1:29–53). A new season of gospel restoration was about to begin that would significantly affect Joseph's life, the lives of future Latter-day Saints, and, indeed, the entire world. Moroni appeared to Joseph three consecutive times that night and twice the following day to tutor the future prophet. Sharing profound guidance and scriptural teachings, the angelic visitor taught Joseph that God would "pour out [his] spirit upon all flesh" and that men and women would "prophesy, [and] your old men shall dream dreams, [and] your young men shall see visions" (Joel 2:28). Moroni informed Joseph "that this was not yet fulfilled, but was soon to be" (Joseph Smith–History 1:41). Joseph learned that dreams could be an important revelatory tool.[1]

JOEL'S PROPHECY

Joel saw that our dispensation would be characterized by blood, fire, war, and pillars of smoke (see Joel 2:30). He also saw a path leading to safety that would come to those who experienced an outpouring of the Spirit. Dreams as a possible source of revelation will become increasingly important as the Dispensation of the Fullness of Times progresses. Like that prophet of old, modern apostles also see great wickedness preceding the Lord's Second Coming along with an outpouring of the Spirit. In a 2003 broadcast for Church educators, President Henry B. Eyring observed:

"We share a consuming concern. . . . All of us are concerned by the signs of the rapidly increasing and spreading wickedness in the world surrounding those young people we love and will love. Terrible evil we hardly knew existed when we were young is being presented every day on screens in almost every home, in what we used to think of as the safe 'family hours' when little children could watch in safety. . . . And the tide of evil never seems to ebb, only to rise, and to rise rapidly."[2]

Dreams can become part of the armor needed for youth, as well as adults, to withstand the fiery darts of the adversary (see Doctrine and Covenants 27:15–18). "[Joel's prophecy] is not poetry, nor is it allegory; it is description of reality as it will be," President Henry B. Eyring declared in August 2004 as he drew attention to the wording of Joel's prophecy. "That scripture does not say that your sons and your daughters *may* claim the gift of prophecy by the Spirit. It says that they will. It doesn't say that your young men *may* see visions. It says that they will. And it will come because the Lord will pour out His Spirit upon all flesh. Not only will the youth you love and serve have the Spirit poured out on them, but so will the people around them and those who lead them."[3]

President Eyring observed that some Latter-day Saints may not notice this increase of prophecy, visions, and dreams that will be "a wonderful outcome which is sure." President Eyring informs us that "some of it will happen so gradually that you may not notice it. Some has already begun across the Church and we may not have seen the blessing developing, or at least we may not have done what we must to help the Lord with these miracles."[4]

"You have read it and heard it many times. But you may not have recognized that it is for us and in these times and that it is a call to courage.... These are words from Joel. It is a promise of an outpouring of the Spirit."[5]

RECOGNIZING DREAMS AS REVELATION

Joseph Smith did not restore an interest in dreams, but rather, he restored or revived an understanding of dreaming as a potential source of divine communication or revelation. By example and word, Joseph taught that the heavens had once again been opened. Men and women could receive revelation as in ancient times. He restored the faith in God necessary for people to again "dream dreams" and recognize those dreams as one source of revelation from God.

At the 2005 "Worlds of Joseph Smith" conference sponsored by the Library of Congress, the themes of restoration and revelation were prominent in many presentations. In his conference presentation, Richard Bushman noted that Latter-day Saints view Joseph Smith as a key figure in a long history of apostasy and restoration.[6] At the same conference, religion scholar Richard Hughes observed that Joseph Smith was not the only restorationist of his time; Alexander Campbell, one of the chief contemporary critics of Joseph Smith, was also a restorationist. Hughes described Campbell as "a child of the eighteenth-century Enlightenment," who "had no use for the romantic notion that God might speak to men and women through dreams and revelations. For Campbell, God spoke only through a book that rational people could read and understand in rational ways."[7] Hughes noted other examples of restorationist groups in Joseph Smith's time including the Shakers and the Oneida Community. Each of those restorationist communities believed that they had a role in restoring the truths of pure Christianity, but the restoration of revelation set Joseph Smith and his followers apart from other restorationists. In his address at the "Worlds of Joseph Smith" conference, President Dallin H. Oaks disclosed, "Revelation is the key to the uniqueness of Joseph Smith's message."[8] In her conference address, historian Jan Shipps explained that through Joseph Smith: "The heavens were opened and the divine once again spoke in a language that humans could understand. Without the reopening of that conversation, Mormonism would likely be just one more restoration movement that started out, as did the Disciples of Christ, claiming to be the only true Church of Jesus Christ, but all too quickly took its place on the religious landscape as an idiosyncratic Protestant denomination."[9]

Joseph knew that revelation was essential to his message and mission when he declared in 1844 that "The doctrine of revelation . . . far transcends the doctrine of no revelation . . . ; for one truth revealed from heaven is worth all the sectarian notions in existence."[10] As religion scholar Terryl L. Givens has observed, Joseph Smith believed that the "cardinal contribution of his calling" was to restore the process of revelation.[11] Restoring a proper understanding of revelation was just one of the many extraordinary things that Joseph Smith accomplished during his earthly ministry.

Joseph Smith made many extraordinary claims during his prophetic career, but as Brigham Young University professor David Paulsen observes, "Of all Joseph's challenges to the theological world, none is more fundamental than his claim to direct revelation from God. This claim challenges every variety of Christian thought and, at the same time, grounds all of Joseph's additional claims."[12] One of those additional claims was that divinely inspired dreams were a "right" of the Saints. Inspired dreams came to many of the early Saints, but not everyone who heard about inspired dreams believed them to be true.

4

REVELATION IN THE FORM OF DREAMS

Educated Americans—ministers, newspaper editors, and physicians—of Joseph Smith's day scorned belief in supernatural gifts.[13] According to Bushman, in the minds of clergymen in the early 1800s, the only acceptable form of divine intervention was the "gift of grace . . . all else was unholy, unscriptural, and irrational."[14] Erastus Snow, an early member and Church apostle, reinforced this concept when he observed:

"So far as this generation is concerned it has been since the Prophet Joseph came forth and declared his belief in revelations, visions and angels that the powers of darkness have operated by external and supernatural manifestations, and as the power of God increased with the people and extended throughout the earth and was felt by other nations besides this, the Evil One manifested his power among men to a greater extent. When the Prophet Joseph appeared, announcing his belief in these things, there was a general unbelief among religious sects in regard to them. Professed Christians disclaimed any belief in manifestations from heaven, had no faith in visions or angels, and considered the claims of any man to be absurd who professed to have communication with the unseen world. Those who had faith in visions and dreams were looked upon as superstitious beings."[15]

In March 1839, Joseph Smith explained to Isaac Galland that divinely inspired dreams are one of various spiritual gifts that may be granted to all worthy Disciples of Christ: "We believe that we have a right to revelations, visions, and dreams from God, our heavenly Father; and light and intelligence, through the gift of the Holy Ghost, in the name of Jesus Christ, on all subjects pertaining to our spiritual welfare; if it so be that we keep his commandments, so as to render ourselves worthy in his sight."[16]

Joseph believed the Bible to be the word of God and that the word of God continued in modern times to be revealed to all worthy followers of Christ. Receiving inspired dreams as revelation was part of the Biblical tradition, and Joseph believed that he was called as a prophet to restore all things—including dreams (see Matthew 17:11; Doctrine and Covenants 77:9, 14–15). Moreover, the Book of Mormon contains a history that supported Joseph's faith in dreams. The Book of Mormon also contains several other non-Biblical examples of divinely inspired dreamers—establishing dreaming as a possible legitimate form of revelation.[17] The fact that Joseph recorded his dreams and recounted them in his sermons demonstrates the spiritual significance that he often accorded to them. Emma Smith, Brigham Young, Wilford Woodruff, and many other early Church members also received what they considered revelatory dreams.

In Joseph's day, the concept of dreams as revelation enjoyed some support among individuals largely removed from organized religion. The established clergy and educated class believed dreaming was a form of revelation that had an unreliable reputation at best, and a devilish reputation at worst. Even though dreams were not Joseph's primary means of receiving revelation, he helped to restore the credibility of revelatory dreams. Just three weeks after entering the Salt Lake Valley, Brigham Young taught (in a newly built bowery on what would soon become Temple Square) that "when a man has a dream or vision of eternal things, it is an evidence of its truth as much as though he saw it with his own eyes."[18]

THE LORD'S USE OF DREAMS

Throughout recorded history, the Lord has used dreams as a means to communicate with His children. Elder James E. Talmage noted that "in the earlier dispensations, the Lord frequently communicated through dreams and visions, oftentimes revealing to prophets the events of the future even to the latest generations. . . . Lehi received through dreams his instructions to leave Jerusalem; and on many subsequent occasions the Lord communicated with this patriarch of the western world by dreams and visions."[19]

Though dreams may occur less frequently than other forms of

revelation, they are still prevalent and happen from time to time to bless the Saints. From multiple dreams recorded in the scriptures, we can be assured that the power of heavenly messengers to produce certain impressions upon our minds during sleep for the purpose of conveying important messages is real. Prophets of old and modern prophets have always known the importance of dreams and that God is the source of inspired dreams.

Prophets have always valued revelatory dreams. President Spencer W. Kimball identified his predecessor President Wilford Woodruff as "one of the great spiritual giants of this dispensation." The evidence President Kimball gave for this distinction was that "the Lord gave [President Woodruff] many dreams and visions."[20] Indeed, one characteristic of a prophet may be that he receives and recognizes revelatory dreams. Elder Robert D. Hales observed, "For all of us, our personal revelations reflect the pattern of revelation received by prophets."[21] Just as prophets can receive revelatory dreams to lead the Church, we can receive dreams to assist and guide us in our personal lives.

Many modern apostles have testified that dreams can be inspired. President Hugh B. Brown of the First Presidency noted that dreams can be revelatory when he suggested, "Now, revelation may come through dreams or visions, the visitation of angels, or, on occasion such as with Moses, by face-to-face communication with the Lord."[22] In addition, President Marion G. Romney of the First Presidency bore witness of dreams as revelation when he testified, "I know . . . and bear witness to the fact that revelation from the Lord comes through the spoken word, by personal visitation, by messengers from the Lord, through dreams, and by way of visions, and by the voice of the Lord coming into one's mind."[23] The Lord can give revelation in the form of dreams. They can be an important form of communication to prophets and to individual Latter-day Saints alike.

DEFINING DREAMS AS REVELATION

Elder Gerald N. Lund, while serving as a member of the Seventy, explained that "The English word 'revelation' comes from the Latin word *revelatus*. This word is formed from the prefix *re-*, which means 'to draw back' or 'to remove,' and the noun *velum*, which is 'a covering' or 'a veil.' Thus, *reveal* literally means 'to uncover,' 'to remove the veil.' In other words, revelation in its more generic sense means to make something previously hidden visible to the eye or clear to the understanding."[24]

With Elder Lund's definition in mind, dreams can be thought of as revelation because they often uncover something that was previously hidden from us. Many who have revelatory dreams say that having a spiritual dream is like watching a scene in a movie. Author Margaret Pope defined dreams this way:

"The Lord has many ways to communicate with his children through the Holy Ghost via the gifts of the Spirit. Frequently, in every age, truths, warnings, comfort and conversions are accomplished by visions or dreams. They are always found in the true church (Moroni 7:30–38). . . . When one has a dream or vision it is as if he were witnessing the scene personally. . . . Many visions simply represent the messenger or messengers. . . . These kinds of experiences are indelibly implanted in the heart and mind even though the actual person seen is rarely present. A dream at times may resemble a television viewing—or it may give one the experience of being there. Living it. Personal involvement."[25]

An inspirational dream can indelibly implant its memory upon the heart and mind of the recipient as if the person was conscious and living the experience rather than just witnessing it in the slumber of the night. Dreams can come as revelation during the night which is remembered when we awaken in the morning.

DREAMS VS. VISIONS

Sometimes it is difficult to distinguish the difference between a dream and a vision because dreams can represent a vision that occurs during the night after a person is asleep. Elder Bruce R. McConkie, of the Quorum of the Twelve, defined the difference between dreams and visions as follows: "All inspired dreams are visions, but all visions are not dreams. Visions are received in hours of wakefulness or of sleep and in some cases when the recipient has passed into a trance; it is only when the vision occurs during sleep that it is termed a dream."[26] (See 1 Samuel 28:6, 15.)

Inspired dreams can be synonymous with visions, but not all visions are received in dreams. Elder James E. Talmage, of the Quorum of the Twelve Apostles, clarified a difference between dreams and visions:

"Visions and dreams have constituted a means of communication between God and men in every dispensation of the Priesthood. In general, visions are manifested to the waking senses whilst dreams are given during sleep. In the vision, however, the senses may be so affected as to render the person practically unconscious, at least oblivious to ordinary occurrences, while he is able to discern the heavenly manifestation. In the earlier dispensations, the Lord frequently communicated through dreams and visions, oftentimes revealing to prophets the events of the future even to the latest generations. . . . Most of the visions and dreams recorded in scripture have been given through the ministering Priesthood; but there are exceptional instances of such manifestations unto some, who, at the time, had not entered the fold."[27]

Another definition that is helpful when trying to understand dreams is that a dream is an experience of the mind that occurs while we are asleep but is remembered after awakening. Latter-day Saint psychologist Errol R. Fish suggests that dreams have "wonderful potential" because "while asleep, the Spirit can put thoughts, pictures, and stories into our minds." Dr. Fish tells of a client whose father had abandoned his family when the client was a baby. After his father left, the child was devoid of any other father figure while he was growing up. Even as a grown man, the client would see fathers and sons together and be envious of their relationships. As time went on, the client often wondered what it would feel like to be held in the arms of his own father. Dr. Fish suggested to this man that "the Lord might be willing to satisfy his wish by means of a dream, but that the Lord usually wants us to ask." As a result of that suggestion, the client prayed for a dream and received one that he felt was inspired. One night he dreamt "he was [being] held in the arms of his own father, as real as if he had lived it—which he reported was immensely satisfying."[28] Dreams can sometimes seem as real to the dreamer as if they had actually experienced them. Such dreams can be manifestations from the Lord wherein He communicates through the gift and power of the Holy Ghost.

The veil between heaven and earth can appear to be thin when dreams and visions are received from the Lord. President Charles W. Penrose of the First Presidency instructed:

"We know the channel of communication is opened up between the heavens and the earth, and that the people of the nineteenth century, by taking a proper course and exercising faith in the right way, and being humble enough to carry into effect the commandments which the Lord gives when he does manifest himself unto them, can obtain communication from on high by the gift and power of the Holy Ghost, by dreams and visions, and by the visible manifestation of God's power in the midst of his people."[29]

As President Penrose instructed, in some instances dreams are not only manifestations of the Lord, but they are also a manifestation of His power. Elder Henry W. Naisbitt of the Seventy remarked, "If we would cultivate this spirit, if we would listen to its teachings, it would come to us in many ways, in visions, in dreams and manifestations of the power of God."[30] Dreams and visions are one way God can communicate with us.

In dreams, we may see things that can appear revelatory to us when we awaken. President Spencer W. Kimball once wrote to his son, "I have come to realize that the Lord does not expect to reveal to us generally in actual daylight vision as he did to Joseph Smith in the grove. Sometimes it will come in open vision, sometimes in dreams."[31] President Wilford Woodruff concurred when he wrote, "The Lord has many ways in which he communicates with us. Frequently, as has been the case in every age, truths, principles, warnings, etc., are communicated to the children of men by means of dreams and visions. . . . It is a communication to man."[32] Dreams and visions are important channels that the Lord uses to communicate with us.

INSPIRED DREAMS ARE A SPIRITUAL GIFT

Gifts of the Spirit were restored to The Church of Jesus Christ of Latter-day Saints. Revelations, prophecy, testimony, and dreams are part of the foundation on which the Lord has built His church. President Boyd K. Packer explained: "The spiritual gifts described in the Book of Mormon are present in the Church today—promptings, impressions, revelations, dreams, visions, visitations, miracles. You can be sure that the Lord can, and at times does, manifest Himself with power and great glory. Miracles can occur."[33] Elder Orson F. Whitney also noted how dreams had blessed early missionaries in this dispensation. In an April 1910 general conference address, he shared:

"The Spirit of the Lord is the source of all spiritual gifts, but He 'divideth to every man severally as He will.' God can reveal the truth in a dream, and has done so on many occasions. When my grandfather, Heber C. Kimball, with Orson Hyde, Willard Richards and others, went to England in 1837, to introduce the Gospel there, they found many people prepared to receive them. Whole villages were converted. The Lord had prepared the way before them. And how had He done it? He had given to some of the people dreams, in which they had seen these very men landing on the shores of England, and when they came to them with the Gospel message these humble factory or farm hands knew they were servants of God, because they had seen them in dreams. It was their privilege to receive the message that way."[34]

Dreams are one of the ways the Lord can send messages to His children. As we keep His commandments, He can answer our prayers and give us guidance through our dreams. President Harold B. Lee promised:

"The Lord will guide us if we live right. The thing that all of us should strive for is to so live, keeping the commandments of the Lord, that He can answer our prayers, the prayers of our loved ones, the prayers of the General Authorities, for us. . . . If we will live worthy, then the Lord will guide us—by a personal appearance, or by His actual voice, or by His voice coming into our mind, or by impressions upon our heart and our soul. And oh, how grateful we ought to be if the Lord sends us a dream in which are revealed to us the beauties of the eternity or a warning and direction for our special comfort. Yes, if we so live, the Lord will guide us for our salvation and for our benefit."[35]

Revelatory dreams from our Heavenly Father are rare, but they can be given for the benefit of his righteous children. Inspired or revelatory dreams should be treasured if they are received, but they should not be expected. Some righteous Church members may have only one such experience in their lifetime, while other members may have none. The presence, or absence, of revelatory dreams is not an indication of God's love for us.

Messages in inspirational dreams come in a form that each individual will understand. Elder Franklin D. Richards of the Quorum of the Twelve Apostles once instructed, "Just as sure as there are honest hearts there, the Lord will stir them up by dreams or manifestations of some sort, until they get to know the truth in their own languages."³⁶ Dreams come in our own language and are for our benefit. Communication can come from our Father in Heaven through dreams giving individual guidance as to what we should do in a given situation. President Charles W. Penrose was surprised that he was given guidance and direction in his dreams. In the October 1922 general conference, President Penrose shared:

"And the blessing that the Lord bestows sometimes upon people, of giving them communications by dream at night, or vision by day, are for themselves. I can testify that the Lord has done that for me, but I have not made known that which was given to me for my own comfort and my advice and my benefit. I have had dreams which I have to acknowledge were divine, because they were fulfilled to the very letter—clearly given and clearly made manifest, and clearly brought into actual being—but they were for me and for my guidance and direction, and sometimes they were of such a nature that they appeared to me to be almost trivial, to think that the Lord would reveal to me certain things that were of very small moment. They only affected me and those with whom I was associated in the ministry, they came to pass in very deed, but I have not had them put on record nor had them published or spread abroad. I did not think that would be right."³⁷

From President Penrose's testimony, we can deduce that dreams are generally for the benefit of the dreamer. Dreams given as a spiritual gift are personal in nature and should not be shared with the general public. They are not intended for general guidance and direction.

Many General Authorities have testified of having inspired dreams. Elder Richard G. Scott of the Quorum of the Twelve Apostles talked often about his dreams and also about the nature of dreams in general. In the April 2012 general conference, he taught that revelation can come through dreams and explained how the Lord can use dreams. Elder Scott instructed:

"Revelation can also be given in a dream when there is an almost imperceptible transition from sleep to wakefulness. If you strive to capture the content immediately, you can record great detail, but otherwise it fades rapidly. Inspired communication in the night is generally accompanied by a sacred feeling for the entire experience. The Lord uses individuals for whom we have great respect to teach us truths in a dream because we trust them and will listen to their counsel. It is the Lord doing the teaching through the Holy Ghost. However, He may in a dream make it both easier to understand and more likely to touch our hearts by teaching us through someone we love and respect."[38]

Elder Scott encouraged Latter-day Saints to write down a narrative of the dreams they felt were "inspired communication in the night. . . . Inspiration carefully recorded shows God that His communications are sacred to us. Recording will also enhance our ability to recall revelation. Such recording of direction of the Spirit should be protected from loss or intrusion by others."[39]

Some dreams are inspired of the Lord. He uses these dreams to communicate important messages with us. In order to remember as much of the dream as we can, we are encouraged write the details of the dreams down as soon as we awaken. Dreams are a spiritual gift that can bless our lives and allow us to help others.

This volume is a collection of recorded dreams. Many of the dreams were received or related by modern prophets and apostles. Revelatory dreams are important because they can serve many beneficial purposes. They can teach, warn, testify, and strengthen us. We hope that reading this book will enhance your ability to recognize and learn from revelatory dreams.

CHAPTER 2

Inspiration, Indigestion, or Imagination

DETERMINING WHEN DREAMS ARE REVELATION

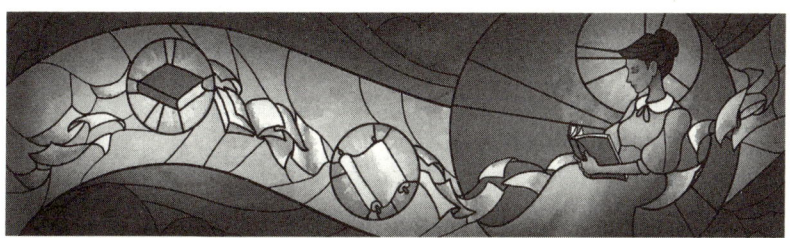

The question is not if Latter-day Saints will have revelatory dreams. The questions for Latter-day Saint dreamers are which dreams are from Heavenly Father and how can they know if a dream is inspiration, indigestion, or imagination? Some general guidelines that dreamers can apply to identify the source of dreams and determine whether a dream is a spiritual gift are included in this chapter. Not all dreams can be considered revelation. While serving as a member of the Seventy, Elder Gerald N. Lund clarified:

"Not all dreams are revelatory in nature. . . . The subconscious mind continues to function while we sleep, sometimes in very normal expressions of our thoughts and feelings. . . . It would be safe to say that the vast majority of our dreams do not constitute revelation from the Lord, and it would be a concern if we looked for spiritual meaning in every dream of the night."[1]

But there are certainly times when we dream and wonder if it is the Holy Ghost precipitating the dream rather than that which we are involved in during our waking hours.

One reason it is hard to determine whether our dreams are revelation is because they differ greatly from other types of revelation. Unlike inspiration that comes as thoughts or feelings, in dreams "we receive information through the visual images we experience in our minds,"[2] and the source of these visual images is sometimes difficult to determine.

DREAMS COME FROM A VARIETY OF SOURCES

Early in the history of The Church of Jesus Christ of Latter-day Saints, deducing the source of dreams was discussed as the Prophet Joseph Smith taught in church. On July 2, 1839, the Prophet made some remarks during a meeting with the Quorum of the Twelve Apostles, teaching them how to recognize and know the source of a dream or vision. He said, "Lying spirits are going forth in the Earth. There will be great manifestation[s] of spirits, both false and true."[3]

Joseph Smith taught that there are certain prerequisites to distinguishing between a divinely inspired dream and a dream from another source. Like all gospel blessings, receiving the blessing of divinely inspired dreams requires righteous living. Joseph Smith taught that dreams could be inspired, but he recognized that not all dreams are of such a variety; he thus taught principles that enabled his followers to discern the difference.

Dreams do come from many sources. Even little children know that dreams can be good or bad. Children have nightmares, but also sing with Cinderella, "A dream is a wish your heart makes."[4] As adults, we too have good and bad dreams, and even prophets—both modern and ancient—have been troubled by some of their dreams. Job had nightmares and proclaimed that the Lord "scarest me with dreams, and terrifiest me through visions" (Job 7:14). When a dream is not a nightmare, it should not always be ascribed as inspiration from the Spirit of the Lord.

President David O. McKay experienced frequent upsetting dreams when his "nerves [were] upset or if [he] had eaten too heartily at a meal before going to bed." In one repetitive dream, President McKay found himself trying to catch a burglar who was "getting out of a window or turning a corner," and President McKay couldn't "catch him and usually called out for help with what he referred to [as] 'a very unearthly noise.'" His wife would awake, nudge her husband, and say his name. He would associate hearing his wife say his name with the dream and continue to sleep. Others became aware of President McKay's dream when they were with him. One time when he was sharing a room with President Heber J. Grant, President McKay awoke to "a thunderous tone saying, 'David! . . . Turn over!'" He also had this same dream one night on a Pullman train. When he awoke, he did not think anyone had heard him call out in his sleep. However, the next morning when the porter was putting up the bed, President McKay said, "Good morning, George. How are you this morning?" The porter replied, "Alright, Cap. How are you? . . . You sure had 'em!" President McKay knew that the porter had heard him calling out in his dreams and did not want to ask the porter anything else.[5]

Though some dreams open up the spiritual world, other dreams can come from undesirable sources. President Joseph F. Smith observed that some people "may have visions and dreams; but except they are faithful and pure in heart, they become an easy prey to the adversary of their souls, and he will lead them into darkness and unbelief more easily than others. The devil himself can appear like an angel of light." He further taught that, "The trouble is, we know so little of the truth ourselves and we live by it so poorly that almost any little jackanapes* in the country may rise up and claim he has had a vision, or some marvelous dream, and however absurd or untrue it may be, he may find believers and followers among those who profess to be Latter-day Saints."[6]

Brigham Young also recognized that not all dreams come from the Lord. He reported seeing the effects of "some anomalous [irregular or unusual] sleep." Many times in his youth, he observed people lying on benches, on the floor of the meetinghouse, or on the ground at camp meetings from ten minutes to an hour catnapping, without, as he said, "a particle of pulse about them." He asked some of these dreamers what they had seen in their dreams, visions, or trances:

"Brother, what have you experienced?"

"Nothing."

"What do you know more than before you had this; what do you call it—trance, sleep or dream? Do you know any more now than before you fell to the earth?"

"Nothing more."

"Have you seen any person?"

"No."

"Then what is the use or utility of your falling down here in the dirt?"[7]

President Young knew that such dreams are not from God.

Levi Hancock, an early Church missionary, received a false dream shortly after the Prophet Joseph Smith called him to serve a mission. Levi departed on his missionary journey, but when snow made traveling difficult, he returned home. When the prophet rebuked him for not pressing forward, Levi explained that he was not to blame, for he had made his decision not to continue because of a troubling dream. Joseph reportedly responded, "Don't let that

---

* A jackanape is "an impudent or conceited fellow" or "a saucy or mischievous child" (https://www.merriam-webster.com/dictionary/jackanapes).

trouble you. I have had dreams as bad as you ever had. You do as I now tell you to and you will come out all right."[8]

For many, it is difficult to determine whether a dream's message is true or false. There are counterfeit dreams just as there are counterfeit angels (see Doctrine and Covenants 129). One counterfeit source of dreams may be our own emotions. President Boyd K. Packer warned, "The spiritual part of us and the emotional part of us are so closely linked that it is possible to mistake an emotional impulse for something spiritual."[9] As President Packer suggests, our dreams can be created by our own emotional responses to things that have happened during the day.

Dreams can also be precipitated by our activities while we are awake. Several Old Testament prophets received dreams from sources that were not divine in nature. The prophet Jeremiah warned, "Let not your prophets and your diviners [dreamers], that be in the midst of you, deceive you, neither hearken to your dreams which ye cause to be dreamed" (Jeremiah 29:8). Jeremiah indicated that the source of our dreams might be our own minds. The prophet Zechariah was plagued by false dreams, and he warned, "For the idols have spoken vanity, and the diviners have seen a lie, and have told false dreams" (Zechariah 10:2).

President Charles Penrose agreed with Jeremiah and Zechariah that there are various uninspired sources of dreams. He quoted the ancient King Solomon saying, "In the multitude of dreams and words, there be divers vanities" (Ecclesiastes 5:7) and then added, "I have dreamed a great deal that was nothing but vanity and followed by a vexation of spirit."[10] That which we are involved in during our waking hours may precipitate dreams that have nothing to do with inspiration from the Holy Ghost. President Harold B. Lee agreed that there are many uninspired sources of dreams: "I'm not going to tell you that every dream you have is a direct revelation from the Lord—it may be fried liver and onions that have been responsible

DREAMS AS REVELATION

for an upset or disorder."[11] Religious scholars George Reynolds and Janne M. Sjodahl explained:

"It has been demonstrated that a person asleep may receive impressions from extraneous sources, although the reflective or reasoning organs are at rest. The smell of flowers may cause him to dream that he is walking in a garden. Sleeping in a smoky room may create the impression of a conflagration and a hot water bottle at his feet may cause him to dream that he is standing on a volcano."[12]

Such dreams are of little importance. President Wilford Woodruff noted, "We have had a great many dreams—I have had in my life and I suppose you have more or less—which amount to nothing. I will tell you something about what I have [made] reference to: A man eats a hot supper when he goes to bed; he gets the nightmare; he is chased by a bear. . . . Yet I have had dreams of a very different character."[13]

Knowing if a dream is a spiritual gift can be perplexing, and there have been times when good-meaning people have interpreted dreams as being inspiration but in reality, those dreams have not been from the Lord. Sometimes such a mistake has caused problems in people's lives. Elder Gerald N. Lund told of one such example. A woman came up to him after he gave an address on sources of revelation. The woman told Elder Lund that his address was the first church meeting she had been to in more than six years and that she had come only at the urging of a friend. She had quit going to church because of a dream that took place soon after the death of her first child. She and her husband had been unable to have children for several years after their marriage. When she had finally become pregnant, they looked forward with great joy to having a child; however, shortly before the baby was due, the woman started to hemorrhage. Her husband rushed her to the hospital barely in time to save her life, but the baby was lost. After the baby's funeral, a sister from this couple's ward came to visit. This neighbor told the grieving mother that she had had a dream the previous night in which it had been revealed to her that if the woman's husband had taken the time to give his wife a priesthood blessing before he had rushed her to the hospital, the baby would have lived. "That was when I stopped going to Church," the woman told Elder Lund. "My husband is a faithful priesthood holder, but all he could think about that night was saving my life. I decided that if God would let my child die under such circumstances, I wanted nothing more to do with him. . . . But what that woman told me wasn't from the Lord, was it?" Elder Lund shook his head and said no.[14] This uninspired dream caused years of bitterness.

INSPIRED DREAMS ARE FOR OUR OWN BENEFIT

Most often, spiritual dreams are given for our own benefit or for the benefit of those we have stewardship over. Elder Robert D. Hales humorously instructed: "As we receive the inspiration of the Holy Ghost for ourselves, it is wise to remember that we cannot receive revelation for others. I know of a young man who told a young woman, 'I've had a dream that you are to be my wife.' The young woman pondered that statement and then responded, 'When I have the same dream, I'll come and talk to you.'"[15] Because we are entitled to dreams only for ourselves and those in our stewardship, seldom will the Lord give us a dream that involves inspiration for those over whom we have little responsibility. President George Albert Smith spoke of this principle in 1945:

"Setting one's self up as a receiver of dreams and visions to guide the human family is not on the Lord's side of the line; and when men, as they have sometimes done in order to win their success along some line or another, have come to an individual or individuals and said, 'I have had this dream and this is what the Lord wants us to do,' you may know that they are not on the Lord's side of the line. The dreams and visions and revelations of God to the children of men have always come through his regularly appointed servant.

You may have dreams and manifestations for your own comfort and for your own satisfaction, but you will not have them for the Church unless God appoints you to take the place that he gave to his prophets of old and in our day, and unless you have been divinely commissioned to do the thing he wants you to do."[16]

President Dallin H. Oaks further defined this concept:

"We should understand what can be called the principle of 'stewardship in revelation.' . . . Only the president of the Church receives revelation to guide the entire Church. Only the stake president receives revelation for the special guidance of the stake. The person who receives revelation for the ward is the bishop. For a family, it is the priesthood leadership of the family. Leaders receive revelation for their own stewardships. Individuals can receive revelation to guide their own lives. But when one person purports to receive revelation for another person outside his or her own stewardship—such as a church member who claims to have revelation to guide the entire Church or a person who claims to have a revelation to guide another person over whom he or she has no presiding authority according to the order of the Church—you can be sure that such revelations are not from the Lord."[17]

GENERAL GUIDELINES

Mistaking the source of a dream is not uncommon, and uninspired dreams have often caused mischief for Latter-day Saints. President Charles W. Penrose taught, "From time to time through the whole history of the Church every now and then somebody has started up with a dream or a vision or a revelation of some kind, and endeavored to lead other people away from the straight path."[18]

Brigham Young observed that "there are certain keys to prove" that a dream is from the Lord.[19] Here are some general guidelines that can be used to determine the source of our dreams:

INSPIRATION, INDIGESTION, OR IMAGINATION

1. SPIRITUAL DREAMS CAN STRENGTHEN FAITH

Living a righteous life can aid us in understanding if a dream is from the Holy Ghost. Dreams are not given to bring someone to faith; rather, spiritual dreams are an addition to a testimony that has already been developed. President Boyd K. Packer said, "[We should not] expect revelation [including through dreams] to replace the spiritual or temporal intelligence we already have received—only to extend it."[20]

President Brigham Young explained that in order to distinguish between truth and error and to properly interpret a dream or vision, one must be living a righteous life.[21] Information obtained from spiritual dreams can be considered wisdom, knowledge, and hidden treasure. Observing the Word of Wisdom can be an essential key to obtaining knowledge and understanding of one's dreams. BYU religion professors Joseph Fielding McConkie and Craig J. Ostler explain that the Word of Wisdom "is not simply a health law. There would be little purpose in extending someone's life if it were not replete with light and truth. To avoid cancer, for example, as marvelous as that may be, is not as important as being able to dream dreams, entertain angels, or get answers to your prayers."[22] Those who keep the commandments may receive dreams from the Holy Ghost that can change lives.

A recipient of a dream must have the Holy Ghost's assistance in order to determine the source of a dream. Heavenly messengers have the power to make impressions upon the mind during our sleep to convey important messages.[23] In order to understand those messages, there are certain requirements of worthiness. Simple questions can be asked by those who receive such impressions to ascertain whether the source is the Holy Ghost. An experience President Harold B. Lee had as a stake president can be applied to those who purport having received a spiritual dream. A man in President Lee's stake had been excommunicated for immorality. This man's brother came to President Lee and proclaimed, "'I want to tell you that my brother wasn't guilty of what you charged him with.'" President Lee replied,

"'Would you mind if I ask you a few personal questions?'

"He said, 'Certainly not.'

"'How old are you?'

"'Forty-seven.'

"'What priesthood do you hold?'

"He said that he thought that he was a teacher.

"'Do you keep the Word of Wisdom?'

"'Well, no.' He used tobacco, which was obvious.

"'Do you pay your tithing?'

"He said, 'No'—and he didn't intend to as long as that blankety-blank-blank man was the bishop of the Thirty-Second ward.

"[President Lee] said, 'Do you attend your priesthood meetings?'

"He replied, 'No, sir!' and he didn't intend to as long as that man was bishop.

"'You don't attend your sacrament meetings either?'

"'No, sir.'

"'Do you have your family prayers?' and he said no.

"'Do you study the scriptures?' He said well, his eyes were bad, and he couldn't read very much."

President Lee then explained:

"In my home I have a beautiful instrument called a radio. When everything is in good working order we can dial it to a certain station and pick up the voice of a speaker or a singer. . . . But after we have used it for a long time, the little delicate instruments . . . begin to wear out. When one of them wears out, we may get some static. . . . Another wears out, and if we don't give it attention, the sound may fade in and out. And if another one wears out—well, the radio may sit there looking quite like it did before, but because of what has happened on the inside, we can hear nothing.

"Now, . . . you and I have within our souls something like . . . a counterpart of those radio tubes. We might have . . . a 'go-to-sacrament-meeting' tube, a 'keep-the-Word-of-Wisdom' tube, a 'pay-your-tithing' tube, a 'have-your-family-prayers' tube, a 'read-the-scriptures' tube, and . . . the master tube of our whole soul . . . the 'keep-yourselves-morally-clean' tube. If one of these becomes worn out by disuse or inactivity—if we fail to keep the commandments of God—it has the same effect upon our spiritual selves that a worn-out tube has in a radio.

"Now, then, . . . fifteen of the best-living men in the Pioneer Stake prayed last night. They heard the evidence and every man was united in saying that your brother was guilty. Now you, who do none of these things, you say you prayed and got an opposite answer. How would you explain that?"

The man replied, "'Well, President Lee, I think that I must have gotten my answer from the wrong source.'"[24]

Those who do not keep commandments they have covenanted to obey do not typically receive inspired revelation.

In addition to being worthy, a dreamer must possess faith in order to understand messages conveyed by the Holy Ghost. Although the Holy Ghost may give an inspired dream to an unworthy recipient, that person may not adhere to the dream. Dreams themselves do not convert. If a dreamer has not previously secured a testimony or does not act on the dream's information to cultivate the Spirit, the dream's message may be null and void. President Wilford Woodruff explained, "There are a great many things taught us in dreams that are true, and if a man has the Spirit of God he can tell the difference between what is from the Lord and what is not. . . . Whenever you have a dream that you feel is from the Lord, pay attention to it."[25] Dreams do not produce faith; instead, they act as a catalyst for men and women to take the necessary steps in prayer to obtain a witness of the gospel's truthfulness.

Another way to tell if a dream is from a divine source regards our ability to understand the message we have been given. To receive the interpretation of a dream or to understand a dream, our motives must be pure. President Henry B. Eyring further explained, "If you want to receive the gifts of the Spirit, you have to want them for the right reasons. Your purposes must be the Lord's purposes. To the degree your motives are selfish, you will find it difficult to receive those gifts of the Spirit that have been promised to you. That fact serves both as a warning and as helpful instruction. . . . God is offended when we seek the gifts of the Spirit for our own purposes rather than for His."[26]

2. SPIRITUAL DREAMS CONCERN IMPORTANT MATTERS

Dreams that come from the Holy Ghost will not be about trivial matters, such as what shirt to buy, what dress to wear, or what cereal to eat for breakfast. Such unimportant issues are not within the framework of the Spirit's communication. In Doctrine and Covenants 58:26–27, we are told that the Lord simply does not care when suitable alternatives are acceptable. President Boyd K. Packer instructs, "We are expected to use the light and knowledge we already possess to work out our lives."[27] President Dallin H. Oaks affirms, "I suggest that there is *not* a right and a wrong to *every* question. To many questions, there are only two wrong answers or two right answers. . . . I believe the Lord expects us to use the intelligence and experience he has given us to make these kinds of choices."[28] When we can make up our own minds on matters of inconsequence, the Lord will not send a dream to instruct us.

On the other hand, President Boyd K. Packer observed, "Some answers will come from reading the scriptures, some from hearing speakers. And, occasionally, when it is important, some will come by very direct and powerful inspiration."[29] A dream is a very direct and powerful form of inspiration; therefore, dreams that come from the Holy Ghost usually deal with important events and have purpose. A faithful man or woman may have dreams about what he is involved with in his daily life. President Brigham Young instructed:

"The Lord will not condemn any man for following counsel,

and keeping the commandments; and a faithful man will have dreams about the work he is engaged in. If he is engaged in building the Temple, he will dream about it; and if in preaching he will dream about that, and not, when he is laboring on the temple, dream that it is his duty to run off preaching, and leave his family to starve; such dreams are not of God."[30]

One of the reasons that dreams are hard to identify as revelation is because many dreams only apply to a specific time or situation.[31]

3. SPIRITUAL DREAMS ALIGN WITH COMMANDMENTS

For a dream to be revelation, its message must be in agreement with commandments the Lord has already revealed. The Lord will never give a dream whose message goes against His commandments. As President Boyd K. Packer explained, not all dreams come from God: "The evil one has the power to tap into those channels of revelation and send conflicting signals which can mislead and confuse us. There are promptings [including dreams] from evil sources which are so carefully counterfeited as to deceive even the very elect."[32] One safeguard against such deception is to remember that our Father in Heaven will never give us a dream that will go against counsel given by His prophets. In Deuteronomy 13:3–4 the Lord instructs: "Thou shalt not hearken unto the words of that prophet, or that dreamer of dreams: for the Lord your God proveth you, to know whether ye love the Lord your God with all your heart and with all your soul. Ye shall walk after the Lord your God, and fear him, and keep his commandments, and obey his voice, and ye shall serve him, and cleave unto him."

A dream will not contradict gospel principles, church programs, or procedures that have been established by the First Presidency and the Quorum of the Twelve. President Thomas S. Monson gives us questions we can ask to determine whether any type of revelation is from God. We might ask ourselves these questions about our dreams:

1. Is the dream contrary to instructions from a living Prophet?
2. Is there anything secret?
3. Does it bring harmony and peace of mind?
4. Does it square with the scriptures?
5. What have you done yourself to ask of the Lord?
6. Are you keeping the commandments?[33]

By answering these questions affirmatively, we can know by the Spirit whether the information given in a dream aligns with the Spirit.

President Charles W. Penrose told of a visit from a woman who was a great believer in dreams. She asked him to interpret a dream, and President Penrose's first question was, "'Sister, what did you have for supper last night?'" She answered, "'I had some fried pork and onions.' 'Well,' [he] said, 'that is the interpretation.'" President Penrose went on to explain:

"I do not want you to infer from this that when the Lord gives a dream to anybody, or persons dream something which is enlightening to their souls and comforting to their hearts and seems to be clear and plain, I wish to attribute that to anything else but what they think it is; but I do say and repeat, that nothing is to be received in this Church by way of direction and commandment, outside of the order which God has established in his Church, and which is most wise and beneficent and beneficial. Follow the counsel and advice and commandment revealed through the head of the Church to the Church and we will not go wrong."[34]

When considering the messages we receive through dreaming, we would be wise to follow the counsel President James E. Faust of the First Presidency gave about voices that are contrary to the Spirit of the Lord. If a dream does any of the following, we can be assured that it did not come from the Lord:

- Requires the dreamer to conjure up perceived injustices or abhor challenge and work.

- Offers sensual enticements.
- Lulls the sleeper into carnal security.
- Professes sophistication or superiority.
- Encourages the dreamer to rely on the arm of flesh.
- Puffs the dreamer up with pride.
- Destroys hope.
- Promotes pleasure seeking.
- Tempts the dreamer to spend money for things that are not of worth.
- Encourages the dreamer to labor for that which cannot satisfy.[35]

Even if a dream seems logical or has merit, if it goes against what is already established by prophets, seers, and revelators, a Latter-day Saint may be sure it is not from God. In 1913, the First Presidency stated:

"Be not led by any spirit or influence that discredits established authority and contradicts true scientific principles and discoveries, or leads away from the direct revelations of God for the government of the Church. The Holy Ghost does not contradict its own revealings. Truth is always harmonious with itself. Piety is often the cloak of error. The counsels of the Lord through the channel he has appointed will be followed with safety, therefore, O! ye Latter-day Saints, profit by these words of warning."[36]

4. SPIRITUAL DREAMS MAY BE SYMBOLIC

Often our Father in Heaven's lessons use a different methodology than that used in today's secular education settings. The Lord's methodology is evident in the scriptures, especially in the writings of Isaiah, in the book of Revelation, and in the temple endowment, all of which include symbolism. Dreams from our Father in Heaven are often symbolic in nature.

Symbolism is frequently used in revelatory dreams. The youthful

Joseph of Egypt dreamed that the sun, the moon, and eleven stars bowed down to him. This dream was fulfilled later in his life, but the fulfillment was not, of course, literal; the sun, moon, and stars did not move and bend. Isaiah described a river that overflowed the land of Judah. This symbolic prophecy was fulfilled (though not literally) when Assyria invaded and conquered Judah. Also, consider the dream interpreted by Daniel of a statue composed of various materials (Daniel 2:31–45). The statue represented ancient nations.[37] Dreams are often symbolic rather than pictorial. The difference in these two terms is described in the portrait of Christ presented in Revelation 1:12–16. In verse 16, he is described as holding seven stars and having a sword issuing from his mouth. These verses contain a series of symbols representing various aspects of Christ's character, not a composite literal image of his person. Symbols in our dreams are ideographic—a coded way of representing tangible concepts.[38]

It might have been easier if scriptural dreams were more simple and straightforward, but if that were the case, the dreams might not be quite as memorable. As President Spencer W. Kimball once observed, "Many men seem to have no ear for spiritual messages nor comprehension of them when they come in common dress."[39] Therefore, the Lord may use common images to press messages upon our minds. Snakes represented apostates in a dream for Wilford Woodruff,[40] flocks of different-colored sheep symbolized individual differences among Latter-day Saints for Brigham Young,[41] and a panther warned Heber C. Kimball of danger.[42] So too in the dreams of modern Latter-day Saints, symbols may be presented so the dreamer might discover messages from our Heavenly Father.

5. SPIRITUAL DREAMS MAY LEAVE DETAILED MEMORIES

With an inspired dream, a dreamer will often be able to remember very vivid details when he or she awakes. A dreamer will be able to describe such things as the people involved, the clothing worn, a building's design, or the exact words used.

For instance, in recounting a dream, Heber C. Kimball described a panther as being jet black and beautiful to look upon, with distinctive ears, a sleek coat, and claws and teeth of silver. Using his description, one can certainly visualize a panther. A biblical example is the statue in King Nebuchadnezzar's dream. The materials, height, and body parts of the statue are described so completely that anyone might draw an image that could be highly detailed. One last example comes from Anthony Uzodimma Obinna, a Nigerian Latter-day Saint. In November 1965, he was visited in a dream by a tall person who was carrying a walking stick in his right hand who asked Obinna whether he had read about Christiana in *A Pilgrim's Progress*, by John Bunyan. "I told him that I had forgotten it and he told me to read it again. After a few months the same personage appeared to me again and took me to a most beautiful building and showed me everything in it. That personage appeared to me three times." He later saw and recognized that same building—the Salt Lake Temple—in an old issue of the *Reader's Digest*.[43] The clarity and details of his dreams assisted Brother Obinna in recognizing Christ's church when it was introduced to him. Dreams that are not from the Holy Ghost generally lack such minute details.

6. SPIRITUAL DREAMS MAY COME IN THE EARLY MORNING

Another key to understanding if a dream comes from the Holy Ghost may be when it comes during sleep. In 1993, Elder Richard G. Scott shared an experience he had with a "disturbing dream." He related that when he awoke, he "ached physically, was saturated with perspiration, and [his] heart was pounding. Every sense was sharpened. . . . The transition from sleep to wakefulness was imperceptible." Elder Scott commented that he had come to recognize that a state of semi-sleep is an indication of a significant spiritual experience in a dream.[44]

Most often, spiritual dreams come to us when we are in between sleeping and awaking. That transitional phase can be a time of dreaming, when we are neither totally asleep nor totally awake. In a 2003 broadcast for church educators, President Henry B. Eyring observed, "Again, this may be personally peculiar, but my dreams at the end of the night often are the prelude to what it is I'm going to be taught. I've learned to wake up and try to figure out what was on my mind—if not dreams in my mind and in my sleep—because I just expect to be taught at the beginning of the day."[45]

President Eyring then gave a personal example of this principle of the timing of dreams. He explained that the morning before he participated in the broadcast, he awoke at 4:30 a.m. He said he was not surprised to wake up. He did not hear a voice, but a very clear impression came to him: "Now remember the main thing to tell teachers is that if they will love the students, they will feel the Savior's love for them and he will teach them individually what to do for each student." In this experience, President Eyring was told what to do right at the start of the day. Sharing that experience was sort of a precursor to the general instructions he was going to give. During this same broadcast, Elder Richard G. Scott noted, "We've noticed that among the senior brethren, it seems like the early morning hour is a time where the Spirit can communicate very powerfully and very directly, and [I] would suggest that as an aid to those of you who want to increase the direction of the Spirit in your teaching and in your lives."[46]

7. SPIRITUAL DREAMS MAY BE ACCOMPANIED BY SPIRITUAL FEELINGS

When a person awakens from a spiritual dream, he or she often has a spiritual feeling. Joseph Smith once said, "A person may profit by noticing the first intimation of the spirit of revelation. . . .

INSPIRATION, INDIGESTION, OR IMAGINATION

When you feel pure intelligence flowing unto you it may give you sudden strokes of ideas, that by noticing it, you may find it fulfilled the same day or soon; *i.e.*, those things were presented unto your minds by the Spirit of God will come to pass."[47] After awaking from an inspired dream, dreamers may have sudden strokes of ideas and know that those ideas are not their own but, rather, come from the Spirit. A dreamer may find that a dream has enlightened the mind, quickened understanding, or spoken peace to the soul, and often this enlightenment, understanding, or peace may come in the early morning hours.

All spiritual gifts, including dreams, are naturally uplifting because of the additional enlightenment we receive. One way to know if a dream comes from our Heavenly Father is to pay attention to the feelings that accompany the experience. God's nature is to be sacred, enlightening, sensible, natural, holy, dignified, and uplifting. Parley P. Pratt once said, "The gift of the Holy Spirit adapts itself to all these organs and attributes." He insisted that the Holy Ghost could quicken our intellectual faculties and increase, enlarge, expand, and purify our passions and affections. Other feelings that Elder Pratt described as coming from the Holy Ghost include inspiration, development, cultivation, joy, kindred feelings, affections, virtue, kindness, goodness, tenderness, gentleness, charity, beauty, form, health, vigor, animation, social feeling, invigoration, strength, and tone.[48] All of these attributes are positive in nature. When a person has experienced a spiritual dream, he or she will generally have such feelings after awaking.

Another test of whether a dream was inspired by the Holy Ghost is to ask if your feelings have become more sensitive. President Ezra Taft Benson stated that the Lord often prompts us through our feelings. The Holy Ghost can cause our feelings to become more tender and sensitive. Consequently, after experiencing a spiritual dream we may find ourselves radiating the influence of the Spirit, whom we have communed with in our dreams. We may have a greater capacity to love and be compassionate and also have the ability to comprehend spiritual things more fully.[49]

8. SPIRITUAL DREAMS CAN FEEL REAL

President Charles W. Penrose noted in general conference, "Dreams are very peculiar things. I have had some recently. They were very clear and plain. I have dreamed several times that I had passed out of the body and was in the other world, and I saw things and heard things. . . . Just what the cause of it was I cannot tell."[50] President Penrose experienced in a dream hearing and seeing through spiritual senses. Joseph Smith said, "All things whatsoever God [in] his infinite wisdom has seen fit and proper to reveal to us, while we are dwelling in mortality, . . . are revealed to us in the abstract, and independent of affinity of this mortal tabernacle; but are revealed to our spirits precisely as though we had no bodies at all."[51] That communication is through spiritual senses that can be as acute as our physical senses. Elder Parley P. Pratt taught that throughout history, God has revealed important information through dreams. He described that during slumber our spiritual senses can be vitalized in ways that are not displayed in our waking hours. Our spirits have the capacity to hear, see, feel, and talk. While we are asleep, Elder Pratt observed, "the spiritual organs are susceptible of converse with Deity, or of communion with angels, and the spirits of just men made perfect."[52]

In a spiritual dream, we may experience feelings, thoughts, or sights and also feel something that resembles physical contact. Elder Orson F. Whitney told of a dream in which he was physically embraced by the Savior. Gazing into His face, Elder Whitney realized the Savior was taller than he was. He awoke with a sob in his throat.[53] Likewise, Joseph F. Smith had a dream wherein he was able to feel warmth from touching the Prophet Joseph Smith's stomach with his own.[54] Others have felt a handshake in their dreams.

CONCLUSION

Most assuredly, dreams can be given to Latter-day Saints as a spiritual gift. Though many desire such experiences, they are not received simply by asking. Our Father in Heaven and Savior are willing to entreat, prompt, encourage, and patiently wait for us to recognize precious spiritual guidance from them, but they will not coerce, control, or dominate.[55]

President Joseph F. Smith once said, "Show me Latter-day Saints who have to feed upon miracles, signs and visions in order to keep them steadfast in the Church, and I will show you members of the Church who are not in good standing."[56] President Smith made that statement based on personal experience. When he was a boy, he would frequently ask the Lord to show him marvelous things so that he might receive a testimony. Though such manifestations were withheld from him, the Lord did show him truth—line upon line, precept upon precept, here a little and there a little until He had made known to President Smith the truth of the gospel "from the crown of [his] head to the souls of [his] feet, and until doubt and fear had been absolutely purged" from him.[57] The Lord did not have to send an angel, nor did He have to speak with the trump of an archangel or give a detailed dream. Instead, by the whisperings of the still small voice and the Spirit of the living God, he gave Joseph F. Smith a testimony.

No amount of marvelous manifestations or dreams will ever accomplish what the still small voice of the Holy Ghost does in giving us a sure witness that Jesus is the Christ, that The Church of Jesus Christ of Latter-day Saints is God's kingdom here on earth, and that the Book of Mormon is truly scripture. As President Joseph F. Smith once said, "It is obedience, humility, and submission to the requirements of heaven and to the order established in the kingdom of God upon the earth, that will establish men in the truth."[58]

CHAPTER 3

Scriptural Dreams

And he said, Hear now my words: If there be a prophet among you, I the Lord will make myself known unto him in a vision, and will speak unto him in a dream.
—NUMBERS 12:6

I have heard what the prophets said . . . saying, I have dreamed, I have dreamed. . . . The prophet that hath a dream, let him tell a dream.
—JEREMIAH 23:25, 28

The scriptures show that our Father in Heaven sometimes communicates to his children through dreams. The Lord can speak "in a dream, in a vision of the night, when deep sleep falleth upon men, in slumberings upon the bed, . . . openeth the ears of men, and sealeth their instruction" (Job 33:15–16).

While revelatory dreams are rare (there are only two dozen examples in all of the Standard Works), the scriptures confirm that revelation can originate in dreams.[1] In the Old Testament—which has the greatest number of scriptural dreams of any of the Standard Works, we read of revelatory dreams given to Jacob, Laban, Joseph, two men (a baker and a butler) from Pharaoh's court, the Egyptian pharaoh, King Abimelech, Nebuchadnezzar, Daniel, and others.[2] Surprisingly, in the New Testament, all of the dreams recorded are found within the book of Matthew. In the opening pages of the Book of Mormon, Lehi identifies himself as a visionary dreamer and receives several dreams from the Lord. Lehi's first two dreams cause him to leave Jerusalem and then send Nephi and his brothers back to Jerusalem to obtain the brass plates from Laban. Lehi also has a doctrinally significant dream regarding the tree of life. (It should also be noted that there are no dreams recorded in either the Doctrine and Covenants or the Pearl of Great Price.)

Scriptural dreams have had a profound effect on people living in previous dispensations. They provided comfort, warning, instruction, and were the difference between life and death for some individuals, and they continue to influence us today. This chapter lists dreams included in the Standard Works of The Church of Jesus Christ of Latter-day Saints. Each dream includes a short title, the name of the dreamer, the scriptural reference, and a brief synopsis.

OLD TESTAMENT

"SARAH IS ABRAHAM'S WIFE"
Abimelech (Genesis 20:1–18)

Abimelech, a Philistine king from southern Israel, is placed in a compromising situation when Abraham, who fears for his life, tells the king that Sarah is his sister. It is not clear why the king wants to take Sarah to wife. The situation is complicated by the fact that Sarah is with child—the promised heir of Israel. The Lord comes to Abimelech in a dream at night warning him about "the woman which thou has taken; for she is a man's wife" (v. 3). Instructions are given in the dream not to touch her and to restore the prophet his wife. Once Abimelech knows the truth, he is swift to return Sarah unharmed to Abraham.

"A LADDER TO HEAVEN"
Jacob (Genesis 28:10–22)

Jacob, son of Isaac and Rebekah and the grandson of Abraham, travels from Beersheba to Bethel. Using stones for a pillow, he dreams of a ladder that reaches to heaven with angels ascending and descending. He understands that the ladder leads to the gate of heaven. The Lord stood above the ladder and extended the Abrahamic covenant to him. Jacob is promised the land of Canaan, numerous posterity, and that the Messiah would come through his lineage.

"LEAVE HARAN"
Jacob (Genesis 31:10–21)

Jacob serves Laban, his mother's uncle, for fourteen years in exchange for his two wives, Leah and Rachel. In the course of Jacob's servitude to Laban, he is blessed with children and the Lord multiplies his flocks and those of Laban. Jacob is counseled in a dream "to return unto the land of thy fathers" (v.3), and he wastes no time. He consults with his wives, gathers his servants, his livestock, and all that belongs to him and departs for Canaan.

"TAKE NO RETRIBUTION"
Laban (Genesis 31:22–24)

Full of rage and vengeance after learning that Jacob has departed, Laban pursues Jacob for seven days and overtakes him on the eastern borders of Canaan at Mt. Gilead. Being accompanied by a number of his people, Laban might have used violence had he not been divinely warned in a dream to not impede his nephew's journey. Because of the dream, Laban allows Jacob and his daughters to escape into the borders of Canaan, but not before he speaks harsh words of false accusations and charges.

"SHEAVES OF WHEAT"
Joseph (Genesis 37:1–8)

While in the land of Canaan, seventeen-year-old Joseph, the son of Jacob and Rachel, has two dreams, the imagery of which varies. The first dream finds Joseph and his brothers binding sheaves in a field. Joseph's sheaf rises up while the sheaves of his brothers bow to his sheaf.

"THE SUN, MOON, AND STARS"
Joseph (Genesis 37:9–11)

In his second dream, Joseph dreams that the sun, the moon and eleven stars give obeisance to him. The meaning of the two dreams are one and the same. Obeisance, an act of reverence by bowing in honor, is given to young Joseph. The fact that he conveyed the dreams to his family suggests that he felt the dreams had significance and were sent by God, but doing so elicited his brothers' envy.

"INTERPRETING A BUTLER'S DREAM"
An Egyptian Butler (Genesis 40:1–15, 23)

Joseph was falsely accused and thrown into prison after attempted entrapment by his employer's wife. Despite his unfortunate circumstances, he did all within his power to help and serve others. Joseph exhibited the gift to interpret dreams. He was placed in charge of a butler and baker, who shared a dream with him and asked for the interpretation. The butler was told within three days the pharaoh would restore him to his former position. After Joseph's prophecy came true, the butler failed to give any credit to Joseph or even to remember him.

DREAMS AS REVELATION

"INTERPRETING A BAKER'S DREAM"
An Egyptian Baker (Genesis 40:16–22)

After interpreting the butler's dream, Joseph was asked to do the same for the pharaoh's chief baker. The baker was not as fortunate as the butler, and did not receive good news. In interpreting the baker's dream, Joseph explained that in three days, the pharaoh would have him hanged from a tree, and it was so.

"OF CORN AND COWS"
An Egyptian Pharaoh (Genesis 41:1–57)

The Egyptian pharaoh had two similar dreams that troubled him. In the first dream, seven fat cows were eaten by seven skinny cows. In his second dream, seven good ears of corn were devoured by seven bad ears of corn. After his magicians were unable to interpret his dreams, he summoned Joseph from prison. With assistance from God, Joseph correctly interpreted the pharaoh's dreams and taught the pharaoh that seven years of plenty would be followed by seven years of severe famine.

"BARLEY BREAD AND VICTORY"
An Israelite Man (Judges 7:13–15)

Gideon, a military hero who delivered Israel from Midianite oppression, learns of a dream that foreshadows his victory.

"GIVE THY SERVANT AN UNDERSTANDING HEART"
Solomon (1 Kings 3:5–15)

The Lord appeared to King Solomon in a dream and asked what he could give to Solomon. Solomon asked to receive "an understanding heart to judge thy people, that I may discern between good and bad" (v. 9). It pleased the Lord that Solomon "asked this thing, and has not asked for thyself long life; neither hast asked riches for thyself, nor hast asked the life of thine enemies; but hast asked for thyself understanding to discern judgment," and he granted Solomon's request (vv. 11–12).

"THE STONE CUT WITHOUT HANDS"
Nebuchadnezzar (Daniel 2:1–48)

Daniel's youthful obedience resulted in God giving him "understanding in all visions and dreams" (Daniel 1:17). King Nebuchadnezzar learned of Daniel's remarkable ability to know "of things both of heaven and in the earth" (Doctrine and Covenants 88:79) and asked him to reveal the dream and its interpretation. Daniel then pleaded with the "God of heaven concerning [the] secret" dreams that troubled Nebuchadnezzar (Daniel 2:18). The Lord showed Daniel a great image followed by a stone cut from the mountain without hands that destroyed the image. The stone, which represents the latter-day kingdom of God, grew and filled the entire earth (see Doctrine and Covenants 65:2). The Lord gave him assurance that he could boldly declare to Nebuchadnezzar: "The dream is certain, and the interpretation thereof sure" (Daniel 2:45). Not only did Daniel reveal the content of Nebuchadnezzar's dream but he rendered an interpretation that was acceptable to the King.

"DOWNFALL OF A KING"
Nebuchadnezzar (Daniel 4:4–27)

King Nebuchadnezzar received a troubling dream that his magicians and astrologers were unable to explain. The king summoned Daniel, who proclaimed the meaning of the dream, which was that the king would fall from power and lose his mind. Daniel also boldly called the king to repentance.

"FOUR BEASTS"
Daniel (Daniel 7)

Daniel's dream centered on the image or figure of four beasts. The beasts were compared to a lion with eagles' wings, a bear, a leopard with four heads, and a fourth beast that was indescribable. The beasts represented "four kings [or kingdoms], which shall arise out of the earth" (v. 17). He saw "the Son of man" (Christ) come to "the Ancient of days" (Adam) (v. 13).

NEW TESTAMENT

"TAKE UNTO THEE MARY THY WIFE"
Joseph (Matthew 1:18–25)

Joseph was a direct descendent of King David and best known for being Jesus's stepfather. Joseph, being a just man, had a mind to go against the prevailing practice of his day to not put away his espoused wife publically when she was found with child. As he contemplated his decision, an angel of the Lord appeared to him in a dream instructing him that the child was a son and his name was to be "Jesus: for he shall save his people from their sins" (v. 21). The angel counseled Joseph to take Mary as his wife. Upon rising from sleep, Joseph did as the angel instructed.

"DO NOT RETURN TO HEROD"
Wise Men from the East (Matthew 2:11–12)

Wise men traveled to Jerusalem from the east in order to worship Jesus. After presenting Jesus with gifts of gold, frankincense, and myrrh, they were warned by God in a dream that they were to return to their country without meeting with King Herod.

"FLEE TO EGYPT"
Joseph (Matthew 2:13–14)

After the wise men departed, an angel of the Lord visited Joseph, Jesus's stepfather, in a dream. Joseph was directed to take Mary and Jesus and flee into Egypt because King Herod sought to take Jesus's life. Joseph was informed that he was to remain in Egypt until directed by the angel to return.

SCRIPTURAL DREAMS

"RETURN TO ISRAEL"
Joseph (Matthew 2:19–21)

Joseph, Mary, and Jesus lived in Egypt until King Herod died. Following Herod's death, an angel of the Lord appeared unto Joseph in a dream and commanded him to return with his family to the land of Israel.

"GO TO GALILEE"
Joseph (Matthew 2:22)

After returning his family to the land of Israel from Egypt because of a dream he received from an angel of the Lord, Joseph received an additional dream telling him to move his family to Galilee.

"A WARNING FOR PILATE"
Pilate's Wife (Matthew 27:17–19)

After Jesus was arrested in Gethsemane, the chief priests and elders of the people conspired to put Jesus to death and delivered him to Pontius Pilate, the governor of Judaea. Pilate's interrogation proved fruitless, and he found no fault in Jesus. Looking for an alternative solution, Pilate appealed to the tradition to release a prisoner of the people's choosing at Passover. To Pilate's surprise, the people voted to release Barabbas, a criminal. Pilate's wife counseled Pilate to have "nothing to do with that just man: for I have suffered many things this day in a dream because of him" (v. 19). We do not know the imagery or details of her dream, but it obviously troubled her.

BOOK OF MORMON

"LEAVE JERUSALEM"
Lehi (1 Nephi 2:1–3)

Lehi, an Israelite prophet who was called to preach repentance to the inhabitants of Jerusalem about 600 years before the birth of

Christ, was commanded by the Lord in a dream to take his family and leave Jerusalem because people sought to take his life.

"OBTAIN THE BRASS PLATES"
Lehi (1 Nephi 3:2–4)

After fleeing from Jerusalem, Lehi was commanded in a dream that Nephi and his brothers were to return to Jerusalem and obtain plates of brass from Laban that contain Old Testament scriptural text and genealogical information.

"THE TREE OF LIFE"
Lehi (1 Nephi 8:2–38)

The prophet Lehi received a dream, which he defined as a vision, regarding the tree of life. The numerous symbolic elements of his dream included a dark and dreary wilderness, a man in a white robe, a large and spacious field, a tree with exceedingly white fruit that made partakers happy, a river of water, a rod of iron, a strait and narrow path, numberless people at varied locations, a mist of darkness, a great and spacious building, and a fountain. In subsequent chapters (1 Nephi 11–14), Nephi received an understanding and interpretation of his father's doctrinally important dream.

"DEPART OUT OF THE LAND"
Omer (Ether 9:1–3)

After being overthrown by secret combinations, Omer, a Jaredite king, was warned in a dream that he should leave.

THE DOCTRINE AND COVENANTS
There are no dreams recorded.

THE PEARL OF GREAT PRICE
There are no dreams recorded.

CHAPTER 4

Dreams in Joseph Smith's Family

Dreams given to members of Joseph Smith's family helped prepare them for the challenges and trials that they would face in coming years. An anticipation of the gospel was planted in their hearts by inspired dreams which made the Restoration that much more precious to them. When young Joseph shared his visions and revelations, his family members were ready to believe and sustain him.

The Prophet Joseph was raised in an extended family who believed in divinely inspired visions and dreams. LDS scholar Richard Lloyd Anderson argues that Joseph Smith "was immersed in genuine spirituality central in the lives of his grandparents, parents, and many of their brothers and sisters."[1] Their spiritual experiences served to bind the family in a common purpose. One night, for example, Solomon Mack, Joseph's maternal grandfather, saw a light and heard a voice calling his name. This experience was instrumental in Mack's conversion to Christ.[2]

Prior to Joseph's birth, his aunt Lovisa (one of Solomon Mack's

DREAMS AS REVELATION

daughters) was bedridden with a terrible sickness during which she was blessed with a vision or a dream.[3] Her subsequent words of exhortation had a deep effect on the faith of her younger sister Lucy who attended to her throughout her illness. Lucy, who later married and became the prophet's mother,[4] also received dreams that prepared her to support her son in his work.[5] Lucy's dreams greatly comforted her and prepared her mind and heart to receive the restored gospel.[6]

Lucy's husband, Joseph Smith Sr., also received a series of inspired dreams that prepared him to embrace the restored gospel and his son's prophetic calling. His dreams (which were received before the spring of 1820) were recorded by his wife, and at least two of them appear to relate to his son's future mission.[7] Dreams helped prepare Joseph Smith Sr. to accept what his son learned directly from the Savior—that the religions of the world were in a general state of apostasy. Scholar Richard L. Bushman explains that Joseph Senior's dreams show both "a profound skepticism about the authenticity of the churches" and "a visionary yearning to find God and salvation." Thus, he was "open to forms of religion that the educated Protestant clergy considered outlandish or heretical"—which is perhaps a fitting description of the religious truths restored through his son.[8]

The Prophet Joseph did not record what effect his family's dreams had on his beliefs. Certainly, his confidence in dreams as divine manifestations was initially rooted in the experience and faith of his mother and father.[9] In the words of historian Mark L. McConkie, "What better place to raise a prophet than in the home of a prophet [and a prophetess]?"[10] Indeed, the dreams of the Prophet's immediate and extended family turned their hearts to each other and to the Lord, preparing them to accept and support Joseph Smith Jr. as the Lord's ordained prophet.

In early Church records, there are references to several dreams attributed to Joseph Smith Jr.[11] They were recorded by Joseph himself, his clerks, or others who interacted with him. For the most part, Joseph's dreams include no explanation, by either him or the recorder, concerning their purpose or interpretation. Yet, we know that Joseph viewed dreams as a legitimate channel of revelation, as evidenced in the fact that he recorded his dreams and used them in his public sermons.

"TRAVELING IN AN OPEN, BARREN FIELD"
Joseph Smith Sr. (Related by Lucy Mack Smith)

[This dream was received prior to Joseph Smith's First Vision.]

One night my husband retired to his bed, in a very thoughtful state of mind, contemplating the situation of the Christian religion, or the confusion and discord that were extant. He soon fell into a sleep, and before waking had the following vision, which I shall relate in his own words just as he told it to me the next morning:

"I seemed to be traveling in an open, barren field, and as I was traveling, I turned my eyes towards the east, the west, the north, and the south, but could see nothing save dead, fallen timber. Not a vestige of life, either animal or vegetable, could be seen; besides, to render the scene still more dreary, the most deathlike silence prevailed; no sound of anything animate could be heard in all the field.

"I was alone in this gloomy desert, with the exception of an attendant spirit, who kept constantly by my side. Of him I inquired the meaning of what I saw, and why I was thus travelling in such a dismal place. He answered thus: 'This field is the world which now lieth inanimate and dumb, in regard to the true religion, or plan of salvation; but travel on, and by the wayside you will find on a certain log a box, the contents of which, if you eat thereof, will make you wise, and give unto you wisdom and understanding.'

"I carefully observed what was told me by my guide, and proceeding a short distance, I came to the box. I immediately took it up, and placed it under my left arm. Then with eagerness I raised the lid, and began to taste of its contents; upon which all manner of beasts, horned cattle, and roaring animals, rose up on every side in the most threatening manner possible, tearing the earth, tossing their horns, and bellowing most terrifically all around me, and they finally came so close upon me, that I was compelled to drop the box, and fly for my life. Yet, in the midst of all this I was perfectly happy, though I awoke trembling."

From this forward my husband seemed more confirmed than ever in the opinion that there was no order or class of religionists that knew any more concerning the kingdom of God, than those of the world, or such as made no profession of religion whatever.

SOURCE: Lucy Mack Smith, *Lucy's Book*, 294–96.

"A FRUIT SO DELICIOUS"
Joseph Smith Sr. (Related by Lucy Mack Smith)

In 1811, we moved from Royalton, Vermont, to the town of Lebanon, New Hampshire. Soon after arriving here, my husband received another very singular vision, which I will relate:—

"I thought," said he, "I was travelling in an open, desolate field, which appeared to be very barren. As I was thus travelling, the thought suddenly came into my mind that I had better stop and reflect upon what I was doing, before I went any further. So I asked myself, 'What motive can I have in travelling here, and what place can this be?' My guide, who was by my side, as before, said, 'This is the desolate world; but travel on.' The road was so broad and barren that I wondered why I should travel in it; for, said I to myself, 'Broad is the road, and wide is the gate that leads to death, and many there be that walk therein; but narrow is the way, and straight is the gate that leads to everlasting life, and few there be that go in thereat.' Travelling a short distance further, I came to a narrow path. This path I entered, and, when I had travelled a little way in it, I beheld a beautiful stream of water which ran from the east to the west. Of this stream I could see neither the source nor yet the termination; but as far as my eyes could extend I could see a rope, running along the bank of it, about as high as a man could reach, and beyond me was a low, but very pleasant valley, in which stood a tree such as I, had never seen before. It was exceedingly handsome, insomuch that I looked upon it with wonder and admiration. Its beautiful branches spread themselves somewhat like an umbrella, and it bore a kind of fruit, in shape much like a chestnut bur, and as white as snow, or, if possible, whiter. I gazed upon the same with considerable interest, and as I was doing so, the burs or shells commenced opening and shedding their particles, or the fruit which they contained, which was of dazzling whiteness. I drew near, and began to eat of it, and I found it delicious beyond description. As I was eating, I said in my heart, 'I cannot eat this alone, I must bring my wife and children, that they may partake with me.' Accordingly, I went and brought my family, which consisted of a wife and seven children, and we all commenced eating and praising God for this blessing. We were exceedingly happy, insomuch that our joy could not easily be expressed. While thus engaged, I beheld a spacious building standing opposite the valley which we were in, and it appeared to reach to the very heavens. It was full of doors and windows, and they were all filled with people, who were very finely dressed. When these people observed us in the low valley, under the tree, they pointed the finger of scorn at us, and treated us with all manner of disrespect and contempt. But their contumely we utterly disregarded. I presently turned to my guide, and inquired of him the meaning of the fruit that was so delicious. He told me it was the pure love of God, shed abroad in the hearts of all those who love him, and keep his commandments. He then commanded me to go and bring the rest of my children. I told him that we were all there. 'No,' he replied, 'look yonder, you have two more, and you must bring them also.' Upon raising my eyes, I saw two small children standing some distance off. I immediately went to them, and brought them to the tree; upon which they commenced eating with the rest, and we all rejoiced together. The more we [ate], the more we seemed to desire, until we even got down upon our knees, and scooped it up, eating it by double handfulls. After feasting in this manner a short time, I asked my guide what was the meaning of the spacious building which I saw. He replied, 'It is Babylon, it is Babylon, and it must fall. The people in the doors and windows are the inhabitants thereof, who scorn and despise the Saints of God, because of their humility.' I soon awoke, clapping my hands together for joy."

Source: Lucy Mack Smith, *Lucy's Book*, 296–98.

"I WAS NOW MADE QUITE WHOLE"
Joseph Smith Sr. (Related by Lucy Mack Smith)

"I thought I was walking alone; I was much fatigued, nevertheless, I continued traveling. It seemed to me that I was going to meeting, that it was the Day of Judgment, and that I was going to be judged.

"When I came in sight of the meetinghouse, I saw multitudes of people coming from every direction, and pressing with great anxiety towards the door of this great building; but I thought I should get there in time, hence there was no need of being in a hurry. But, on arriving at the door, I found it shut. I knocked for admission and was informed by the porter that I had come too late. I felt exceedingly troubled and prayed earnestly for admittance.

"Presently I found that my flesh was perishing. I continued to pray, still my flesh withered upon my bones. I was in a state of almost total despair, when the porter asked me if I had done all that was necessary in order to receive admission. I replied that I had done all that was in my power to do. 'Then,' observed the porter, 'justice must be satisfied; after this, mercy hath her claims.'

"It then occurred to me to call upon God, in the name of his Son Jesus; and I cried out, in the agony of my soul, 'Oh, Lord God, I beseech thee, in the name of Jesus Christ, to forgive my sins.' After which I felt considerably strengthened and I began to mend.

The porter or angel then remarked that it was necessary to plead the merits of Jesus, for he was the advocate with the Father, and a Mediator between God and man.

"I was now made quite whole and the door was opened, but on entering, I awoke."

SOURCE: Lucy Mack Smith, *Revised and Enhanced History*, 89–90.

"YIELDING TO THE GOSPEL"
Lucy Mack Smith

While we were yet living in the town of Tunbridge [Vermont], my mind became deeply impressed with the subject of religion, which probably was occasioned by my singular experience during my sickness at Randolph. I commenced attending Methodist meetings and endeavored to persuade my husband to attend with me. . . .

As soon as his father and Brother Jesse[12] heard that we were attending Methodist meetings, they were much displeased. . . . Accordingly, my husband requested me not to go, as he considered it hardly worth our while to attend any longer, and it would prove of but little advantage to us, and it gave our friends such disagreeable feelings.

I was very much hurt by this, but did not reply to him then. I retired to a grove of handsome wild cherry trees not far distant and prayed to the Lord that he would influence the heart of my husband that it might be softened so as to receive the true gospel whenever it was preached, or that he might become more religiously inclined. After praying some time in this manner, I returned to the house much depressed in spirit, which state of feeling continued until I retired to my bed. That night I had the following dream:

I thought that I stood in a large and beautiful meadow, which lay a short distance from the house in which we lived, and that everything around me wore an aspect of peculiar pleasantness. The first thing that attracted my special attention in this magnificent meadow was a very pure and clear stream of water which ran through the midst of it; and as I traced this stream, I discovered two trees standing upon its margin, both of which were on the same side of the stream. These trees were very beautiful. They were well proportioned, and towered with majestic beauty to a great height. Their branches, which added to their symmetry and glory, commenced near the top and spread themselves in luxurious grandeur around. I gazed upon them with wonder and admiration, and after beholding them a short time, I saw one of them was surrounded with a bright belt that shone like burnished gold, but far more brilliantly. Presently, a gentle breeze passed by, and the tree encircled with this golden zone bent gracefully before the wind and waved its beautiful branches in the light air. As the wind increased, this tree assumed the most lively and animated appearance and seemed to express in its motions the utmost joy and happiness. If it had been an intelligent creature, it could not have conveyed by the power of language the idea of joy and gratitude so perfectly as it did; and even the stream that rolled beneath it shared, apparently, every sensation felt by the tree, for, as the branches danced over the stream, it would swell gently, then recede again with a motion as soft as the breathing of an infant, but as lively as the dancing of a sunbeam. The belt also partook of the same influence, and, as it moved in unison with the motion of the stream and of the tree, it increased continually in refulgence and magnitude until it became exceedingly glorious.

I turned my eyes upon its fellow, which stood opposite; but it was not surrounded with the belt of light as the former, and it stood erect and fixed as a pillar of marble. No matter how strong the wind blew over it, not a leaf was stirred, not a bough was bent, but obstinately stiff it stood, scorning alike the zephyr's breath, or the power of the mighty storm.

I wondered at what I saw, and said in my heart, What can be the meaning of all this? And the interpretation given me was that these personated my husband and his oldest brother, Jesse Smith; that the stubborn and unyielding tree was like Jesse; that the other, more pliant and flexible, was like Joseph, my husband; that the breath of heaven, which passed over them, was the pure and undefiled gospel of the Son of God, which gospel Jesse would always resist, but which Joseph, when he was more advanced in life, would hear and receive with his whole heart and rejoice therein; and unto him would be added intelligence, happiness, glory, and everlasting life.

SOURCE: Lucy Mack Smith, *Revised and Enhanced History*, 58–60.

"TWO SNAKES LOCKED FAST TOGETHER"
Joseph Smith Jr. (Related by Miles Romney)[13]

<June 13, 1844>

Joseph Smith the Prophet and Seer gave out An Appointment to preach in the Seventy Hall. About A Week before he was Martyred At Carthage Jail

And When the Meeting Was Convened He Arose and said he did not feel A Disposition to preach being very much oppressed in Spirit So he Appointed George J. Adams to speak in his place . . . After he had done the P[reaching?]/ Prophet Arose and Stated the Reason why he did not speak he felt much oppressed

But he would Relate a Dream that he had the night before Which was in Substance as follows

I ~~He~~ was Riding out by the temple in his Carriage. He had not gone far Whith my g[u]ardian Angel along with ~~him~~ me Which was Always the Case ~~they~~ we had not gone far before ~~they~~ we espeyed [spied] Two Large Snakes So fast Locked together that either of them had no power

I then enquired of my guide what they meant

~~He said,~~ He Answered Them Snakes, that you see Represents Doctor Foster and C[h]auncey Higbee they are your enemies and

Desire to Destroy you But you see they are so fast locked together that they have no power and Can do you no harm

SOURCE: Miles Romney Report.

"RIDING UP MULHOLLAND STREET"
Joseph Smith Jr. (Related by Miles Romney)

[William Law, called by the Lord in 1841 (Doctrine and Covenants 124:91) to serve as Joseph Smith's second counselor in the First Presidency, later turned against the Prophet and published the *Nauvoo Expositor* with his brother Wilson and others. Miles Romney reported hearing Joseph Smith relate the following dream, and it is written in Joseph's voice.]

<June 13, 1844>[14]

He I then Dreamt again that he I was Riding Up Mulholland Street [in Nauvoo, Illinois] But he I had not his my Conducter along with him me As Always was the case before this time. When he I Came to the edge of the Priare [prairie] Who Should he I see Approaching him me But Wm and Wilson Law Saying . . Ah . . Ah . . Ah . . now we have got you at Last We will secure you and put you in a Safe place. And Without any Ceremony, Dragged Me out of my Carriage. And Let me to the Edge of the Wood W[h]ere they had prepared a Deep Pit for the Purpose They put <me> Down into it Then Turned and went Away.

They had not been gone long . . When I heard them Calling out with all their Might . . Joseph . . Joseph . . Joseph . . Come to our help I repl[i]ed . . You have put me into this Deep pit And I can not get out

I then made a spring And I Caught hold of the grass which was growing at the edge of the pit with my fingers and pulled myself up saw has I could see on the priare And at Little Distance I there beheld that A large snake had twisted itself around Wilson Law and grabbed him by the arm A little above the elbow and was fast strangling him, A little further, I, saw That a great Bear had Laid hold a <William

Law> ~~him~~ and was tearing him to pieces At this time I heard my name Called Joseph, Joseph, What in goodness are you Doing here

I Looked up and Saw my g[u]ardian Angel coming <bounding> over the fence, I said my enemies hath put me here

He Said take hold of my hand I did so He jerked me out of the pid And said follow me And he Led me of[f] in an oppisite Direction

I then Awoke

This is the Dream

And the interpretation you can give for yourselves

Miles Romney A hearer

Source: Miles Romney Report.

"I SAW MYSELF DRIVEN FROM CARTHAGE"
Joseph Smith Jr. (Related by Dan Jones)

[The following incident occurred in Carthage Jail. The actual dreamer is unknown.]

Amusing conversation on various interesting topics engaged us till late; after prayer, which made Carthage prison into the gate of heaven for awhile, we lay promiscuously on the floor the last words spoken were, by the Prophet,— "For the most intelligent dream tonight bretheren;" and the first words spoken next morning were by him also enquiring for the same. None, save one, were told which was listened to by all as follows— "Portrayed before my mind was Gov. Ford and troops on their way across the prairie to Nauvoo, the prisoners had plead in vain to return with him, although promised by him to go; with a letter of importance I saw myself driven from Carthage, galloping through the masses of medley soldiers, half Indians and semi barbarians, I hurried across the prairie, had gone down on a boat from Nauvoo towards Quincy, but while landed at Warsaw awoke, in the midst of powder, smoke, death, and carnage."

The Prophet reply'd it was ominous of future events, nor did he believe the Governor would ever take him to Nauvoo alive.

Source: Dan Jones, "The Martrydom of Joseph Smith and His Brother Hyrum," 98.

"ONE OF JOSEPH SMITH'S LAST DREAMS"
Joseph Smith Jr. (Related by W. W. Phelps)

In June 1844, when Joseph Smith went to Carthage and delivered himself up to Governor Ford, I accompanied him, and while on the way thither, he related to me and his Brother Hyrum the following dream.

He said: "While I was at Jordan's in Iowa the other night, I dreamed that myself and my brother Hyrum went on board a large steamboat lying in a small bay, near the great ocean. Shortly after we went on board there was an alarm of fire, and I discovered that the boat had been anchored some distance from the shore out in the bay, and that an escape from the fire, in the confusion, appeared hazardous: but, as delay was folly, Hyrum and I jumped overboard, and tried our faith at walking upon the water.

"At first we sank in the water nearly to our knees, but as we proceeded we increased in faith, and were soon able to walk upon the water. On looking towards the burning boat in the east, we saw that it was drifting towards the wharf and the town with a great flame and clouds of smoke; and, as if by whirlwind, the town was taking fire, too, so that the scene of destruction and horror of the frightened inhabitants were terrible.

"We proceeded on the bosom of the mighty deep and were soon out of sight of land. The ocean was still; the rays of the sun were bright and we forgot all the troubles of our mother earth. Just at that moment I heard the sound of a human voice, and turning around, saw my brother Samuel H. approaching towards us from the east. We stopped and he came up. After a moment's conversation he informed me that he had been lonesome back there, and had made up his mind to go with me across the mighty deep.

"We all started again, and in a short time were blest with the first sight of a city, whose gold and silver steeples and towers were more beautiful than any that I had ever seen or heard of on earth. It stood, as it were upon the western shore of the mighty deep we walking on, and its order and glory seemed far beyond the wisdom of man. While we were gazing upon the perfection of the city a small boat launched off from the port, and, almost as quick as thought, came to us. In an instant they took us on board and saluted with welcome, and with music such as is not of earth. The next scene, on landing, was more than I can describe; the greeting of old friends, the music from a thousand towers, and the light of God Himself at the return of three of His sons, soothed my soul into quiet and a joy that I felt as if I were truly in heaven. I gazed upon the splendor; I greeted my friends. I awoke, and lo, it was a dream!

"While I meditated upon such a marvelous scene, I fell asleep again, and behold I stood near the shore of the burning boat, and there was great consternation among the officers, crew and passengers of the flaming craft, as there seemed to be much ammunition or powder on board. The alarm was given that the fire was near the magazine, and in a moment, suddenly, it blew up with a great noise, and sank in the deep water with all on board. I then turned to the country east, among the bushy openings, and saw William and Wilson Law, endeavoring to escape from the wild beasts of the forest, but two lions rushed out of a thicket and devoured them. I awoke again." I will say that Joseph never told this dream again, as he was martyred about two days after. I relate from recollection as nearly as I can.

SOURCE: W. W. Phelps, *Joseph Smith's Last Dream*, 1–9.

"MY OLD FARM IN KIRTLAND"
Joseph Smith Jr.

<June 27, 1844> [Carthage Jail] . . .

Joseph related the following dream which he had last night:

"I was back in Kirtland, Ohio, and thought I would take a walk out by myself, and view my old farm, which I found grown up with weeds and brambles, and altogether bearing evidence of neglect and want of culture. I went into the barn which I found without floor or doors, with the weather boarding off, and was altogether in keeping with the farm. While I viewed the desolation around me, and was contemplating how it might be recovered from the curse upon it, there came rushing into the barn a company of furious men, who commenced to pick a quarrel with me. The leader of the party ordered me to leave the barn and <the> farm, stating it was none of mine, and that I must give up all hope of ever possessing it. I told him the farm was given me by the Church, and although I had not had any use of it for some time back, still I had not sold it, and according to righteous principles it belonged to me or the Church. He then grew furious, and began to rail upon me and threaten me, and said it never did belong to me nor the Church. I then told him that I did not think it worth contending about; that I had no desire to live upon it in its present state, and if he thought he had a better right I would not quarrel with him about it, but leave; but my assurance that I would not trouble him at present did not seem to satisfy him, as he seemed determined to quarrel with me, and threatened me with the destruction of my body. While he was thus engaged, pouring out his bitter words upon me, a rabble rushed in and nearly filled the barn, drew out their knives, and began to quarrel among themselves for the premises; and for a moment forgot me, at which time I took the opportunity to walk out of the barn about up to my ankles in mud. When I was a little distance from the barn I heard them screeching and screaming in a very distressed manner, as it appeared they had engaged in a general fight with their knives. While they were thus engaged the dream or vision ended."

SOURCE: "History, 1838–1856, volume F-1," 177–78.

"WARNED OF GOD TO COME IMMEDIATELY"
Samuel H. Smith (Related by Lucy Mack Smith)

I [Lucy Mack Smith] came to the man and asked him how far it was to Kirtland. He started up and exclaimed, "Is this Mother Smith?"

"Yes, sir," I said. "We would like to know whether there is any chance of procuring teams to take our goods to Kirtland."

"And is it possible that this is Mother Smith?" said he. "I have sat here three days and nights looking for you. Do not give yourself any uneasiness. Brother Joseph is expected here every hour, and in less than twenty-four hours there will be twenty teams on hand to take the goods from here to houses that are waiting to receive them."

When he mentioned Joseph's name I started, for I just began to realize that I was so soon to see my husband and three oldest sons. As I turned from the stranger, the first thing that met my eyes was Samuel coming towards me. We met in tears of joy, but before I could speak to him, Joseph came up and caught hold of my other hand. "Mother," said Samuel. "I was warned of God in a dream to come immediately to this place to meet the company from Waterloo, and I was afraid that some dreadful thing had befallen you. Indeed, I feared that you were dead and that I should only meet your corpse."

Joseph also seemed overjoyed to find me in so good health and said, "I was myself in great fear for your life, for Brother Humphrey came to Kirtland three days since and told me he thought there was great danger of your wearing yourself out before you got here. He said you had been a perfect servant to the company all the way along, but Mother, I shall now take you away from them and you shall have no more to do with it."

SOURCE: Lucy Mack Smith, *Revised and Enhanced History*, 272–73.

CHAPTER 5

Dreams of the Savior

In the scriptures, the Savior affirms that we "shall see my face and know that I am" (Doctrine and Covenants 93:1). It should come as no surprise, then, that the Savior would appear to men and women in dreams. The children of God in all nations have His promise that He can manifest Himself to them. The Book of Mormon teaches, "He manifesteth himself unto all those who believe in him, by the power of the Holy Ghost; yea, unto every nation, kindred, tongue, and people, working mighty miracles, signs and wonders, among the children of men according to their faith" (2 Nephi 26:13). Certainly, the Lord is no respecter of persons when it comes to whom He will manifest Himself unto. This chapter attests to the fact that our Savior, Jesus Christ, can appear in dreams to those who believe in him according to their faith.

Of all the dreams included in this book, those of the Savior are among the greatest in importance and consequence. The Savior teaches in the Doctrine and Covenants that "to some is given by the Holy

Ghost to know that Jesus Christ is the Son of God, and that he was crucified for the sins of the world" (Doctrine and Covenants 46:13). That knowledge—to know that Jesus Christ is the Son of God—is worth more than all the riches in the world. That Jesus forgives us of our sins, mends our broken hearts, raises us up from beds of affliction, and calms our troubled souls are illustrated in this chapter.

For those who have experienced dreams of Jesus Christ, there is a surprising similarity from one dream to another. Often an encounter with the Savior in a dream speaks of a kiss or an embrace where the recipient is wrapped in the warmth of His arms in an indescribable emotion of love that penetrates to the very soul of the dreamer. The Savior's embrace leaves a lingering feeling of inexpressible joy and love for all mankind. Dreams of the Savior often communicate to the recipient that Christ knows of the dreamer's trials, heartaches, difficulties, and challenges. Some dreams of the Savior recount the events of His ministry, including His Atonement and crucifixion, while other dreams of the Savior give comfort, warning, chastisement, or encouragement. Dreams of the Savior are a cherished gift.

"I SHALL NEVER FORGET THAT SMILE"
Melvin J. Ballard

"When I was doing missionary work with some of our brethren, laboring among the Indians, seeking the Lord for light to decide certain matters pertaining to our work there, and receiving a witness from Him that we were doing things according to His will, I found myself one evening in the dreams of the night, in that sacred building, the Temple. After a season of prayer and rejoicing, I was informed that I should have the privilege of entering into one of those rooms, to meet a glorious Personage, and as I entered the door, I saw, seated on the raised platform, the most glorious Being my eyes ever have beheld, or that I ever conceived existed in all the eternal worlds. As I approached to be introduced, he arose and stepped towards me with extended arms, and he smiled as he softly spoke my name. If I shall live to be a million years old, I shall never forget that smile. He took me into his arms and kissed me, and pressed me to His bosom, and blessed me, until the marrow of my bones seemed to melt! When He had finished, I fell at His feet, and as I bathed them with my tears and kisses, I saw the prints of the nails in the feet of the Redeemer of the world. The feeling that I had in the presence of Him who hath all things in His hands, to have His love, His affection, and His blessings was such that if I ever can receive that of which I had but a foretaste, I would give all that I am, all that I ever hope to be, to feel what I then felt!"

SOURCE: Bryant S. Hinckley, *The Faith of Our Pioneer Fathers*, 226–27.

"HE TOOK ME IN HIS ARMS"
Mary Stevenson Clark

I had a dream of seeing the Saviour. He took me in His arms. We sat in a circle. He blessed and kissed us. It was only the members who accepted the Gospel that sat in the circle. I told Mother my dream. She said it was a good dream and for me to be a good girl. I was about 7 years old.

SOURCE: Mark L. McConkie, *Remembering Joseph*, 213.

"YOU HAVE DONE IT UNTO ME"
(Related by J. Richard Clarke)

"Many years ago in a small town in the southern part of the state of Utah, my great grandmother was called to be the president of the Relief Society. During this period of our Church's history there existed a very bitter and antagonistic spirit between the Mormons and the Gentiles.

"In my great grandmother's ward one of the young sisters married a gentile boy. This of course did not please either the Mormons or the Gentiles very much. In the course of time this young couple gave birth to a child. Unfortunately the mother became so ill in the process of childbirth that she was unable to care for her baby. Upon learning of this woman's condition, great grandmother immediately went to the homes of the sisters in the ward and asked them if they would take a turn going into the home of this young couple to care for the baby. One by one these women refused and so the responsibility fell completely upon her.

"She would arise early in the morning, walk what was a considerable distance to the home of this young couple where she would bathe and feed the baby, gather all that needed to be laundered and take it with her to her home. . . . One morning she felt too weak and sick to go. . . . However, as she lay in bed she realized that if she didn't go the child would not be provided for. [With the help of the Lord,] she mustered all her strength and went. [When she returned home, exhausted, she] collapsed into a large chair and immediately fell into a deep sleep. She said that as she slept she felt as if she were consumed by a fire that would melt the very marrow of her bones. She . . . dreamed that she was bathing the Christ child and glorying in what a great privilege it would have been to have bathed the Son of God. Then the voice of the Lord spoke to her saying, 'Inasmuch as ye have done it unto the least of these, ye have done it unto me.'"

SOURCE: J. Richard Clarke, "Love Extends beyond Convenience," 81.

"YOU ARE WORTHY"
(Related by Liriel Domiciano)

As a youthful convert to the Church in São Paulo, Brazil, Liriel Domiciano would often shed tears as she would hear broadcasts or recordings of the Mormon Tabernacle Choir. On March 21, [2004,] the 22-year-old singer, who has achieved fame and popularity in her homeland as a recording artist under her first name Liriel, performed as a soloist with the [Tabernacle Choir] during its nationwide broadcast. It was, for her, the fulfillment of a dream. . . .

Liriel found The Church of Jesus Christ of Latter-day Saints through a family friend who, when Liriel was young, would come to the house to work and occasionally care for the children.

"This girl, whenever she was in our home and was near me, I always felt some special spirit about her," Liriel recalled. "She always sang songs from the Primary, and the music I still remember. Then she began to talk to my mother about the Church. She asked my mother to pray and said if she would pray with a pure heart and real intent, that God would answer her prayers and tell her that the Church was the true Church."

The mother believed those words and prayed. Then, she went to sleep and dreamed of being near the Salt Lake Temple by a garden of beautiful flowers. In the dream, a man in the distance called to her to come to him. "This was not a common man; she knew that. It was Christ Himself. And He called her to come into the temple. My mother said, 'No, I'm not worthy to go in the temple.' 'You come; you are worthy, and I will show you inside.' And when she went inside, He asked her to take off her shoes and He showed her through the temple—everything that was beautiful within the walls of the temple. This was a response to her prayer, that she had this dream, and she felt like this was the answer to her prayer asking if the Church was the right direction to take her family."

Liriel's mother did not share that experience with her daughter until she was 14. Liriel said, "I didn't have one doubt that my mother was telling me the truth. . . . I thought, 'Why didn't she tell me about this dream before? I would have entered the Church before the age of 14.'"

SOURCE: R. Scott Lloyd, "Longtime dream to sing with choir," 6.

"SHE PRAYED HE WOULD NEVER LOOK AWAY"
(Related by Linda and Richard Eyre)

A friend of ours had a dream that she has never forgotten. Unlike most dreams that fade, this one somehow grows stronger. In it she was sitting on a mountainside overlooking a blue lake and listening to one who stood, speaking, holding his audience spellbound. She became aware that it was Christ, that he was giving the Sermon on the Mount. The feeling she remembers is one of awe and of fear: fear that he would look at her, that his eyes would meet hers, and that he would see into her, through her, discovering all her faults. She prayed that he would not look.

And then he did look at her, directly into her eyes. In an instant her fear was transformed into love. She knew that he saw all that she was, all that was inside her. But she also knew he would always love her. She was warmed and softened and lifted by his gaze. She prayed that he would never look away.

SOURCE: Linda and Richard Eyre, *Teaching Children Charity*, 39.

"APPROVED OF THE LORD"
Charles N. Lund

[November, 1857]

A short time after my baptism, I dreamed one night I was standing at the place where I was baptized and I saw the Savior coming in the clouds of heaven, and as I looked at him I saw him wave his hand, and then the heavens rolled together like a scroll. This dream impressed me that what I had done was approved of the Lord.

I did not then know all that the gospel is and what it will do for people, but in fifty years I have learned much. From the hour of receiving it, I have never doubted nor wavered, and bear testimony today to its wonderful truth and saving power.

SOURCE: "Conversion and Testimony of the Late President C. N. Lund," 59–60.

"THE CITY ETERNAL"
David O. McKay

In 1921 [President] David O. McKay (1873–1970) . . . made a world tour of the missions of the Church. While aboard a ship nearing Apia, Samoa, he had a beautiful [dream]. President McKay wrote:

"Towards evening, the reflection of the afterglow of a beautiful sunset was most splendid! The sky was tinged with pink, and the clouds lingering around the horizon were fringed with various hues of crimson and orange, while the heavy cloud farther to the west was sombre purple and black. These various colors cast varying shadows on the peaceful surface of the water. Those from the cloud were long and dark, those from the crimson-tinged sky, clear but rose-tinted and fading into a faint pink that merged into the clear blue of the ocean. Gradually, the shadows became deeper and heavier, and then all merged into a beautiful calm twilight that made the sea look like a great mirror upon which fell the faint light of the crescent moon!

"Pondering still upon this beautiful scene, I lay in my berth at ten o'clock that night, and thought to myself: Charming as it is, it doesn't stir my soul with emotion as do the innocent lives of children, and the sublime characters of loved ones and friends. Their beauty, unselfishness, and heroism are after all the most glorious!

"I then fell asleep, and beheld in vision something infinitely sublime. In the distance I beheld a beautiful white city. Though far away, yet I seemed to realize that trees with luscious fruit, shrubbery with gorgeously-tinted leaves, and flowers in perfect bloom abounded everywhere. The clear sky above seemed to reflect these beautiful shades of color. I then saw a great concourse of people approaching the city. Each one wore a white flowing robe. . . . Instantly my attention seemed centered upon their Leader, and though I could see only the profile of his features and his body, I recognized him at once as my Savior! The tint and radiance of his countenance were glorious to behold! There was a peace about him which seemed sublime—it was divine!

"The city, I understood, was his. It was the City Eternal; and the people following him were to abide there in peace and eternal happiness.

"But who were they?

"As if the Savior read my thoughts, he answered by pointing to a semicircle that then appeared above them, and on which were written in gold the words:

> *'These Are They Who Have Overcome The World—*
> *Who Have Truly Been Born Again!'*

"When I awoke, it was breaking day over Apia harbor."

SOURCE: David O. McKay, *Cherished Experiences*, 101–2.

"THE SAME SENSE OF LOVE"
George F. Richards (Related by Spencer W. Kimball)

"The Lord has revealed to men by dreams something more than I ever understood or felt before." I heard this more than once in quorum meetings of the Council of the Twelve when George F. Richards was president. . . . He said, "I believe in dreams, brethren. The Lord has given me dreams which to me are just as real and as much from God as was the dream of King Nebuchadnezzar . . . or the dream of Lehi who through a dream led his colony out of the old country across the mighty deep to this promised land, or any other dreams that we might read in the scriptures.

"It is not out of place for us to have important dreams," he said. "And then more than 40 years ago I had a dream which I am sure was from the Lord. In this dream I was in the presence of my Savior as he stood mid-air. He spoke no word to me, but my love for him was such that I have not words to explain. I know that no mortal man can love the Lord as I experienced that love for the Savior unless God reveals it to him. I would have remained in his presence, but there was a power drawing me away from him.

"As a result of that dream, I had this feeling that no matter what might be required of my hands, what the gospel might entail unto me, I would do what I should be asked to do even to the laying down of my life. . . .

"If only I can be with my Savior and have that same sense of love that I had in that dream, it will be the goal of my existence, the desire of my life."

SOURCE: Spencer W. Kimball, "The Cause Is Just and Worthy," 119.

"MAKE EVERY SACRIFICE NECESSARY"
George F. Richards

"Last night I dreamed of seeing the Savior and embracing him. The feelings I cannot describe, but I think it was a touch of heaven. I never expect anything better hereafter. The love of man for woman cannot compare with it. May we be faithful and make every sacrifice necessary . . . to live in His presence forever."

SOURCE: Lucile C. Tate, *LeGrand Richards*, 47.

"IT WAS A MOST WONDERFUL THING"
LeGrand Richards (Related by Lucile C. Tate)

Soon after [the October 1925] general conference Bishop [LeGrand] Richards faced President Frank Y. Taylor of Granite Stake with these words: "You heard what President Grant said. Financially I am as able as any man in my ward to go on such a mission, and I am not the kind of man to pass the buck. So if you want me to go, I am willing to do it."

"I will take up the matter with President Grant," President Taylor responded.

DREAMS OF THE SAVIOR

He did, and with no hesitation President Grant said, "Send him." A short-term mission call to the Eastern States soon followed, with instructions to leave on January 6, 1926. . . . After the long train journey to New York City, they reported first to the mission president, B. H. Roberts, a member of the First Council of the Seventy. . . . [Elder Richards was assigned to serve in New Bedford, Massachusetts and experienced both success and rejection.]

. . . Before the elders left for a mission conference in Boston, however, others showed great sincerity and real promise as repeat visits were made and the gospel was more fully taught to them. The conference was to be presided over by Church President Heber J. Grant, and President B. H. Roberts would of course be there. There was a good deal of anticipation of a spiritual feast. . . . At the conference he would also learn of his mission release. It was disappointing, however, that after the public announcements made and the encouragement given to the people, attendance at the meetings was poor and there were few strangers there. New Bedford had a better showing than most of the branches. There was no explanation for the poor attendance except that many members were not sufficiently committed to make the trip and that people in general were "simply not hunting for the truth."

That night Elder Richards stayed in the home of a member in Lynn, Massachusetts. With the disappointment of the poorly attended meetings fresh in his mind, he drifted off to sleep and had this dream, which he recorded the next evening, Monday, May 10, 1926.

> I had a very beautiful dream last night. I dreamed that while we were met together in priesthood meeting, the Savior appeared [in a pillar of light], and immediately we began to sing "Hosanna, Hosanna, Hosanna to our Lord." It was a most wonderful feeling, and I awakened with the thought that, though the world doubted his coming, I had actually lived to see it. It was a sweet and beautiful climax. I do hope I

will be worthy of him when he does appear, for I do know he shall come.

SOURCE: Lucile C. Tate, *LeGrand Richards*, 124–25, 136–37.

"A LESSON MY FATHER COULD UNDERSTAND"
(Related by Leon Hartshorn)

Leon Hartshorn relates a poignant story about how his father's belief in Christ was increased:

"My father was a good man. He took good care of my mother for numerous years while she was ill before she passed away. He taught his children to be honest and upright. He always paid his tithing, but he did not attend Church. My father had worked in the mines much of his life, in an environment that did not usually invite the Spirit of God, and perhaps for this reason he did not think that he could be fully active and enjoy the full blessings of activity in the gospel.

"When I had been married two or three years, I returned to my father's home for a visit. As we sat down together, he said to me, 'Son, I've had a dream. I dreamed I was standing on the edge of a cliff, and the Savior came riding toward me on a horse. He had a rope tied to the saddle and wrapped around the saddle horn. He reached the rope out to me and said, "Bob, I want you to lower me and my horse down this cliff." I replied that this was impossible; there was no way one man could lower the weight of a horse and rider down a cliff. He responded, "Bob, lower me and my horse down the cliff." So I took the end of the rope and lowered them down the cliff. To my surprise, it was not difficult at all. When the horse and rider arrived at the bottom of the cliff, he looked up and said, "Bob, drop the rope." I dropped it, and he wound it around the saddle horn again. Then looking up at me from the bottom of the cliff, he said simply, "Bob, it's just that easy for you to live my commandments if you will try."' It was a lesson my father could understand, a lesson in his own language of horses, riders, saddles, and ropes. Thereafter he would try whatever he was asked to do in the Church and was very active during the last twenty-five years of his life."

SOURCE: Stephen E. Robinson, *Believing Christ*, 79–80.

"A HOUSE FILLED WITH THE GLORY OF GOD"
Daniel Tyler

On [27 July 1846], the other companies [of the Mormon Battalion] arrived at Francisco's rancho. When within four or five miles, the author recognized the place and surrounding country, having seen it in a dream prior to the Battalion's discharge. At the time of this remarkable dream, the intention of the Battalion was to take the southern route *via* Cajon Pass, reaching the Great Salt Lake from the South. . . .

First, I thought a man clothed in white came to my tent door, having a bottle in his hand, filled with a liquid resembling olive oil. Reaching it to me he said: "take this and drink of it; it is the pure love of God, that casteth out all fear and causeth men to draw nigh unto God." I drank two swallows, and returned the bottle. The eyes of my understanding were then opened and I was filled with the glory of God throughout my whole system. I saw that we traveled northward and subsequently eastward, instead of south and east as anticipated. On arriving at this rancho, I thought we had passed all of the wild animals that sought to destroy us or impede our progress, which it appeared were numerous and strong, the last being a lion, which I instructed the company to pass without halting or seeming to notice.

On arriving at the creek, I dismounted and drank of the water, and received strength to pursue my journey, which many feared I would be unable to do. I was then caught away in the spirit to the valley of the Great Salt Lake, and saw myself with many others in a holy Temple, where the Twelve Apostles presided. The house was filled with the glory of God, and in a room adjoining the main one in which I sat was Jesus, the Redeemer of the world. I did not see Him, but knew He was there. Lucifer also appeared, claiming to be the Christ, and offering free salvation to all who would accept him as their ruler without any church obligations. He was finely dressed, in black, and very genteel, until he discovered that no one paid any attention to his sophistry, when he became enraged and threatened to "tear down the Temple and destroy the kingdom of God," when, as commanded, he left the house. All was calm as a summer's morning and no one seemed to fear any of the threats made or to believe he would have power to do any harm. . . .

When I awoke and found that it was only a dream, the reality of facts did not seem to lessen, but I found my whole being filled with joy and rejoicing, a thrill of gladness pervading my soul from my crown to the ends of my fingers and toes. As to the wild beasts, they represented the many obstacles thrown in our way to hedge up our departure, prominently among them being the Californians selling us animals stolen from their fellows . . . When the officers saw so few re-enlist we were also threatened with being pressed into the service; at least it was rumored that such a move was under serious consideration.

On overtaking Captain Allred's company, I predicted that we would have no further trouble from those sources, which proved literally true, for no further attempt at claiming animals or other trouble of like nature, came in our way. On arriving at the creek I purposely fulfilled a portion of my dream, by alighting from my horse, lying down and taking a good drink at the very place seen in the dream, and received health and strength in so doing.

Many of my comrades will doubtless recollect the relation of the foregoing dream and vision.

SOURCE: Daniel Tyler, *Concise History of the Mormon Battalion*, 306–8.

DREAMS OF THE SAVIOR

"WILL YOU EVER DOUBT AGAIN?"
Rulon S. Wells

While on my way to my mission field, crossing the ocean on the Steamship Dakota, I went down into the salon of the ship one day, and lay upon one of the cushioned benches surrounding the eating tables, where I fell asleep. While asleep the Lord appeared to me in a dream and I saw Him standing before me; and by His side was William W. Taylor, one of the other missionaries, a son of President John Taylor, a boy like myself going upon his first mission. He stood by the side of the Savior, and the Savior extended His hand to me and grasping my hand, holding it tight, looked at me in the face and said: "Will you ever doubt again?" Brother Taylor, who stood beside Him said: "I believe that is enough for him." With that, the Lord let go of my hand and I awoke.

SOURCE: Rulon S. Wells, in Conference Report, April 1940, 41.

"I WAS ASLEEP AT MY POST"
Orson F. Whitney

[Brother Whitney related the following experience that occurred while on his mission:]

"Then came a marvelous manifestation, an admonition from a higher Source, one impossible to ignore. It was a dream, or a vision in a dream, as I lay upon my bed in the little town of Columbia, Lancaster County, Pennsylvania. I seemed to be in the Garden of Gethsemane, a witness of the Savior's agony. I saw Him as plainly as I have seen anyone. Standing behind a tree in the foreground, I beheld Jesus, with Peter, James and John, as they came through a little wicket gate at my right. Leaving the three Apostles there, after telling them to kneel and pray, the Son of God passed over to the other side, where He also knelt and prayed. It was the same prayer with which all Bible readers are familiar: 'Oh my Father, if it be possible, let this cup pass from me; nevertheless not as I will, but as Thou wilt.'

"As He prayed the tears streamed down His face, which was toward me. I was so moved at the sight that I also wept, out of pure sympathy. My whole heart went out to Him; I loved Him with all my soul, and longed to be with Him as I longed for nothing else.

"Presently He arose and walked to where those Apostles were kneeling—fast asleep! He shook them gently, awoke them, and in a tone of tender reproach, untinctured by the least show of anger or impatience, asked them plaintively if they could not watch with Him one hour. There He was, with the awful weight of the world's sin upon His shoulders, with the pangs of every man, woman and child shooting through His sensitive soul—and they could not watch with Him one poor hour!

"Returning to His place, He offered up the same prayer as before; then went back and again found them sleeping. Again He awoke them, readmonished them, and once more returned and prayed. Three times this occurred, until I was perfectly familiar with His appearance—face, form and movements. He was of noble stature and majestic mien—not at all the weak, effeminate being that some painters have portrayed; but the very God that He was and is, as meek and humble as a little child.

"All at once the circumstance seemed to change, the scene remaining just the same. Instead of before, it was after the crucifixion, and the Savior, with the three Apostles, now stood together in a group at my left. They were about to depart and ascend to Heaven. I could endure it no longer. I ran from behind the tree, fell at His feet, clasped Him around the knees, and begged Him to take me with him.

"I shall never forget the kind and gentle manner in which He stooped, raised me up, and embraced me. It was so vivid, so real. I felt the very warmth of His body, as He held me in His arms and said in tenderest tones: 'No, my son; these have finished their work; they can go with me; but you must stay and finish yours.' Still I clung to Him. Gazing up into His face—for He was taller than I—I besought Him fervently: 'Well, promise me that I will come to you at the last.' Smiling sweetly, He said: 'That will depend entirely upon yourself,' I awoke with a sob in my throat, and it was morning.

"'That's from God,' said Elder Musser, when I related to him what I had seen and heard. 'I do not need to be told that,' was my reply. I saw the moral clearly. I have never thought of being an Apostle, nor of holding any other office in the Church, and it did not occur to me then. Yet I knew that these sleeping Apostles meant me. I was asleep at my post—as any man is who, having been divinely appointed to do one thing, does another.

"But from that hour, all was changed. I never was the same man again. . . . I did not give up writing, . . . but not to the neglect of the Lord's Work. I held that first and foremost; all else was secondary."

SOURCE: Orson F. Whitney, *Through Memory's Halls*, 82–83.

"SACRIFICE AND OBEDIENCE BRING FORTH HONOR AND IMMORTALITY"
Jabez Woodard

Lausanne, September 16th, 1852

Dear President Richards:

Nearly two years have passed away since I left parents, wife and children to join the Italian mission. During that long period I have experienced many changes in these foreign lands.

One day I sat down in a solitary place, and melancholy thoughts began to occupy my mind. Then a strange sensation swept over my spirit. Did I fall asleep and dream, or did the visions of futurity beam around? The world seemed spread out before me, and revolution after revolution passed over the nations.

I saw Jerusalem inhabited by happy multitudes. The children were playing in the streets, and old men leaning upon their staves. The curse brooded no longer over Judah's ancient land, for the midnight shades of sin and sorrow were replaced by the brightness of the Millennial morn.

Jesus had visited the earth again, and all nature smiled as if conscious of her Creator's presence. Myriads of noble beings came from tower and temple, and stood near the holy city. Then the Savior came forth, and every eye rested upon His glorious countenance, while every knee bowed in reverence. He raised His right hand, and, pointing to Calvary, thus addressed the mighty host which worshiped at His feet: "Two thousand years ago I died upon that Mount for the sins of the world, but now my Father hath given me the crown of universal empire. Thus shall it be known through all His vast creations that *sacrifice and obedience bring forth honor and immortality.*"

Then I started as from a trance, and lo! instead of the palm trees and flowers of the "pleasant land," I was surrounded by the rocks and snows of the Alpine wilds. But all was not fled, for those words, "sacrifice and obedience bring forth honor and immortality," left a soothing balm upon my spirit which will never be forgotten.

Yours in the New and Everlasting Covenant,

JABEZ WOODARD

SOURCE: Eliza R. Snow, *Biography and Family Record of Lorenzo Snow*, 228–29.

CHAPTER 6

Dreams of Missionary Work and Conversion

Elder Orson F. Pratt of the Quorum of the Twelve Apostles taught that missionary work can be associated with spiritual dreams. He promised missionaries that "the power of the Lord God of Israel will be with you to a far greater extent than what has been poured out in days that are passed; and the way will be open before you, and the Lord will visit the hearts of the people before you arrive among them, and make manifest to them by visions and dreams that you are the servants of God, before they shall see your faces." He continued, "And you will receive heavenly visions to comfort you, and dreams to give you knowledge of the things of God, if you prove faithful before him. I will prophesy this in the name of the Lord God of Israel; and you will find that his power will be more conspicuously made manifest through your administrations on these missions than has ever taken place since the rise of this Church."[1]

This chapter chronicles dreams involved with the process of

conversion. Dreamers include missionaries, investigators, and others. In many dreams, investigators were given specific information regarding the missionaries who would teach them—even before they knew of the significance of the missionaries' message. Elder Orson Pratt taught:

"What do they want with the Elders? They want to be baptized. Who told them to come and be baptized? They say that men came to them in their dreams, and spoke to them in their own language, and told them that away yonder was a people who had authority from God to baptize them; but that they must repent of their sins, cease their evil habits and lay aside the traditions of their fathers, for they were false. . . .

"It is not confined to hundreds, but thousands testify that men have appeared individually in dreams, speaking their own language. . . . These men tell their descendants what their duties are, what they should do, and how they should hunt up this people, repent of their sins, be baptized, etc. And the parties who have been thus instructed time and time again, have fulfilled the commandments that they received, and some of them have come hundreds of miles to be baptized."[2]

Dreams in this chapter also show the Lord revealing the truth of the Book of Mormon to first-time readers. In these dreams, we can see the Lord giving a witness to the truthfulness of that book of ancient scripture.

Elder Pratt promised that dreams could be given to missionaries to them help share the gospel. He assured missionaries that "you were promised that the angels should go before you, and open the hearts of the people to receive you; and when you have gone among a strange people, some of them have recognized you through the dreams and visions given them from the Almighty, and they have said: 'I know you are a servant of the Lord, for you were shown to

DREAMS OF MISSIONARY WORK AND CONVERSION

me in the night vision.' These and other blessings are given to us on condition that we are diligent and faithful."[3]

This chapter illustrates that Elder Pratt's words were prophetic.

"I HAVE SEEN YOU IN A DREAM"
(Related by Samuel O. Bennion)

At another conference I attended . . . an elder bore his testimony in a priesthood meeting, in which he related the following incident: He was out tracting one day, and as he approached the home of a certain lady, she said to him: "Come in, you are the man I saw in my dream." She was a Turkish woman; her father was a Mohammedan [Muslim]. She had been in this country perhaps ten or fifteen years. She related unto him how she had been praying earnestly for the truth and the Lord had shown her in the dreams of the night this elder; so that when he walked up to her door, stood on the steps with that book in his hand, she recognized him and said: "Come in, for I have seen you in a dream."

SOURCE: Samuel O. Bennion, in Conference Report, June 1919, 128.

"WHAT THE LORD WANTS ME TO DO"
(Related by Joe J. Christensen)

A few years ago, while serving as president of the Missionary Training Center in Provo, Utah, I had a delightful visit with one of the missionaries who came into my office. He was obviously older than the average young elder. He was about twenty-five years of age. He told me of his conversion.

When he was sixteen, he was baptized into the Church in Europe along with his mother. His father did not object to his wife's and son's joining the Church, even though he was not interested. He was a banker and wanted his son to prepare himself for a profession in the same area.

The young man loved studying the scriptures, but occasionally had some difficulty when his father would interrupt him when he was studying his seminary course and say, "Don't waste your time studying those things. Study your regular school courses so that you can be accepted at the university."

The elder said, "One night later on, when I was about eighteen, I had a dream. I dreamed that I had been called on a mission to Japan. I felt so good about it. I really wanted to go. The next day, when I told my parents about my dream, my dad strongly objected. He said, "Oh, no! Don't waste two years of your life on a mission. You need to get on with your university studies."

Since he was too young to leave for a mission at that time anyway, he did go on with his university studies. He chose to come to Brigham Young University. He majored in finance and banking for his undergraduate degree and stayed to complete a master's degree in business administration.

He was hired by an international banking firm in Germany and was doing very well as a promising junior executive, but the idea of filling a mission would not leave his mind, and so he went to visit with his bishop and stake president. When he told his stake president of the vivid dream he had years before about going on a mission to Japan, his stake president chuckled and said, "Well, I don't think you will be going to Japan. Missionaries from here generally are called to some other country on the continent, and a few go over to the British Isles."

When he received his call and his father heard of it, he came and tried to change his son's mind because he thought that a two-year interruption would be a disaster for his son's professional career. One of the bank executives came down from Frankfurt and tried to discourage him from leaving, saying something like, "My boy, do you know how much this will cost you in salary and opportunity loss? You ought to sit down and figure it out."

The elder said that he did that, and he had determined that the mission would cost him a very large amount of money—more than 150,000 dollars. Then tears came to his eyes, and he said, "But President, if it were to cost several times that amount, I would still be here, because I know that serving a mission is what the Lord wants me to do."

That elder was one of the few I remember who left the Missionary Training Center speaking what Japanese he had learned with a German accent. He was called to Japan. He served a successful mission, and I am confident that when he finished he found many international businesses that would like to hire a junior executive who can speak English, German, and Japanese—the major languages of the economic free world. Even if he didn't earn an extra cent, he still knew that he had done what the Lord wanted him to do.

SOURCE: Joe J. Christensen, "Good Memories Are Real Blessings," 43–44.

"I'D BETTER DO AS I'M PROMPTED"
Emile C. Dunn

[Emile C. Dunn served as a missionary in Tonga, 1920–1924, and returned to serve twice as president of the Tongan Mission, 1936–1946 and 1948–1950.]

[While serving as a missionary in] Rarotonga I had one of the most interesting experiences. I called a missionary to go to Aitutaki and told him to get everything ready for the boat the next morning and then I would come and get him and take him up to the boat to go to Aitutaki. During the night I dreamed that I went out to another branch and got another missionary, brought him in and put him on the boat and told the first missionary to stay home. After I'd had that dream I woke up and thought, "Well, I'd better do as I'm prompted." So I told the missionary, "You won't go this time. You can work out in Ngatangia and we'll pick up the missionary out there and send him over there, because he's good at Scouting." So I picked him up and put him on the boat.

He was halfway over to Aitutaki when I was called in to the telephone office by the president of the mission and he said, "Brother Dunn, as to that missionary that you need over there in Aitutaki, will you please send Elder So-and-so?" I said, "He's halfway over there, Brother." So that was kind of an inspiration to me. I call it inspiration.

SOURCE: Emile C. Dunn and Evelyn H. Dunn oral history, 50–51.

"I HAVE BEEN EXPECTING YOU"
(Related by Alvin R. Dyer)

A farmer in Pennsylvania met us at the farm gate to say, "I have been expecting you. I have seen you in my dreams." After a day and night of giving them a message of the restoration, I witnessed this family of five request baptism, which was accomplished by damming the creek in back of their barn.

SOURCE: Alvin R. Dyer, in Conference Report, October 1971, 151.

"ON THE TWENTIETH OF MARCH"
Brother and Sister Benjamin Estill (Related by James W. LeSueur)

Dreams and visions seem to have guided a family to where they would hear the truth and to have led them into important service, in the instance of Brother and Sister Benjamin Estill of Mesa, Arizona.

They were living in Kansas City, Missouri, but they did not feel satisfied, and were desirous of having their family bought up in a better way. They fasted and prayed that the Lord would guide them.

On the night of October 2, 1930, they were both impressed by a dream of similar nature. In their dreams they saw a man offer them employment and a railroad ticket that would take them to the west, where they should live. Each one dreamed that this offer would be made them on the twentieth day of the next March.

While working at the stockyards in Kansas City, helping to unload cars of sheep for an owner from Buckeye, Arizona, the man asked Brother Estill if he would like to work for him. He took a railroad ticket from his pocket and offered it to Brother Estill saying that the man who came with him was not returning and that he might as well use the return ticket.

Remembering the dream, Brother Estill went home and asked his wife the day of the month and what was to happen on that day. She replied, "The twentieth of March, the day you were to have fare offered you to go west."

"Well, here is the ticket," said Brother Estill.

He arrived in Phoenix on March 26, and made inquiry at the Chamber of Commerce regarding a place to find work, as his employer had sold out. He was referred to President J. R. Price of the Phoenix Stake, who called up Mesa, where Brother J. J. Huber answered and said Brother Estill could live with him and receive employment. President Price told him he thought he was to come west to do temple work, a thing entirely new to him. While working for Brother Huber, Brother Estill saw Latter-day Saint family life at its best, and his prejudice began to leave him. He attended services, and eventually it dawned upon him that he was to come west to join the Church and help to save his kindred dead.

He sent for his family, and they all joined the Church.

SOURCE: James W. LeSueur, "For a Wise Purpose," 357.

"HE WAS TOLD TO BE BAPTIZED"
Heinrich Eyring (Related by Henry B. Eyring)

Heinrich [Eyring], my great-grandfather, had lost both of his parents and a great worldly inheritance. He was penniless. He recorded in his history that he felt his best hope lay in going to

America. Although he had neither family nor friends there, he had a feeling of hope about going to America. He first went to New York City. Later he moved to St. Louis, Missouri.

In St. Louis one of his co-workers was a Latter-day Saint. From him he obtained a copy of a pamphlet written by Elder Parley P. Pratt. He read it and then studied every word he could obtain about the Latter-day Saints. He prayed to know if there really were angels that appeared to men, whether there was a living prophet, and whether he had found a true and revealed religion.

After two months of careful study and prayer, Heinrich had a dream in which he was told he was to be baptized. A man whose name and priesthood I hold in sacred memory, Elder William Brown, was to perform the ordinance. Heinrich was baptized in a pool of rainwater on March 11, 1855, at 7:30 in the morning.

SOURCE: Henry B. Eyring, "A Priceless Heritage of Hope," 22.

"MESSENGERS WILL COME FROM FAR, FAR AWAY"
(Related by Vaughn J. Featherstone)

We had a young missionary couple in Texas, LeRoy Wilcox and his wife, who tracted over thirteen thousand homes and kept track of what happened. It was a very interesting account. At one home a little lady came to the door. They introduced themselves as missionaries from the Church. She said, "You might as well come in. For ten years I have been searching for the true church, and I haven't found it yet. I might as well listen to you."

After they had finished the first discussion, she said, "I have a whole lot of friends and they know that I've been searching for the true church. Every once in a while, almost every month, I get a call from one or the other of them and they say, 'Have you found the true church yet? When you find it, let us know; because we know that you will recognize it.'"

Brother and Sister Wilcox completed the visit with the usual testimony and prayer. As they got up to leave, for some reason Brother Wilcox said, "We want you to know that we have come from far, far away to give you this message."

She looked startled and asked, "Did you say far, far away?"

He said, "Yes."

"How far?"

"Over sixteen hundred miles—from Orem, Utah."

She said, "That is far away. You know, about two years ago a woman appeared to me in a dream and she said, 'You will find the true church. Messengers will come from far, far away.'" What a blessing!

Almost that same week the Wilcoxes had another experience wherein they quoted Moroni 10:4—"And when ye shall receive these things. . . ." They went through the whole passage. When they had finished, the woman they were visiting said, "I have been searching for that scripture. I heard that in a dream. I was told that I would find the truth wherever I would find that scripture. Where is it? Will you let me read it?"

They opened the Book of Mormon, and she read it two or three times. She soon joined the Church.

SOURCE: Vaughn J. Featherstone, *Commitment*, 82–83.

"HE SAW TWO FOREIGN MISSIONARIES"
Opapo Fonoimoana (Related by Carl Fonoimoana)

Not much is known about his early life in Fogatuli, Savaii, the village in Samoa where he [Opapo] was born in 1859. Even in a poor land, Fogatuli was a poor village; and Opapo's family had an especially difficult handicap to overcome. The mother, Malia Toa, belonged to a prominent family in Fogatuli, but the father, known only as Fonoimoana, was a stranger from Uvea (now Wallis Island, about five hundred miles to the west) who had been caught by a storm and driven ashore. Of Tongan ancestry, Fonoimoana was regarded all his life with slight suspicion in that village.

The first significant event in Opapo's life was a dream he had as a young man. In it, he saw two foreign missionaries come into his village, walk directly to his *fale* (hut), and sit down. That's where the dream ended; but when two Latter-day Saint missionaries entered his house a few years later, he recognized them as the men in his dream, and the Spirit strongly confirmed to him that their message was true.

Source: Carl Fonoimoana, "Opapo: The Power of His Faith," 64.

"TWO YOUNG MEN IN MY DREAM"
Grace Mays Hale

[After wondering which Church was right for me] I prayed: "God, if there is a church on earth that is right for me, help me to find it. I cannot find it by myself." Thus, I left my burden with the Heavenly Father and fell asleep.

How much later I do not know, but I was aroused by three loud raps on our front door. I started to get out of bed to answer the door . . . Sitting on the edge of the bed I fell asleep and dreamed. In my dream I opened the door. Two young men were standing there. One, tall and dark-haired, had his hand on the latch of the screen. The other was at the edge of the porch just at the top of the steps. He only smiled, but the young man at the door was speaking to me when another quite masculine voice interrupted and said to me, "Watch this young man, for once you meet him your life will never be the same again." The young man leaned toward me and said, "Mrs. Hale, I know this is true."

I awoke, still sitting on the side of the bed in the dark. I had not moved from this position. Like Sarah of old, I laughed as I got back into bed. It was funny, something a fortune teller would say—a tall dark stranger would bring a change into my life! I was well past the half-century mark, had a husband, a home, two grown sons, and four grandchildren. My life seemed pretty well settled.

It was not clear to me what the words "Watch this young man" meant. Were they a warning or an admonition? . . . I was drifting off to sleep again when the same voice I had heard at the door was saying, "Would you know this young man if you should see him again?" I answered, "Yes, I would know his voice anywhere." I felt that his voice was his most distinctive quality.

I thought of this dream occasionally during the following days, not because I attached any importance to it but because it was so vivid and had seemed so real. . . . I was puzzled but not otherwise impressed, for I had never been a believer in dreams.

The morning of September 22, 1963, there was a knock at the door, and when I opened it I was astonished to see standing there the two young men I had seen in my dream. They introduced themselves as Elder Duane Finley and Elder Barry Anderson, missionaries of The Church of Jesus Christ of Latter-day Saints. I was very busy that morning and ordinarily would have dismissed any stranger as rapidly as possible, but these two were not exactly strangers. I had seen them once before in a dream. So I stood on the porch and talked to them a few minutes, concealing my amazement as well as I could. Perhaps there was some quality showing through my manner or my voice that struck a responsive chord, for they told me later that they had a feeling of unusual interest that was different from the usual contact. Whatever the reason, a rapport was established between us at this brief meeting.

They started to leave and I felt panicky—I might never see them again if I let them go now! . . . I just *had* to investigate the mystery; I had to find out why I had seen them in a dream! They had reached the sidewalk when I called to them, "If you will come back in thirty minutes, you can have lunch with us." They both smiled pleasantly and said they would be back. . . .

So when the elders arrived I forced myself to take a very resolute attitude towards them. I refused to listen to the record they had prepared to play. I told them I had decided that I could never be a Mormon and that they should not waste any more of their time with me. For a moment they were speechless; each looked solemnly at the other and then sorrowfully at me. Elder Finley began to talk; he was preaching the gospel to me. During his speech he leaned toward me and said in a voice that vibrated with deep conviction, "Mrs. Hale, I know this is true!" The very voice and the words I had heard in the dream! I was amazed! . . .

[After additional study and prayer, Grace Mays Hale was baptized as a member of The Church of Jesus Christ of Latter-day Saints.]

SOURCE: Hartman Rector Jr. and Connie Rector, *No More Strangers*, 4:48–52.

"DO YOU BELIEVE WHAT YOU ARE READING?"
John F. Heidenreich

One night I had a spiritual dream. It was as vivid as life. I had never before had such an experience or have I since. . . . In my dream I came into a beautifully furnished room in a contemporary style. There was a man lying on a couch with a book in such a way that it hid his face from my vision and I could not identify him. I knew he was reading the Book of Mormon. I did not see the title on the book but somehow I knew it to be the Book of Mormon.

I said to the man, "Do you believe what you are reading?"

He replied, "No, I don't believe it. I think it is the most fantastic thing I ever read."

I became annoyed at this rude fellow who hadn't the courtesy to rise from the couch to acknowledge my presence, so I spoke to him abruptly:

"I know the book is true and I can tell you why it has to be true." . . . I thought to myself: "That's my answer; I must memorize those words. They didn't come from me; they came from the throne of God."

I went over the sentence several times to be sure to remember it. As I was repeating the sentence the man on the couch lowered his book from his face. I saw who he was. It was me! I awakened and could not remember a word of the precious sentence. I was greatly distressed because I felt in the sentence may have been the secret to my dilemma. I couldn't quite accept the Book of Mormon and I couldn't reject it. It was like a splinter under the skin rubbing on my clothing. Some days later the meaning of the dream snapped into my mind.

In the dream the man of faith I would someday become, was talking to the man that I was, this rude, faithless man on the couch!

The golden sentence was lost from my memory but there came an assurance that in time it would be given to me. About this time I read in Ether 12:6 a statement that seemed to lift up off the page as though it had been especially written for me: "Wherefore, dispute not because ye see not, for ye receive no witness until after the trial of your faith." The kind of assurance we call full knowledge or absolute certainty comes only after the trial of our faith.

SOURCE: John F. Heidenreich, "An Acorn Becomes an Oak."

"WE HAVE COME TO BRING YOU THE TRUE GOSPEL"
(Related by Milton R. Hunter)

A missionary related an experience that illustrates one method that God has used to bring the searchers after truth into his true church. He stated that he and his companion had knocked on a door. A woman opened the door immediately, enthusiastically invited them in, and said to them, "You young men have come to my home today in answer to my prayers.

"For a long time I have been dissatisfied with the church to which I belong, feeling that it does not contain many of the doctrines that Christ taught while here upon the earth. I felt that it was not the true church that was founded originally by our Savior. I prayed earnestly and asked our Father in heaven to send somebody to me who would bring me the true gospel plan of salvation and make it possible for me to find the true church.

"After doing so, I had a dream that two young men knocked on my door and when I let them in they said to me, 'We have come to bring you the true gospel of Jesus Christ.' I recognize that you two young men are the same two young men I saw in my dream, and as in my dream, you announced yourselves by saying, 'We have come to bring you the gospel of Jesus Christ.' I know that you are the servants of our Master and that you will teach me his gospel."

The two missionaries were surprised at the reception but happy to have the privilege of teaching this good woman the gospel. She eagerly received it and soon thereafter was a baptized member of The Church of Jesus Christ of Latter-day Saints.

SOURCE: Milton R. Hunter, "The Miracle of Missionary Work," 51.

"YOU PLANTED A SEED"
Jenn (Related by Ann M. Dibb)

Several years ago Kristi and Jenn were in the same high school choir class in Hurst, Texas. Although they didn't know each other well, Jenn overheard Kristi talking with her friends one day about religion, their various beliefs, and favorite Bible stories. Recently, upon reconnecting with Kristi, Jenn shared this story:

"I felt sad that I didn't know anything about what you and your friends were talking about, and so for Christmas I asked my parents for a Bible. I received the Bible, and I started reading it. This began my religious journey and my search for the true Church. . . . Twelve years passed. During that time I visited several churches and attended church on a regular basis but still felt that there was something more. One night I fell on my knees and begged to know what to do. That night I had a dream about you, Kristi. I hadn't seen you since we had graduated from high school. I thought my dream was strange, but I didn't attribute it to anything. I dreamed about you again for the next three nights. I spent time thinking about the meaning of my dreams. I remembered that you were a Mormon. I checked the Mormon website. The first thing I found was the Word of Wisdom. My mother had passed away from lung cancer two years previously. She had been a smoker, and reading about the Word of Wisdom really hit home with me. Later I was visiting my father's house. I was sitting in his living room, and I started to pray. I asked to know where to go and what to do. At that moment a commercial for the Church came on television. I wrote down the number and called the same night. The missionaries called me three days later, asking if they could deliver a Book of Mormon to my home. I said, 'Yes.' I was baptized three and a half months later. Two years later I met my husband at church. We were married in the Dallas Temple. Now we are the parents of two beautiful little children.

"I wanted to thank you, Kristi. You set such a wonderful example throughout high school. You were kind and virtuous. The missionaries taught me the lessons and invited me to be baptized, but *you* were my third missionary. You planted a seed through your actions, and you truly have made my life better. I have an eternal family now. My children will grow up knowing the fulness of the gospel. It is the greatest blessing that any of us can be given. You helped bring that into my life."

SOURCE: Ann M. Dibb, "I Believe in Being Honest and True," 117–18.

"YOU ARE WANTED AT PRESTON"
Heber C. Kimball (Related by Orson F. Whitney)

While laboring [as a missionary] in [Walkerfold, England], Heber had a dream in which Willard Richards appeared to him and said: "You are wanted at Preston, and we cannot do without you any longer."

"The next morning," says he, "I started for Preston where I found that I was anxiously expected by the brethren."

SOURCE: Orson F. Whitney, *Life of Heber C. Kimball*, 143.

"I SAW YOU IN A DREAM THREE DAYS AGO"
Solomon F. Kimball (Related by W. J. Kohlberg)

While on a Wisconsin train bound for my native Illinois home, anticipating a happy meeting with my parents, brothers and sisters, after a first and lengthy absence, I fell asleep, just before reaching the junction where I was to change cars:—dreamed of home, and did not awake until the train was near the boundary line of Iowa, and I, further away from home than ever. I got off at the first station, with the intention of taking a train back, but before doing so, I met a man who was instrumental in leading me to the place where, for the first time, I attended a "Mormon" meeting. That meeting later resulted in more than I had anticipated—my mountain home among the Saints.

After hearing awful tales about the "Mormons" and reading for two and a half years all that I could find, for and against the Church, I determined to know things for myself, bade my pleading parents, friends, and relatives goodbye, and left my home in tears with a promise of converting either myself or some of the "Mormons."

I arrived in Salt Lake City on New Year's morning, 1903, an absolute stranger. The first residence I entered was that of Solomon F. Kimball, at 274 6th Street, where to my surprise I was greeted and welcomed as one he had seen before. I had never seen Brother Kimball before, and I wondered, till he said: "I saw you in a dream three days ago." This statement together with a subsequent prediction of my conversion to "Mormonism," and my accomplishment of a great work, almost overcame my surprise—because of my skepticism concerning "Mormon" dreams and prophecies—but his further telling me of my past experience in the East, and my reason for coming West, turned my surprise into greater wonder. . . .

On a sunny morning, the second day in the beautiful month of May, 1903, faith and evidence led me to the waters of baptism. Later I was confirmed with knowledge, and filled with conviction, through the gift of the Holy Ghost. Since then, amid storms and sunshine, I have had ecstatic experiences and mountain-high evidence that so-called "Mormonism" is the restored gospel of Christ."

SOURCE: W. J. Kohlberg, "Editor's Table: Messages from the Missions," 573.

"A LIGHT SHINING IN DARKNESS"
Madeline

Madeline, her clothes under her arms, ran down the stairs and into the kitchen where her mother was preparing breakfast. Mother looked up to say good morning to her little girl, but when she saw how pale and breathless Madeline was, she asked, "What's the matter? Are you sick?"

"No," answered Madeline, but at the moment she could say no more. She sank down onto a stool near the fireplace and stared into the flame. She wondered how she could ever put into words the strange dream she had just had, and what her mother would think if she could.

It had seemed in her dream that she was a young lady sitting on a small strip of meadow close to the vineyard and that as she watched to make sure the goats didn't tramp on the vines and eat them, she glanced down at a Sunday School book in her lap. As she looked up again, she was startled to see three strange men. . . .

One of the men said, "Don't be frightened. We have come from a place far from here to tell you about the true and everlasting gospel."

Then the men told her that an angel had directed a boy to find an important book of gold hidden in the earth. They said that someday she, Madeline, would be able to read this book, and then, because of it, she would gladly leave her home, cross the great ocean, and go to America to live. . . .

Long after everyone else was asleep that night, Madeline could hear the murmur of her parents' voices. The last thing she remembered before she went to sleep was hearing her mother insist, "But we already have the true gospel, so there couldn't be any real meaning to that story Madeline told us." . . .

The very next year [1850] Lorenzo Snow, who later became the fifth president of the Church, was called to open a mission in Italy. . . . Shortly afterward, on a Saturday afternoon, Madeline's father went home early from his work of building a chimney for a neighbor. He told his family that three strangers were coming to bring an important message. "I must dress in my best clothes and go welcome them," he said.

He found the men he was looking for on Sunday morning and invited them to go home with him. As they walked up over the winding paths and through the dangerously narrow mountain passes, Madeline's father told them of the dream his daughter had had many years before.

When they reached his small rock home, they found Madeline sitting on a little strip of meadow close to the vineyard. She looked up from the Sunday School book she was reading into the faces of three men. They told her they had come to give her people the message contained in a wonderful book of gold that had been taken out of the earth, and said that she could now read this book.

That evening Madeline's neighbors came to meet the strangers and hear their message. Some of the men found it so unusual and exciting that they stayed up all night to learn more about the newly revealed truths that had been brought to them by these missionaries of The Church of Jesus Christ of Latter-day Saints. . . . Twenty families eventually accepted the gospel, and . . . Madeline's dream became a reality.

SOURCE: "Madeline's Dream," *The Friend*, 2–4.

"THIS MAN HAS THE TRUTH"
Daniel Mich

Brother Daniel Mich, a full-blooded Indian of the Patzicia [Guatemala] Branch, told of a dream where seven men were beckoning him to follow, each one taking a different road. He had just been visited by the missionaries and despite the vicious stories being told, he was praying to know the truth of their message. In his dream he saw a tall, stately, white-headed man who introduced himself as David O. McKay, a prophet of God, who told him the way to the right road. When later his Elders showed him a photograph of President McKay, he immediately recognized him as the prophet of his dream.

SOURCE: L. Brent Goates, *Harold B. Lee*, 291.

"I'M GOING TO UTAH TO SAVE MY PARENTS"
Mr. Miller

Three years ago my mother died. She had been a good woman, always seeking for light, but never quite satisfied with her religion. When she had been dead for about a year, she came to me one night in a dream. Her long, thick hair hung down her back unkempt; her face was drawn as with sorrow; her eyes were red with much weeping; and still she wrung her hands and wept. When I awoke in the morning the dream was fixed in my mind. When I went to sleep again at night it was repeated. And night after night, my mother came to me, always as at first, unkempt, sorrowing, weeping.

The dream worried me at first; and when it was so oft repeated,

I grew distracted. "What does my poor mother want me to do?" I asked myself, "Why is she so distressed?"

Mother had taught me prayer when I was a little child. So now I prayed earnestly to God to let me understand what I was to do for my sainted mother. A few days later, when I came to my boarding house, the landlady said; "Those men have left some more of their vile tracts, today. They are in your room."

On reaching my room I found them: "*Faith, Repentance, and Baptism,*" and this one, "*Salvation for the Dead.*"

I sat down at once and began to read. . . . I almost devoured this tract, "*Salvation for the Dead.*" It was the thing I wanted. It was what my mother wanted. "I'm going to Utah to save my parents," I said to myself that night. "I have no money, but if I have to walk half the way, I shall go there where the holy temples are built!"

That night my mother did not come.

I began to hunt up our genealogy; and by spending much time and all my earnings, I have traced our family line back to the year, 1700. When I had finished this work, my mother visited me once again. This time she was dressed in white. Her hair was in smooth braids above her brow. A smile of peace was on her face. And when I cried out, "Oh, mother, am I doing right?" she clasped her hands joyfully and vanished. I know that what I am doing pleases her, and I shall go on to a finish . . . there is no guess work about it. "Mormonism" is true! I know it is true! And I would die rather than give it up!

SOURCE: Annie D. Palmer, "How Elsa Came from Germany," 587–88.

"TOBACCO BARNS ON THE TAR RIVER"
James H. Moyle

Nothing of the kind had ever occurred to me before. I was not much of a dreamer. I was deeply impressed that we should get away from the little spot in which the work had been done ever since the early days when the missionaries were sent from Nauvoo. I had a dream in which I saw the homes and tobacco barns of the people on the Tar River in the extreme eastern part of North Carolina. I knew nothing of the locality, but this dream was so vivid in its details, and so impressive in its suggestion, that when President Morgan advised me they were sending two additional missionaries, Elmer Johnson and J. S. Carpenter, I asked that they be sent direct to the Tar River where, so far as I knew, no member of the Church had ever been. The new missionaries were down there six months or longer before I saw them, during which time they baptized several people, and when they came up for conference, I described the residences and tobacco barns on the Tar River of which I had dreamed, and the missionaries said my description corresponded with the homesteads of the members baptized in the locality in which they had been laboring with such singular success. It was not then common for a missionary to baptize as many in two years' labor as was done in this instance in about six months.

SOURCE: James H. Moyle, "Looking Back Sixty Years," 280–81, 310–12.

"YOU MUST FEED HIM"
Jonathon H. Napela

In 1850, Brigham Young sent ten missionaries to the Hawaiian Islands. Without understanding the language and culture, the missionaries found the work extremely difficult. Eventually they became discouraged, including the mission president. They became so discouraged that five of the ten left to go home. The youngest of the remaining missionaries, Elder George Q. Cannon, was determined to stay. He went to the Lord in prayer. The Lord inspired him to go to Lahaina on Maui. He did so.

As he approached this town, two ladies went screaming into a nearby house and brought out a local gentleman. The previous night, this man had had a dream that a messenger of God was coming to his town and that he must feed him. Elder Cannon was invited to stay and preach in the home of this man, Jonathon H. Napela, who was a very well-educated man and the magistrate of that district (see Alma 10:4).

Subsequently, Elder Cannon and Jonathon Napela became very close friends, like Alma and Amulek in the Book of Mormon (see Alma 10–15). Because of the guiding hand of God and Brother Napela's great help, along with the hospitality and kindness of the Hawaiian Saints, the missionary work began to excel in Hawaii, and the foundation was laid.

Source: Yoshihiko Kikuchi, "Daughter of God," 76–77.

"HE SAW THE BOOK OF MORMON"
Alexander Neibaur (Related by Hyrum L. Andrus)

Alexander Neibaur . . . was born in France of Jewish parents, on January 8, 1808. Educated to be a rabbi, Neibaur chose instead the profession of surgeon and dentist. After his graduation, young Alexander took another major step: he became a Christian and went to England.

One morning very early, a few years later in the city of Preston, his wife was giving the front steps a coat of whitewash when a neighbor called to her, "Have you seen the new ministers from America?"

"No," replied the young woman, still going about her work.

"Well," came the further information, "they claim to have seen an angel."

"What?" rang out an abrupt voice from an inner chamber, as the young Hebrew doctor sprang from his seat and put his head out of the window. "What is that you say?"

When the information was repeated, Brother Neibaur secured the address of the American ministers, and shortly thereafter he was in close conversation with Elders Heber C. Kimball, Willard Richards, and others. Immediately he asked if they had a book, for he had previously seen the Book of Mormon in a dream; and he recognized it when it was shown to him. Taking the book with him, he went home, and read it through in three days.

Following his baptism, Brother Neibaur took passage with the second company of Saints to embark for America. When he arrived at Nauvoo, he established himself in that prospering city as a surgeon and dentist. He became intimately acquainted with the Prophet and was employed to instruct him in the German and Hebrew languages.

Source: Hyrum L. Andrus, "Little Known Friends of the Prophet Joseph Smith."

"EXACTLY WHAT HE HAD SEEN"
(Related by Dallin H. Oaks)

A medical doctor in a village in Nigeria had a dream in which he saw his good friend speaking to a congregation. Intrigued, he traveled to his friend's village on a Sunday and was astonished to find exactly what he had seen in his dream—a congregation called a ward being taught by his friend, who was their bishop. Impressed with what he heard in repeated visits, he and his wife were taught and baptized. Two months later over 30 others in their village had also joined the Church, and their clinic had become the meeting place.

Source: Dallin H. Oaks, "All Men Everywhere," 78.

"YEARS OF WAITING IN NIGERIA"
Anthony Obinna (Related by E. Dale LeBaron)

In Nigeria, Anthony Obinna was a faithful and persistent pioneer. As a lifelong seeker after truth, he relates the following, which occurred in the late 1960s: "One night I was sleeping and a tall man came to me . . . and took me to one of the most beautiful buildings and showed me all the rooms. At the end he showed himself in the crucified form. Then in 1970 I found this book to read. It was the

September, 1958, *Readers Digest*. There was an article entitled, 'The March of the Mormons' with a picture of the Salt Lake Temple. It was exactly the same building I had seen in my dream."

Brother Obinna persistently wrote to Church headquarters and to missions, seeking Church literature and hoping for personal visits from Church representatives. After years of waiting, he wrote the following to the Quorum of the Twelve Apostles on 28 September 1978: "Your long silence about the establishment of the Church in Nigeria is very embarrassing. . . . What could hinder this church from having a foothold here? Did Christ not say, 'Go ye and teach all nations?'" When the Obinna family learned of the revelation on the priesthood, they wrote to the First Presidency: "We are happy for the many hours in the upper room of the temple you spent supplicating the Lord to bring us into the fold. We thank our Heavenly Father for hearing your prayers and ours and [that he] by revelation has confirmed the long promised day. . . . We thank you for extending the priesthood which has been withheld [from] us and to prepare us to receive every blessing of the gospel."

When the missionaries arrived in Nigeria, they found many prepared for the gospel through the teaching and leadership of Brother Obinna. He became the first person to be baptized by the missionaries sent to West Africa, and Sister Obinna became the first Relief Society president in black Africa. The first Latter-day Saint chapel built in Nigeria is in Aboh Mbaise, of the Imo State, near the home of the Obinna family.

SOURCE: E. Dale LeBaron, "Revelation on the Priesthood," 130–31.

"I WILL SHARE THIS MISSION WITH YOU"
(Related by LeGrand Richards)

[A young man said] that all his life he had wanted to go on a mission. His father had wanted him to go, but his father died recently.

He said when he received his call he had a dream in which he saw his father, and he said: "My son, I will share this mission with you."

SOURCE: LeGrand Richards, in Conference Report, April 1934, 87.

"YOU HAVE THE GOSPEL FOR ME"
(Related by LeGrand Richards)

[Two sister missionaries] were walking along the street one day [in the Central American Mission], and a man came up to them and said, "I know who you are. I have seen you in a dream. You have the truth. Will you come to our home and teach it to us?"

SOURCE: LeGrand Richards, in Conference Report, April 1956, 97.

"YOU ARE GOING TO NEED THIS LANGUAGE"
Robert L. Simpson

[This dream was received in about 1938, approximately one month after Robert L. Simpson arrived in New Zealand to serve as a missionary. He returned to New Zealand in the 1950s as mission president and later served as a General Authority.]

In this dream I had returned home from my mission. I was getting off the boat down in Los Angeles harbor from whence I had left, and there was my bishop, my stake president, my mother and dad, all of my friends. As I came down the gangplank of the boat they all started talking to me in Maori, every one of them—my mother, my father, my bishop—all talking in Maori, and I could not understand a word they were saying. I was so embarrassed. I was humiliated. I thought to myself, "This is terrible. How am I going to get out if it? And I started making excuses. Right then I woke up and I sat straight up in bed and the thought came to my mind so forcefully, "You will *have* to do something about learning this language. The Lord has given you a blessing, but you are going to have to do something about it yourself. You are going to need this language when you get through with your mission. You are going to need it." This thought kept ringing through my ears all through that day, so arrangements were made and we had study time allotted each day to learn the Maori language. The Lord blessed me and we were able to bear testimony in the language after a short time.

SOURCE: Robert L. Simpson, "The Lord Is Mindful of His Own."

"A GROUP OF PEOPLE CALLED SAINTS"
Meliton G. Trejo

A great help for missionaries and for Spanish-speaking people everywhere is the translation of the Book of Mormon into Spanish. Meliton Gonzalez Trejo is the man who is most responsible for its first translation. The son of a nobleman, Meliton was born in Garganta la Olla, Spain, in 1843. Well educated as a boy and young man, he was always interested in religion. But nothing he read about various churches satisfied him.

One day, however, he heard a friend mention a group of people, called "saints," who had been led over the Rocky Mountains in America by a prophet. These people, Meliton was told, were living in the Salt Lake Valley. He was so anxious to find out more about them that he asked for and was given permission by the queen to join a military expedition to the Philippine Islands, as he thought this would be a help toward his going to America.

During his stay in the Philippines, Meliton became seriously ill. While recovering, he had time to think more about religion and the "saints" in the Salt Lake Valley. One night after a fervent prayer for guidance, he was directed in a dream to leave the army and journey to Utah. This dream was so sacred to Meliton that he never told the details of it to anyone but President Brigham Young whom he met soon after arriving in Utah. In order to leave the Philippines the young soldier needed money. In time, he was able to secure two thousand dollars in bills that he sewed inside the lining of his vest before he left.

Arriving in Salt Lake, Meliton investigated the Church and soon became a member. He was one of the first missionaries to go to Mexico, and was asked by the General Authorities to translate the Book of Mormon into Spanish. With some help from another man, Meliton Trejo finished the translation in 1886.

SOURCE: "The Church in Spain and Gibraltar," 32–33.

"GO TO THE LITTLE CHAPEL"
(Related by Joseph L. Wirthlin)

I often think of my two grandfathers—one was born in England and the other was born in Switzerland. The one in England at the age of twenty-one was very anxious to find the Church of the Lord Jesus Christ. Yes, he belonged to another church, a great church, but he was not satisfied. He could not understand the matter of baptism. He could not understand the matter of authority. He could not find it.

One Saturday evening on retiring to his bed, he made it a matter of prayer. He asked the Lord if the Church of Jesus Christ was upon the earth could he be directed to it. That night he had a dream, and in the dream he saw not too far from where he lived a road and at the end of it was a little chapel. When he arose Sunday morning, he was so impressed with the dream he immediately dressed and went down the road, and there was the little chapel. In it two men were preaching the gospel of the Lord Jesus Christ, and who were they—two Mormon missionaries! My grandfather immediately joined the Church. There was no question about it in his mind.

I am positively sure that over the world where individuals have a desire to find the true Church, they can find it. They may find it in the way of a dream or they may find it by the missionaries who may come to their homes and teach them the gospel of the Lord Jesus Christ.

SOURCE: Joseph L. Wirthlin, in Conference Report, October 1959, 65.

"FIVE KEYS"
Yellow Face (Related by C. Frank Steele)

This incident dates back a number of years when a dignified Indian who called himself Yellow Face appeared in Cardston [Canada] along with twenty families seeking a good trapping region. . . . [He describes his history:]

"The year before our company came here first I was taken very sick, and was told by some of my Indian people who had been dead for many years that I would soon be better. But I would get sick again and that when I did, I would die, but my family should not think I was dead and bury me, for I was not to be buried until my body was cold all over. When I woke up I called my family together and also the council of five chiefs of which I was a member, and I told them of my dream. They laughed at me as they did not believe me, but I was afraid. Time went on and one day some time afterward, I was taken very sick, and at once feared my dream would come true, so I warned my family not to be in a hurry to bury me even if I died till they were sure I was cold all over.

"I got weaker and weaker until I left my body and I went away among a lot of Indians that I knew were dead; some I knew, and some I did not for they had been dead so long. But they were really not dead at all, and I could not understand it all, and they told me that to die was only to leave the body for your folks to take care of, and I would be where they (the dead) were. But as for me I had to go back and use my body again for several years. They said I was to go among the white people till I found a Book that told of the history of these dead Indians who really were not dead. I asked them how I would know these people who had the Book and they gave me five keys by which I would know the people who had the Book that would tell my live Indian friends all about who they were and about their dead relatives, as follows:

"'First, they will let you camp on their own land, and trap and hunt; second, they will treat you like one of them in business with them; third, they will invite you to their meetings and ask you to speak; fourth, they will ask you to sit with them at their tables to eat; they will visit you at your camp and their men will not bother your women nor molest any of you.

"'When you find this people have them meet in your council and tell you what they believe, and they will tell you about this Book.

"'I then woke up and found my wife and friends had about decided to bury me as I had seemed dead for some time and was cold all over except a small place over my heart. But when I came back and told them where I had been and that our Indian relatives were not dead at all, they wondered at me and when I told them I would pick about twenty families and travel till I found the Book they again wondered, but as they all believed in a God they would follow me. So in due time we made up our company and started and made many camps and traveled many seasons, but it was hard to find a people who answered the five keys till we landed among you as we find few people who are true friends of the Indian.'

"At the close of this story Yellow Face asked the bishop for the Book and a copy of the Book of Mormon was presented to him, and this he immediately placed among his treasures."

SOURCE: C. Frank Steele, "A Delightsome People," 294.

CHAPTER 7

Dreams of Family History and Temple Work

As recorded in the closing book of the Old Testament, the prophet Malachi prophesied: "Behold, I will send you Elijah the prophet before the coming of the great and dreadful day of the Lord: and he shall turn the heart of the fathers to the children, and the heart of the children to their fathers, lest I come and smite the earth with a curse" (Malachi 4:5–6).[1] Malachi's prophecy signifies the importance that the Lord places on sealing families together. Dreams can help link families together and strengthen those everlasting bonds.

This chapter includes dreams that assisted individuals to connect with their ancestors in ways they would not have considered on their own. Upon listening to the promptings of the Spirit, some dreamers received important information regarding family history records they were able to use to seal their families together in a house of the Lord.

President John Taylor asked, "What about the others, they who have died without a knowledge of the Gospel?" And he quickly answered, "They are amply provided for. The Lord has shown us that we must build Temples in which to officiate for them. We have commenced to do so, and our fathers have already commenced to feel after us, manifesting themselves by dreams and visions, and in various ways to those most interested in their welfare."[2]

Many Latter-day Saints have been blessed to find family history records after receiving an informative dream. Elder Franklin D. Richards, an apostle, told how this happens with the intercession of dreams: "How many there are who, when they have gone up and done their little work in the temple, and have wondered how they could get knowledge of any more, have had dreams given to them telling them the very names of persons they ought to do for."[3]

Prophets and apostles have related experiences of family members appearing to them in dreams. While those appearances do not always result in temple work, they are evidence of the hearts of the children being turned to the fathers. President David O. McKay remarked, "I would like to dream about my mother more often." His desire and hope for eternal families was strengthened through reminiscing with his deceased mother. Most of us desire to see family members again who have passed on, but President McKay was blessed with a special gift to draw himself closer to family through his dreams.[4] President James E. Faust, formerly a member of the First Presidency, felt the same way. He said, "As we get older, the pull from our parents and grandparents on the other side of the veil becomes stronger. It is a sweet experience when they visit us in our dreams."[5]

Church members also shared stories of dreams about the building of temples that would someday be instrumental in their lives. Without these holy edifices, Latter-day Saints would be unable to be sealed to their families for eternity. Dreams that reveal future temples can bring great joy into the lives of Church members who are currently without the opportunity to perform sacred ordinances in a temple close to their homes.

In other dreams, deceased family members, through their encouraging presence, remind mortal relatives of eternal promises that await them after this life. The dreams recorded in this chapter can help increase our understanding that dreams can be a legitimate process by which revelation is received. The promise of fathers' and children's hearts being turned to one another can be fulfilled in dreams in unexpected and unpredictable ways as illustrated here.

"A PHOTOGRAPH WAS HANDED TO ME"
Carol Batey

Soon after my conversion to the LDS Church, I received my patriarchal blessing. In it I was counseled to do my genealogy work. This surprised me, for as a black person I had always thought that pursuing genealogy would be hopeless. Slaves were only recorded as nameless property. How could I possibly find the records of my ancestors?

But although I didn't have the experience, time, or funds that Alex Haley[6] had, I did have a patriarchal blessing that encouraged me to uncover my personal roots and see that my ancestors' temple work was done. So I began.

After months of dead ends, one night I had a dream. In the dream, a photograph of my great-great-grandmother that hangs on our living room wall was lifted down and handed to me. I had already searched in vain for her records. Yet the dream was so vivid that the following day I stared urgently at the photograph, wondering what it held for me and why it had appeared to me in the dream.

Many times that day I returned to the picture. Slowly, but firmly, I received the impression that I should write to the

Mississippi archives for information. It didn't seem logical, but I followed the impulse.

One week later I received the copy of a particular census that verified my great-great-grandmother's birth and gave me all the information I needed. I now look forward to performing the saving ordinances for her in the Atlanta Temple.

I used to look at that photograph in my living room and see only my great-great-grandmother. Now that picture reminds me that when I felt that finding information about my ancestors was impossible, a way was shown to me.

SOURCE: Carol Batey, "Finding My Black Ancestors," 54.

"A CHOICE PEOPLE WITH A MAJOR ROLE"
Ezra Taft Benson (Related by Sheri Dew)

One evening a moving experience demonstrated just how close assistance was from the other side. President Benson related: "Soon after retiring I had this impressive dream: Karl G. Maeser stood before me. He was tall, dignified yet pleasing, dressed in a dark suit and white shirt, clean shaven with ruddy face and clear blue eyes. He said to me, 'Brother Benson, what are you doing to promote the sacred work in the temples for my people of Europe? They are a choice people who have played a major role in building up the Kingdom of God in these last days. The sacred ordinances must be performed for them in the temples in order to permit their progress in the spirit world. Will you please do all you can to help bring this about? They are a choice people of our Heavenly Father.' These were his words as nearly as I can recall them. He smiled kindly as he nodded goodbye without further words. The brief message impressed me deeply."

SOURCE: Sheri L. Dew, *Ezra Taft Benson*, 381.

"WRITE A LETTER"
Hubert E. Bowen

I have spent many years in research and on some of my lines have hired genealogists without a great deal of success. After searching many hundreds of books and also hiring others, I decided to go to the Lord in prayer. I prayed for the way to be opened for me to gather Bowen records. That night I had a dream. In this dream I felt impressed that I should write to the mayor of a certain city in Vermont. The next morning I wrote the letter. Not knowing the mayor's name, I just addressed it to the mayor of that city. I asked him if he knew of any Bowen families living in his community or the descendants of any to whom I could write, as I was compiling a record of the Bowen families and trying to trace the genealogy and family history of the many lines back to the original or Puritan ancestor.

The mayor replied, giving me a list of about ten names. Near the bottom of this list was the name of one Bertha McDaniels of East Dorset. A strong impression came to me to write to her. Immediately I wrote to her. She sent in return a record of her own immediate family. Then I sent her family group sheets and asked for the record of her parents, grandparents, and ancestors as far as she had them. This she sent me. I was so amazed to find that she had such a marvelous record that I asked her how it was that she had in her possession such a wonderful genealogy and facts going into the sixteenth and seventeenth centuries not in possession of any of the Bowen genealogists. This was her story:

When Bertha was a little girl, her mother, who has now been dead over forty years, called her to her side and gave her some genealogy and old papers, and told her to keep them, saying that this was the genealogy of her people, and when the right man called for it she was to give it to him. In her letter to me she said, "I suppose you must be that man." She related how her grandmother when she was over eighty years old had given this same genealogy to her mother, and told her to keep it, as it was the record of her people and would some day prove valuable.

The genealogical record this lady sent me proved to be the only known record so far uncovered by genealogists in America tracing an unbroken pedigree back to Richard Bowen, the emigrant, who came to America and settled in Rehoboth [Massachusetts] about 1638. This record has given to me more complete genealogy than I have been able to find in all my research, and more than I had been able to obtain by hiring genealogists to search for me. I thank the Lord for this marvelous manifestation of His goodness to me and the remarkable preservation of these records.

SOURCE: Hubert E. Bowen, "Record Providentially Obtained," 44.

"HELPING GRANDFATHER FIND TWO NAMES"
(Related by Steven R. Covey)

One time I was pouring out my heart in prayer for a particular gift of the Spirit. That night I dreamed that I saw my grandfather who had been deceased about two years. He was looking through his wallet for a couple of lost phone numbers, a couple of lost names. In the dream I was looking over his shoulder, trying to help him. And in the background in another room, where I couldn't see who the person was, a man whom I knew to be a member of our extended family was preaching this incredible sermon about this gift of the Spirit that I was seeking.

Then I woke up, and I just instantly knew what it meant. I knew that the Lord was linking those two things. If I would help my grandfather find those two names, then I would be given that spiritual gift.

The next morning I went downstairs and looked through my grandfather's things, which I would not normally have done, because I thought his line had been thoroughly researched already. But knowing that the Lord had sent me there, I knew that I would find something. I started with my grandfather's immediate family. He had six brothers, just one of whom was still living, and that brother was a temple worker. Glancing down the page, I realized that two of the brothers had gone inactive and had never had their endowments or their sealings done. I called my mom and asked, 'Is it possible that they didn't take care of their brothers?' She said, 'Well, I don't know. Call Uncle Ed at the Provo Temple.' And I called him, and he said, 'You know, I don't think we ever did.'

I am quite certain that probably the very day the final work had been completed, I received in a significant and obvious way the endowment in my life of that gift of the Spirit that I had been seeking.

SOURCE: Steven R. Covey, *Six Events*, 172–73.

"I SAW A PIECE OF PAPER WITH A NAME"
Henry B. Eyring

A few nights ago I had a dream. I saw a piece of white paper with a name on it I did not know and a date I could only partially read. I got up and went to the records of my family. The last name on the slip of paper is from a line which came into my mother's ancestry 300 years ago in a place called Eaton Bray. Someone is anxious for a long wait to end. I have not yet found that person. But I have found again the assurance that a loving God sends help in answer to prayer in this sacred work of redeeming our families, which is His work and His glory and to which we have pledged our hearts.

SOURCE: Henry B. Eyring, "Hearts Bound Together," 80.

"A TEMPLE IN KONA"
Philip A. Harris (Related by Chad S. Hawkins)

The temple in Kailua-Kona is on Hawaii, the state's largest and southernmost island. White marble walls and orderly rows of royal palms contrast with the island's green hills. The temple itself rests on

DREAMS OF FAMILY HISTORY AND TEMPLE WORK

a hillside flanked by Mount Hualalai to the east and overlooking the Pacific Ocean to the west.

As president of the Kona Hawaii Stake, Philip A. Harris prayed to know what the Lord would have him accomplish during his service. He recounted: "One night I dreamt there was to be a temple in Kona. I woke and told my wife. . . . I took my dream to be a direction for me as a stake president that I was to [help] my people to become temple worthy and temple ready."

Knowing the logistics of building a large temple in Kona, he thought that the dream simply meant the people were to be spiritually prepared, not that there would be an actual temple in Kona. Then President Gordon B. Hinckley announced that a number of small temples would be built. And soon, a temple was announced for Kona. "I knew then that in my lifetime I would see the temple here that I had seen in my dream."

SOURCE: Chad S. Hawkins, *The First 100 Temples*, 192.

"WHAT COULD I DO?"
Joseph W. B. Johnson

For Joseph W. B. Johnson, news of [a temple being built in Ghana] is something he has waited 15 years for. He is one of the Church's pioneers in West Africa, having in 1964 started a congregation patterned after the Church after he read LDS literature and the Book of Mormon. He and others in his unofficial congregation were baptized after the missionaries arrived in Ghana in 1978.

Brother Johnson said that he had a dream several years after he was baptized that the spirits of people who had died asked him what he was doing for them. "What could I do?" he pondered, not having access to a temple.

"Now we can start doing the temple work for those of our ancestors," he said after President Hinckley announced the temple.

SOURCE: Steve Fidel, "A temple to be built in Ghana," 3, 5.

DREAMS AS REVELATION

"THE MAN SEEMED PLEASED BUT DID NOT SPEAK"
Spencer W. Kimball (Related by Edward L. Kimball and
Andrew E. Kimball Jr.)

[Elder Spencer W. Kimball] wondered what to do about a strange dream he had had while on the reservation. He had retired, feeling well, and fallen into a peaceful sleep. He dreamed vividly of going to the members of a family he had known well in Safford. He urged them to change their ways and devote themselves seriously to the work of the Lord. As he spoke he wept, realizing that they might reject his message and might resent his interference. One put her fingers over his lips as if to stop him, but he continued with great urgency to plead with them for complete surrender to the Lord's way.

The scene changed slightly and he and one of the women stood apart. Her deceased husband stood near them, pleased at what Spencer was saying to her. The man stood straight, clean, well-groomed, looking taller and straighter and healthier than in life. Spencer slapped him on the shoulder and greeted him. The man seemed pleased but did not speak. As the husband moved slowly away and vanished, Spencer continued to implore the wife to follow a life of Church service.

Spencer awakened from the dream and lay there under a continuing impression of serenity, reviewing the picture of his friend—peace personified, with a face almost transparent, wearing a perfectly fitting dark suit. He got out of bed and recorded the dream. When he finished, his watch showed 2:35.

In retrospect the dream surprised Spencer a little. His friend had been a businesslike shopkeeper, often worried and preoccupied, a good fellow but sometimes lightminded, giving little attention to Church or religion. And after the funeral the wife had dropped all connection with the Church. Years had passed without any contact between Spencer and the family. Nothing he could recall would have triggered this dream; it came like lightning from a clear sky. Although he could almost hear the family laugh together at the huge joke and express resentment at his intrusion, Spencer felt he must contact them.

Just a month later a funeral called him to Arizona. He sought out the woman he had dreamed about and, at her invitation, met with her family. They seemed interested in the dream and what it might mean. He left with a hope that his visit might influence them.

SOURCE: Edward L. Kimball and Andrew E. Kimball Jr., *Spencer W. Kimball*, 259–60.

"I KNOW NOW THAT IT IS TRUE"
Emil Pooley

In Mesa we stayed with a Sister Black. . . . I had a dream that night where I was in the kitchen, sitting reading the Book of Mormon. Someone came in the front door. I looked up, and it was my father who had died some few years before.

I said, "Father, what are you doing here?"

He said, "Son, I'm glad to see you. I have come to bring you a message. You are going to the temple tomorrow. I am very happy for you and your family. It is the right thing to do." (His endowments had been done previously.) And then he continued:

"When you get back home, you tell your mother to join our Church, because I know myself now that it is true. I long for her, and I want her to be with me when it is time for her to come. So, you do that for her." In my dream he left me, and I closed the Book of Mormon.

SOURCE: Emil Pooley, "A Hopi Prophecy Fulfilled," 150–51.

"THE LOAD WAS NOW HIS TO CARRY"
George Albert Smith (Related by Merlo J. Pusey)

[When George Albert Smith was called to be a member of the Quorum of the Twelve Apostles,] this new sense of responsibility spurred him on. He felt that somehow he must now measure up to the standards his father had set. Probably he also experienced, in the absence of his father, a subconscious release from some of the inhibitions that had resulted from the superabundance of Smiths in the church leadership. While his grief was still fresh George Albert had a vivid dream. It seemed that he was approaching President Joseph F. Smith for something in the presence of his father. John Henry said nothing but just sat smiling as the president finally handed George Albert a large package that seemed to contain what he had been asking for. The implication was that George Albert was now in a better position vis a vis the church and that this pleased his father.

Another dream involved his maternal grandfather, Lorin Farr, who dressed in a business suit, seemed to be walking in a beautiful pasture with the spring of young manhood in his step. Being well aware of his grandfather's death, George Albert was surprised when the dream image shook hands with him. But he was soon at ease and walked toward a brook with his grandfather while they engaged in conversation. "There will be a harvest of my family soon," the grandfather said. "After I was awake," George Albert wrote in his journal, "I could feel the warmth of his hand and the thrill of pleasure that I had when I found he could shake hands and had a body of flesh and bone."

Whatever the meaning of his dreams might be, George Albert was increasingly conscious of the passing of the older generation. As the giants disappeared, men like himself took their place. Perhaps his father and grandfather were telling him that a larger part of the load was now his to carry. In any event, his feet seemed to be a little firmer on the path that led into the mists of the future. George

Albert seemed to remember, as he had written to a young missionary, "The troubles of this life will be but the stepping stones upon which you will mount to better things."

SOURCE: Merlo J. Pusey, *Builders of the Kingdom*, 253–54.

"GRANDMA, WHY ARE YOU SO UNHAPPY?"
(Related by Patrick Wong)

"In 1988, while my wife and I were living in Australia, my father died. A year later my mother was gone. When I returned to Hong Kong for her funeral, we agreed that the work for our parents should be done. My younger brother volunteered to do it in the Taiwan temple.

"Two months later, my wife had a dream. She saw my mother, who seemed very unhappy. 'Grandma, why are you so unhappy?' she asked. 'Patrick's brother promised to take care of me, but he hasn't.' 'Don't worry, Grandma. Patrick will take care of you,' my wife promised.

"Believe it or not, I didn't understand what the dream meant when my wife told me about it," Elder Wong says. "However, two weeks later she had another dream, a dream of my father. 'Kathy, tell Patrick I need to get married as soon as possible.' When Kathy told me about that dream I finally understood.

"I immediately called my brother and asked him if he'd been to the temple to do our parents' work. He hadn't. His wife had experienced a miscarriage and was having a difficult time recovering. 'Go and do it, Patrick,' he told me. So within days, we went to the temple in Sydney and had my parents sealed.

"I know this work is essential for our ancestors," Elder Wong concludes emotionally. "My parents wanted their work done so badly. Other ancestors feel the same way. The Hong Kong Temple is part of Heavenly Father's plan. It is a comfort to us, a symbol of the Lord's confidence in the Chinese people here and all around the world, a symbol of the future of the Church."

SOURCE: Kellene Ricks Adams, "A Dream Come True in Hong Kong," 51.

"AN INDIAN CHIEF CAME INTO THE TEMPLE"
Wilford Woodruff

I had a dream one night about our temple in Salt Lake City. I thought the temple was dedicated and organized, and we as the elders of Israel were laboring there for the redemption of our dead, and suddenly there was a door opened in the west, and an Indian chief came into the temple, leading a vast host of his tribe, and took possession of the temple, and I thought they performed more work in one hour than we could do in a day. This made a strong impression on my mind. I am satisfied that, although we have done a little for the Lamanites, we have got to do a great deal more.

SOURCE: Wilford Woodruff, "Remarkable Manifestations," 296.

"LET ALL COME INTO THE TEMPLE WHO SEEK SALVATION"
Wilford Woodruff

[March 12, 1887] "I dreamed last night that the Latter-day Saints were holding a great conference in the Salt Lake Temple. I saw a great rush to finish the Temple. I was called upon to open the conference, and I was given the keys of the Temple to open it. I saw thousands assembling and I met President Young, who asked me what was the matter with the great multitude at the door. Some one answered that the elders did not want to let the people into the Temple. He exclaimed, 'Oh, oh, oh;' he then leaned over to me and said, 'Let all come into the Temple who seek salvation.' I saw several who were dead, among them my wife, Phoebe. I believe there is some special meaning in this dream."

SOURCE: Matthias F. Cowley, *Wilford Woodruff*, 562.

"I SAW TWO ELDERS DRESSED IN WHITE"
Steven B. Wright (Related by M. Russell Ballard)

Two faithful missionaries, Elder Todd Ray Wilson and Elder Jeffrey Brent Ball, lost their lives in Bolivia [in 1989]. . . . With the permission of [Mission] President Steven B. Wright of the Bolivia La Paz Mission, I share this special experience that came to him in a dream: "I saw these two elders dressed in white, standing at the doors of a beautiful building. They were greeting numerous people, who also were dressed in white as they entered the building. It was obvious from their dress that those who entered were Bolivians. I envisioned the temple that will someday be built in Bolivia. Elders Wilson and Ball were ushering those they had prepared to receive the gospel in the spirit world into the temple to witness the vicarious ordinances being performed in their behalf. This dream has been a great comfort to me and has helped me to understand and accept their deaths."

SOURCE: M. Russell Ballard, "Duties, Rewards, and Risks," 33.

CHAPTER 8

Dreams of Warning

Dreams can be given to *exhort* us—"to give warnings or advice: make urgent appeals."¹ This chapter records dreams concerning danger, false teachers or deception. In the history of the Church, dreams warned some Latter-day Saints of the martyrdom of Joseph Smith. One of the reasons for those dreams of warning may have been because of the Prophet's previous ability to thwart hazard. Elder George Q. Cannon explains,

"It was particularly so at the martyrdom of the Prophet Joseph Smith, for he had passed through so many difficulties, and had so many narrow escapes, and so many deliverances from perils of the most menacing character, that the Latter-day Saints had been led to regard him as almost invulnerable, and that his life would be spared to a good old age, if not to the winding up scene. His martyrdom, then, fell as a very unexpected blow upon the people. It was a dreadful shock, for which a great bulk of the Latter-day Saints were unprepared."²

However, Elder Cannon revealed that there were some who were informed of the impending death of Joseph Smith. He shares, "It is true that many were warned, especially those who were abroad among the nations preaching; they had dreams and manifestations of the Spirit concerning the terrible calamity."[3] The Lord can exhort us regarding impending tragedy.

As Elder Joseph Young, a President of the Seventy, explained, "God's work is not like man's; the Lord shows things to come, perhaps in dreams or by visions of the night, and we should learn what is mingled and connected in his designs. We should observe so as to know what is intended, so that we may not run into a snag."[4] The dreams that follow show there are times when the Lord can give dreams of exhortation that can protect the dreamer from difficulty, sin, or problems—if they will follow the counsel received.

Dreams can also provide advance warning regarding those who seek to deceive us. President Joseph F. Smith believed that the message of such dreams would generally be brought by individuals that we have trusted who have died. He felt that the duty to warn might be assigned to loved ones beyond the veil to bring these kinds of messages. He professed, "Our fathers and mothers, brothers, sisters and friends who have passed away from this earth, having been faithful, and worthy to enjoy these rights and privileges, may have a mission given them to visit their relatives and friends upon the earth again, bringing from the divine Presence messages of love, of warning, or reproof and instruction, to those whom they had learned to love in the flesh."[5] And perhaps dreams are sometimes the way information is shared with us on this side of the veil. In the dreams that follow are many examples.

"A DREADFUL FLOOD OF WATER"
Richard Ballantyne

Phineas Young, and his son Brigham, desired the use of my horse-team, including my wagon, to go to McQueen's mill for some flour with which to go west. I consented to let them have it, and as my health was quite poor at the time, I concluded to go with them to improve my health, and was to be ready next morning. During the night, I had a dream which betokened trouble. I thought, in my dream, that myself and some others were rowing a boat up the middle of the great Mississippi river, when suddenly a dreadful flood of water was seen rolling down toward us. The flood seemed to be about twenty or twenty-five feet high, and I thought destruction was inevitable. However, I thought we rowed with all our might to the shore, and as it was about to overwhelm us, I suddenly found myself, as if by some unseen power, with the rest of the company walking safely up the banks of the river. But this dream did not dissuade me from going on the morrow.

We started up the river, on the public road that led to Pontoosuc, and from there reached McQueen's mill, a distance of about twelve miles from Nauvoo. We obtained the flour, and next morning, (being Sunday) we took the homeward journey, and as we passed through Pontoosuc we saw, around the public square, a large number of horses, here and there tied to the fences. We wondered what this could mean, and, on reaching the edge of the town, a woman, probably a friend, standing on the porch of her house, cried, "For God's sake, be off for the mob's in town!" Not thinking that they had seen us, we traveled leisurely along about two miles further, and finding a convenient watering place, we unhitched our horses and watered them in the Mississippi. Just as we were harnessing them to the wagon, we became alarmed on hearing the sound of horses, as if rushing at full speed. Supposing this to be the mob, I seized my gun, but Phineas Young, fearing that the sight of this might endanger our lives, seized it and threw it into the bush, not, however, soon enough to hide it from the mob, for in the very act, they came rushing upon us with cocked revolvers and ordered us to surrender, and with them to return to Pontoosuc. Having seen the gun, they took it, and one of them, on my asking by what authority all this was being done, presented his cocked revolver in my face, and said, with a terrible oath, "this is my authority." Finding it useless to resist, for there was some twenty of them, we turned our team and followed them back to Pontoosuc.

On our arrival in Pontoosuc, our captors halted us on the public square . . . proud of their bloodless victory. It was now about ten o'clock in the morning, and we were kept on the square till sometime after noon. Then we were taken to the wharf, on the river, and lodged in a warehouse till it was growing dark. About a dozen mounted men, armed with rifles and revolvers, now came and took us out of town. . . . We spent a wakeful night, and were much chilled, having no bedding, and although it was July, the night was quite cold.

Just as the first indications of morning appeared in the east, we were all aroused by the rumbling of wagons, and the sound of horsemen, and a few sharp reports from the firing of muskets . . . A body of well armed men from Nauvoo had taken the place before most of its inhabitants were out of bed. . . . The object of our brethren was to take us out of the hands of the mob, without giving our captors time to mature their evil designs. . . . "Old Wimp," for this was the leader's name, said, "Hold on till I go and see what causes this uproar." . . . [He] returned and said in great excitement, "The 'Mormons' are here." . . . Phineas Young sprang out and caught "Old Wimp" by the arm, and pleaded for our lives. With a great oath, the latter said, "I will, if you'll follow me."

Phineas agreed, and no sooner was this said than the command was given, "follow me." . . . We were now destined to be in the hands of this murderous guard for two weeks more. . . . One morning they were nearing our hiding place when the proceedings in our camp were suddenly stopped on sight of a man who came rushing along at full speed, and who, when he reached us, caused great excitement and fear by yelling, "The 'Mormons' are on you." Our captors had just completed arrangements to have each of us shot. The announcement of their murderous purpose had been made to us. The ground had been measured off, and the place was selected where we were to stand. "Old Wimp" had cleared the ground between the place, beside a large tree, where we were to stand, and the position which our executioners were to occupy, a distance of fifty feet. . . . All seemed ready for the order to be given to place us in position, and to prepare their rifles, when this mysterious messenger rushed upon us with his foaming horse.

Their purpose was now changed, their own perilous condition dawned upon them. In the haste and alarm of the moment they proposed to us "if you will save us, we will save you." To this we agreed; then we were instantly started on a hurried march. . . .

About this time, (so we afterward learned,) our brethren, numbering about two hundred, gave up the chase as hopeless, and returned to their homes. In the meantime, all sorts of rumors reached Nauvoo, harrowing up the minds of our friends, and torturing their feelings. Sometimes it was reported that we had been savagely tortured, and put to death; and sometimes, our deaths were reported to have been accomplished one way and then another, until all hopes of ever seeing us again were abandoned. . . . Once they tried to kill us with poisoned whiskey; all but one of us refused to partake, and he was preserved by vomiting it up. At another time similar arrangements to those already narrated had been made to murder us, but they miscarried also.

Last of all, on the morning of Saturday, just two weeks from the time we had left our homes, we demanded our liberty of the guard. We told them we were going home. If they chose to shoot us, they might, but we would stay no longer with prospects of being murdered in cold blood. . . . They let us go, and aided us as far as Warsaw, and, lest the mob should overhaul us by land, a few of them got two skiffs, and rowed us at midnight five miles up the middle of the Mississippi river, landing us at Keokuk, about 2 a.m., on the west side of the river, six miles below Nauvoo. . . .

The unexpected news of our safe arrival spread rapidly over the city and many were the joyful greetings we received. . . . The dream, foreshadowing our deliverance, was fulfilled.

SOURCE: Richard Ballantyne, "With the Remnants at Nauvoo," 274–79.

"GO HOME, YOU ARE NEEDED THERE"
Jacob ("Jake") Hamblin (Related by Louise Lee Udall)

On the evening of August 30, 1886, Jake had made a neat camp on the freight road, a day's journey . . . from Pleasanton. The night had been filled with fitful sleep and troubled dreaming, and he was up early in the morning. After caring for his horses and preparing breakfast, he called to his younger brother Oscar. To urge him on, Jake said, "We'll be home tonight, boy. We're going home." Oscar was bewildered. "But I thought you said this load of freight had to go through today."

"It is rush freight, all right," said Jake, "but it won't get there today. I feel like I ought to go home. I am afraid something has happened. Last night I could hardly sleep for thinking about them, and when I did get to sleep, I would dream. I dreamed the same thing three times. Then I awoke, and it seemed like a voice said to me, 'Go home. You are needed there.' I am afraid something has happened."

And so it was that Jake and Oscar drove into Pleasanton in the evening of the day their father died.

SOURCE: Louise Lee Udall, "Jacob Hamblin," 743.

"I CAN'T GO TO WORK WITH YOU TODAY"
David L. Hardy

The winter of 1979–80 was more severe than usual in our area, and the heavy snowfall in the mountains collapsed the roof on a friend's cabin. The entire roof system, all the way down to the concrete footings, needed rebuilding. I was hired to do the job. . . .

As the weather gradually got warmer, I started taking my little son Kenny with me every day. He was two and a half years old at the time and really enjoyed going to work with his dad. . . .

One night, after taking Kenny with me for four or five weeks, I had a terrible dream. I woke up in a cold sweat after dreaming that he had fallen into the rushing water and drowned. It was so real and scared me so badly that I sat up in bed and found myself shaking.

I couldn't go back to sleep. I spent the rest of the night trying to calm myself down and thoughtfully considering the frightful images that kept turning over and over in my mind. I had the distinct feeling that this dream was a warning not to be disregarded. At the same time, I wondered how I could tell little Kenny that he wouldn't be able to go with me to work on the cabin again. I was concerned about hurting his feelings because I knew how he loved to go to the mountains to work with me.

The next morning I told my wife, Georgia, of the experience and of my feelings, and she agreed that I had better not take him with me to the cabin anymore. But she, too, was concerned about how he was going to handle the disappointment.

Kenny got up early that morning, and as usual, started to dress himself. He came into our bedroom and sat on my lap, and as I was helping him put on his shoes and socks I was still trying to figure out how to tell him he couldn't go with me anymore.

All of a sudden he said, "Dad, I can't go to work with you today."

"Why?" I asked, surprised.

"Cause I will drownd in the river," he said.

Tears of joy came to our eyes as we realized that little Kenny had received the same warning that I had that night.

SOURCE: David L. Hardy, "Warned in a Dream," 37.

"A JET-BLACK PANTHER"
Heber C. Kimball

At this time, I had many dreams from the Lord; one of them I will relate. I dreamed that I entered the house of John F. Boynton, in which there was a panther; he was jet black and very beautiful to look upon, but he inspired me with fear; when I rose to leave the house he stood at the door with the intention to seize on me, and seeing my fear, he displayed his beauty to me, telling me how sleek his coat was, and what beautiful ears he had, and also his claws, which appeared to be of silver, and then he showed me his teeth, which also appeared to be silver. John F. Boynton told me that if I made myself familiar with him he would not hurt me, but if I did not he would. I did not feel disposed to do so, and while the panther was displaying to me his beauty, I slipped through the door and escaped, although he tried to keep me back by laying hold of my coat; but I rent myself from him. The interpretation of this dream was literally fulfilled. The panther represented an apostate whom I had been very familiar with. I felt to thank the Lord for this dream, and other intimations that I had, which, by His assistance, kept me from falling into snares.

SOURCE: Orson F. Whitney, *Life of Heber C. Kimball*, 114.

"JOHNSTON'S ARMY"
Isaac C. Laney

During the early days, when the Saints were threatened by the army, [Isaac Laney] had another dream which was fulfilled. Again it was the sign of an enemy—a large snake coiled and menacing the Valley of Great Salt Lake. The head raised high and seemed watching something in the east. Then it began to sway from north to south and soon the head broke off and flew to the south, then the whole snake broke up, some pieces going north and some south.

We see the fulfilment of this dream in Johnston's army, which was a menace to the city until the outbreak of the Civil War, when the head broke off and left to join the Southern army, the rest breaking up and returning east in disorder, some to join the North and some the South.

SOURCE: I. C. Laney, "Struggles of an 1847 Pioneer," 784.

"SNAKE BITES AND BULLETS"
Isaac C. Laney

The 28th of October, 1838, found [Isaac Laney, my grandfather] with a small number of Saints working at a place called [Hawn's] Mill, in Missouri. It was on this day that the mob came upon them demanding that they sign a treaty of peace and deliver their weapons of war.... Grandfather had little faith in the mob's promise of peace.

October 29 passed peacefully at the Mill, but that night grandfather had a dream which was not in the least reassuring. In the dream he seemed to be passing along a trail where there were a great many snakes. They crawled along the ground, hurled themselves through the air and hung twisting and hissing from the limbs of trees. Dodge and hurry as he might, his body was soon pierced and bleeding from the attacks of the angry snakes. Finally escaping the serpents, he met a man with whom he was acquainted.

"Brother Laney," he said, "you are terribly bitten and it is no use to encourage you, for no one was ever bitten so by snakes and lived."

"Well, then, I'll be the first, for I'm not going to die," was grandfather's answer. . . .

On October 30, the mob, heavily armed, dashed down on the little party at the Mill and began firing. Grandfather, through a clever act of strategy gained possession of three guns, gave two of them to the other men and, placing himself between the mob and the cabins housing the women and children, began firing. . . . Lead was flying around like a hail storm. You may judge how thick was the hail of lead, for while he was preparing to fire, eleven bullets hit the stock of his gun, cutting it off in his hands. . . . He returned to the cabin, [and] told the women and children to run for the woods. As he turned, a bullet struck him in the right armpit and came out the left. This was not the first wound he had received, however, for two bullets had gone through his breast and came out his back and two had passed through his hips.

After the shouted warning to the women and children, Isaac fled for his life, taking a trail leading up a small hill. As he was running up the hill, his body much bent with effort, a large ball struck him in the back near the kidneys, passing lengthwise through his body. . . .

Knowing he must hurry to help or give up his life, Grandfather first sat down to take off his boots, for they were so heavy that it was hard to lift one foot after the other in his weakening condition. He was obliged to split the boots with his knife before he could remove them.

So weak and stiff that it was hard to move, he struggled on, but soon met the man he had seen in the dream. He said, "Brother Laney, it is no use to encourage you, for no man was ever shot as you are and lived." Then followed the identical conversation of the dream, excepting the substitution of "shot" instead of snake bite.

Just a little farther on was the home of friends who took him in. So great was their fear that the mob would follow and kill him, they took up a board and hid him under the floor. Of course, in his condition, he could not stand this long and begged to be taken out. They did so, and after washing and dressing his wounds put him in bed.

His clothes were literally cut to pieces and his body almost as bad, for it had been struck by seven bullets, leaving thirteen scars, six passing through and through, the seventh, that struck him in the back, leaving but one scar. . . . For some time he lay near death, being fed with a spoon, and so weak he could not so much as open or close his eyes. With so many wounds practically all of his blood was lost.

The elders were called in and he was anointed and promised in the name of Jesus Christ he would recover. From this time on he recovered rapidly and was soon chopping logs in Illinois for the homes of the Saints.

SOURCE: I. C. Laney, "Struggles of an 1847 Pioneer," 781–83.

"PLAIN WARNING SIGNS ALONG THE WAY"
(Related by Harold B. Lee)

I know a young woman who was about to fail in her faith because of a sudden sorrow which she was not quite prepared to bridge over after having been a convert of a few years. She had a dream in which she saw herself going back to the church of her previous acquaintance. As she drove along in her car, she came to a road . . . under construction, and after ten tortuous miles returning she found to her amazement that there were plain warning signs all along the way which, if she had observed, would have guided her along a safe detour road and past the shoals of difficulty.

SOURCE: Harold B. Lee, *Stand Ye in Holy Places*, 366.

"THE LORD FAVORED HIM WITH A DREAM"
John McCarthy

Having just returned from a trip to New Zealand and Australia, [President Gordon B. Hinckley] told a story about a group of Saints in Australia who struggled to make the journey to the Salt Lake Valley. They left Australia on the ship *Julia Ann* in 1855, he said. A violent storm in the Pacific Ocean drove the ship onto a coral reef where it broke in two. Five people were drowned.

The dreams of a faithful returning missionary who was on the ill-fated ship led to rescue. The crew of the *Julia Ann* had built a small boat from the wreckage and, as instructed in the dream, sailed west, finding land. They landed in Bora Bora, in the Tahiti group of islands.

President Hinckley said: "A rescue ship was found, and all of those left on the atoll were saved. I wish to say to you that the missionary who had the dream enjoyed the ministering of angels as promised by John the Baptist to Joseph and Oliver. I think he did not hear a voice. I think he did not see a heavenly being, but in the stillness of the night, on that harsh and lonely coral reef, out in the vast Pacific Ocean, the Lord favored him with a dream which led to the rescue of himself and his associates."

SOURCE: Gordon B. Hinckley, "Pres. Hinckley addresses 'My fellow servants,'" 7.

"A BATTLE IN JACKSON COUNTY"
Parley P. Pratt

We then repaired to Lexington, and made oath before Judge Ryland of the outrages committed upon us, but were refused a warrant. The Judge advised us to fight and kill the outlaws whenever they came upon us. We then returned to the place where we breakfasted, and, night coming on, we retired to bed. Having been without sleep for the three previous nights, and much of the time drenched with rain, this, together with the severe wound I had received, caused me to feel much exhausted. No sooner had sleep enfolded me in her kind embrace than a vision opened before me.

I was in Jackson County; heard the sound of firearms, and saw the killed and wounded lying in their blood. At this I awoke from slumber, and awaking Mr. Marsh and the family with whom we lodged, I told them what I had seen and heard in my dream, and that I was sure a battle had just occurred.

Next morning we pursued our journey homeward with feelings of anxiety indescribable. Every officer of the peace had abandoned us to our fate; and it seemed as if there was no alternative but for men, women and children to be exterminated. As we rode on, ruminating upon these things, a man met us from Independence, who told us there was a battle raging when he left; and how it had terminated he knew not.

This only heightened our feelings of anxiety and suspense. We were every instant drawing nearer to the spot where we might find our friends alive and victorious, or dead, or perhaps in bondage, in the hands of a worse than savage enemy.

On coming within four miles of Independence, we ventured to inquire the distance at a certain house; this we did in order to pass as strangers, and also, in hopes to learn some news; the man seemed frightened, and inquired where we were from. We replied, from Lexington. Said he, "Have you heard what has happened?" We replied, "That we had heard there was some difficulty, but of all the participants we had not been informed." "Why," said he, "the Mormons have *riz*, and have killed six men."

We then passed on, and as soon as we were out of sight we left the road and took into the woods.

Taking a circuitous route, through thickets of hazel interwoven with grape vine, we came in sight of Independence, after some difficulty and entanglement, and advanced towards it; but seeing parties of armed men advancing towards us, we wheeled about, and retreating a distance, turned again into the woods, and galloping about a half mile, reached the tents of our friends.

But what was our astonishment when we found our brethren without arms, having surrendered them to the enemy!

The truth was this: The same evening that I dreamed of the battle, a large body of the outlaws had marched to a certain settlement, where they had before committed many outrages, and commenced to unroof dwellings, destroy property, and threaten and abuse women and children. While some sixty men were thus engaged, and their horses quietly regaling themselves in the cornfields of the brethren, about thirty of our men marched upon them, and drove them from the field. Several were severely if not mortally wounded on both sides; and one young man of the Church died of his wounds the next day—his name was Barber.

SOURCE: Parley P. Pratt, *Autobiography of Parley P. Pratt*, 79–80.

"MY FAMILY HAD PREDICTED MY ARRIVAL"
Parley P. Pratt

At 9:00 A.M., a council meeting was held. During it, Parley P. Pratt arrived from Fort Leavenworth with a purse of $5,860. Elder Pratt reported that the battalion was doing well. He mentioned that it was reported in Missouri that President Polk had issued a proclamation "that the Mormons had better not be in haste in going to California, that they should be protected, and paid for all their losses in Missouri and Illinois."

"I rode with all speed, and in less than three days reached home—distance one hundred and seventy miles. Unexpected as this visit was, a member of my family had been warned in a dream, and had predicted my arrival and the day, and my family were actually looking for me all that day. I delivered the money to President

Young and Council, with the list of subscribers, and of the persons for whom it was sent, and again prepared for my departure."

Sources: See Bruce A. Van Orden, "Founding a city, fighting fevers," and Parley P. Pratt, *Autobiography of Parley P. Pratt*, 312.

"I'VE SEEN THAT HOUSE BEFORE"
Frank Snow

While at the dinner table Prest. [Ben E.] Rich [President of the Southern States Mission] told us of a dream which Elder Frank Snow had a few years ago. Bro. Snow at the time he had the dream was living in Idaho. He related it to Bro. Rich when the latter was paying a visit to the Gem State.

The dream is as follows: — Elder Snow dreamed he was called upon a mission to the Southern States, and obeyed the call and reached Chattanooga on a cold wintery day. He also dreamed that he was in a large house in the South and saw Prest. Rich killed. . . .

A few months later Frank Snow [was called on mission to the Southern States and] reached Chattanooga. It was a very cold day and the ground was covered with snow. Elder Snow went to the Mission House. As he approached the House Prest. Rich saw him and opened the door and came out. When Elder Snow saw the president he exclaimed, "This is the first part of my dream."

Elder Snow was assigned to labor in Virginia. Some months after he reached that state the Virginia conference was held in a settlement where a number of Saints lived. Elder Snow with the rest of the Virginia Elders came to the conference. He and his companion reached the settlement the day before the conference was held. As they were walking along a street they came to a house which attracted Elder Snow's attention. He stopped and exclaimed, "I've seen that house before, and I am going in there." And he went in. He shook hands with the folks and told them he had seen them before. . . . Then the folks told Elder Snow that Prest. Rich was going to stay there that night. But Elder Snow told them that Prest. Rich would not stay there.

Prest. Rich came to the settlement and met Bro. Snow who told him not to stay at the house at which he had made arrangements to stay. The President made other arrangements.

The day after Prest. Rich's arrival it was learned that a mob had surrounded the house in the night of which he had first made arrangements to stay. It was also learned that it was the intention of the mob to take Prest. Rich and bear him and probably kill him.

SOURCE: Nephi Jensen Journal, 45–48. Spelling and grammar corrected.

"A MOB AT A SCHOOL HOUSE"
Lorenzo Snow

I traveled and preached during the following summer and autumn, in different parts of Ohio, baptizing quite a number—always traveling on foot, "without purse or scrip," and often meeting with trying and sometimes amusing circumstances.

When at the house of Brother Smith, in Stark County, Ohio, I dreamed one night that arrangements were in progress to mob me. The following evening after I had the dream, as I sat conversing with friends who had called on me, a loud rap at the door preceded the entrance of two well-dressed young men, who politely invited me to accompany them to a school house about one mile distant and to address an audience already assembled. After a little hesitation on my part, they began to urgently request my acceptance of their invitation, when the dream of the preceding night instantaneously flashed across my mind, and I told them I could not comply with their wishes. They still persisted to urge and insist on my accompanying them. When they were convinced that I was immovable in my determination of non-compliance, they not only manifested disappointment, but were exceedingly angry.

The next day I learned that they told the truth so far as a

congregated audience waiting my appearance at the schoolhouse was concerned, but the object was entirely different from that reported by the young men—it corresponded precisely with my dream.

SOURCE: Eliza R. Snow, *Biography and Family Record of Lorenzo Snow*, 16–17.

"SUDDEN CLOUDS OF INTENSE BLACKNESS"
Joseph Standing

A district conference was to be held in Rome, Georgia, in late July 1879. Elders Standing and Clawson, of course, planned to attend. They decided to stop for a few days at a little place called Varnell's Station and accompany the Saints there to conference. On the way, Joseph recounted to his companion the details of a deeply disturbing dream he'd recently had. In the dream, Joseph said, he had gone to Varnell's, "when suddenly clouds of intense blackness gathered overhead and all around me." In the dream he stopped at the home of a Mormon family and was told by the woman of the house, who was influenced "by a sense of great fearfulness," that he could not stay. Joseph awoke suddenly "without... being shown the end of trouble."

The dream deeply troubled Elder Standing. He was "fearful that something terrible was going to happen" and was filled with a sense of impending doom. Neither he nor Elder Clawson was able to interpret the dream. Despite their fears, the young men continued bravely on their journey.

The two young missionaries arrived at Varnell's Station late on the evening of Saturday, July 20, and made their way through the darkness to the home of a local member family. There Joseph's terrible dream began to be fulfilled. The woman of the house, in great agitation, told them they could not stay there. She warned the elders there was a "bitter and murderous" attitude toward them in the neighborhood. They spent a sleepless night at the home of a nonmember who promised to defend them so long as they were under his roof.

Joseph was frightened and anxious, with good reason. He had twice escaped a mob previously, when laboring with Elder John Morgan. He confided to Rudger "his intense horror of being whipped" and declared that "he would rather die than be subjected to such an indignity."

Despite his fears, however, Elder Standing evidently gave no thought to turning back. His deep conviction of the divinity of the cause in which he was engaged impelled him to go on. Neither fears of mob violence, a horror of whippings, nor the terrifying dream of blackness deterred him from his duty. How impressive his moral courage!

The next morning, Sunday, July 21, the two missionaries resumed their journey. Suddenly, on a lonely, densely forested stretch of road, they were apprehended by a mob of twelve men, three on horseback, the rest on foot. The mobsters approached the missionaries with weapons drawn, cursing and shouting profanities. Joseph boldly spoke up: "By what authority do you arrest us upon the public highway here? If you have a warrant of arrest, we would like to see it."

"There is no law in Georgia for Mormons," was the reply. The two missionaries were escorted down the road, threatened and bullied every step they took, and struck with clubs or guns if they did not move quickly enough. Certain they were being led to their deaths, they were told they would be whipped so they would never forget it. "You'll be pretty limber when we finish with you," one of their captors yelled.

What a horrifying experience that must have been for those two brave young souls, particularly for Joseph, who undoubtedly sensed the fulfillment of his horrible dream of darkness.

At first, it appears the mob intended only to beat the missionaries and put them on a train out of the state. "If we ever find you in this part of the country we will hang you by the neck like dogs," the leader of the group snarled.

The mob and their captives stopped by a secluded stream of clear water about fifty yards off the road. Three of the mobsters left, to reconnoiter the road ahead. Those who remained continued to threaten and bully the elders. Finally, the three who had left returned. "Follow us," they ordered. Elder Standing, undoubtedly with thoughts of torture and death in his mind, made some resistance. As quick as thought, one of the mob shot him dead. The leader of the mob then pointed to Elder Clawson. "Shoot that man," he ordered his fellow ruffians. Elder Clawson, certain he, too, would die, collected himself, folded his arms calmly, and said, "Shoot." Someone yelled, "Don't shoot." The guns were lowered, and the immediate danger passed. Clawson was allowed to leave.

SOURCE: Alexander B. Morrison, *Feed My Sheep*, 91–93.

"HE HEARD THE REPORT OF A GUN"
Nathan Terry

After an interesting council, we commenced to descend the difficult cliff to the crossing of the river. While doing so, Brother Nathan Terry said he had a dream the night before, and that it had been on his mind all day, and he believed it meant something. In the dream he saw the company riding along the trail, when he heard the report of a gun. He looked around, and saw one of the company fall to the ground, and he thought he went and put the person on his horse, and they continued their journey.

After descending the cliff, I was some distance in the rear of the company, when suddenly, what appeared like a flash of lightning came over me. It was with great difficulty that I could breathe. Not being able to help myself, I partly fell to the ground.

I lay there some time, when one of the Kanab Indians who was with us came along, saw my situation, and hurried on to the camp.

Brother Terry came back to me after dark. He administered to me in the name of the Lord, when the death-like grip that seemed to have fastened on my lungs let go its hold, and I could again breathe naturally.

Source: Jacob Hamblin, *A Narrative*, 112–13.

"A LOG CABIN FULL OF SERPENTS"
Wilford Woodruff

I will give you an instance of the Lord's protecting care over me while I was a Priest. I had this experience while in Arkansas with my companion, who was an Elder. There was a man in that country who with his wife and five sons had been in Jackson county. His wife died there. The old gentleman was in the faith apparently when he left there. He was driven out, the same as the rest of the Saints were, and some of his sons were whipped with hickory gads in the persecution there. I knew he was in this Arkansas country, and I felt anxious to go and see him, as he was the only Latter-day Saint that we knew anything about in that region.

The night before I got there I had a peculiar dream. I dreamed that an angel appeared to us and pointed out a certain path that we must follow, and that the blessings of God would attend us in following that path. As we went along this path we came to a log cabin with a wall on each side ten or fifteen feet high. This road led right through that building. When I went to the door and opened it, it was full of large serpents. My companion said he was not going into that room for anybody or anything. "Well," says I, "I am, or I'll die trying. The Lord told us to follow that path, and I am going to walk in it, unless I am stopped by some power that I know not of." I stepped into the door. These serpents all arose up ready to jump on me, and there was a very large one in the middle of the floor that made a pass at me. It appeared to me as though I would be destroyed, but when the serpent reached near to me it dropped dead; in fact, they all dropped dead, and they turned black and burst open, after which they took fire and burned up, and both of us went through safely.

The morning after, we arrived at this man's house. His name was Akeman. It was Sunday morning, and we went into the house. Mr. Akeman and his daughter were at breakfast. His sons were settled in cabins around him. We sat down, but there seemed to be a peculiar spirit in the place. I finally stepped up to the mantelpiece, on which I saw a Book of Mormon. I picked it up, and said, "Brother Akeman, you've got a very good book here." He said, "It's a book that came from hell." I then began to understand a little of what lay before us. He had apostatized. He cursed everything and everybody—Joseph Smith, Lyman Wight, the Apostles and a good many others whom he named. He was very angry. I inquired about his sons. He said they were settled around him there.

Well, we took up our valises and left. I looked up one of his sons—the youngest, I believe, and the only one that was in the faith, and he was like a drowning man; but by praying with him we got the Spirit of the Lord in him, and we had a pretty good time with him. We told him of our experience at his father's, and I said we were desirous to have some meetings there if we could. He said he did not know; his father had apostatized and was at war against everything that was Mormon. He told us, however, where an old gentleman lived close by to whom he had loaned the Book of Mormon. He was an aged man and his wife was an aged woman. Their name was Hubbard. We went to see them and they were very glad to receive us.

In the morning my companion said he was going to leave the place. Of course, he was an Elder, and I was only a Priest, and we generally suppose that the lesser should obey the greater; but I said to him, calling him by name, "You are not going to leave here, nor I either; we shall both of us stay here till I see the fulfillment of my dream. It is here, and I am going to stay and see it, and you will, too." It is not natural for me to take a stand of that kind, but I felt led to do it upon that occasion. We stopped there three weeks, and cleared land for father Hubbard, while he fed and housed us.

Three times while we were there I was warned of the Lord to go and warn this Mr. Akeman. The last warning I received from the Lord was on Saturday night of the third week. I went up to his house which was about three quarters of a mile distant, and when I got there his daughter stood in the doorway. I walked in and saluted him. He was walking the room, but did not say anything to me. I told him the Lord had sent me to pay him a visit. Then he made some exclamation that was rather profane. I sat down and commenced warning him. I told him that he had apostatized from the Gospel of Christ; he had had the Priesthood and he was pursuing a course that would send him to destruction, and the judgments of God would overtake him. Well, he raged like a demon. That is about all I said to him. I certainly did not stay long, but I delivered my message. When I left the house he followed me, and when he came to where I was he fell dead at my feet as though he had been struck with a thunderbolt from heaven. . . . The next day I attended his funeral. But he had raised a mob and had sent word for them to come and drive us out of the country or hang us, and they had sent warnings to us to leave. The consequence was, there were some fifteen or twenty deaths during my stay there. Men were taken with what was called pleurisy. . . . One of these men sent for me, and I went and saw him. Two men were holding him. . . . I said to myself, "If your eyes were open, you would see the angel of death standing by your side." He died while I was there. After this my partner left me, and I went alone to Memphis, Tennessee, and met with Brothers Patten and Parrish.

SOURCE: Wilford Woodruff, in *Collected Discourses, 1896–1898*, 5:234–35.

CHAPTER 9

Dreams of Instruction

President Wilford Woodruff explained that one purpose of dreams of instruction is to teach gospel principles. "The Lord does communicate some things of importance to the children of men by means of visions and dreams as well as by the records of divine truth. And what is it all for? It is to teach us a principle. We may never see anything take place exactly as we see it in a dream or a vision, yet it is intended to teach us a principle," he said.[1] The dreams in this chapter show that dreams can provide new insights, understanding, and enlightenment.

One difficulty with receiving this kind of revelation is that the dreamer may not recognize or value the source. In a nineteenth-century missionary tract, Elder Parley P. Pratt, an apostle, discussed this tendency to discount dreams as a source of instruction when he wrote: "In this situation [dreams], we frequently hold communion with our departed father, mother, brother, sister, son or daughter; or with the former husband or wife of our bosom, whose affection for us, being rooted and grounded in the eternal elements, or issuing from under the sanctuary of Love's eternal fountain, can never be lessened or diminished by death, distance of space, or length of years."[2]

Elder Harold B. Lee noted that "if we will learn not to be so sophisticated that we rule out that possibility of impressions from those who are beyond sight, then we too may have a dream that may direct us as a revelation."[3]

Subjects discussed in such dreams can give new understanding to various aspects of the gospel of Jesus Christ. This new understanding may be accompanied by a softening of the heart or a change of attitude. Dreams of instruction may open the eyes of dreamers and their families to new possibilities. Sometimes dreamers may be encouraged by the Spirit regarding what to do in temporal matters.

By studying the dreams in this chapter, we may increase our understanding of dreams as they instruct and prepare us. As Elder Heber C. Kimball observed, "If you want to grow and thrive, and want to have the Spirit of the Lord, and the Holy Ghost to be with you, and have dreams and visions, and gold and silver, and herds and flocks, wives and children, and every other good thing, go ahead in every duty, and never falter one moment, and tell the Devil to kiss your foot."[4]

"SNOW-WHITE BIRDS"
George Brimhall

George Brimhall, having already served 19 years as president of BYU, determined to establish a recognized teachers college. He had hired three professors: one with a master's degree from Harvard, one with a doctorate from Cornell, and the other with a doctorate from Chicago. They hoped to transform the college into a full-fledged university. They determined that practicality and religion, which had characterized the school, must now give way to more intellectual and scientific philosophies.

The professors held that "the fundamentals of religion could and must be investigated by extending the [empirical] method into the spiritual realm," and they "considered evolution to be a basic, spiritual principle through which the divinity in nature expressed itself." The faculty sided with the new professors and the students rallied to them.

Horace Cummings, superintendent of Church schools, became concerned because they were "applying the evolutionary theory and other philosophical hypotheses to principles of the gospel and to the teachings of the Church in such a way as to disturb, if not destroy the faith of the pupils," and he wrote, "Many stake presidents, some of our leading principals and teachers, and leading men who are friends of our schools have expressed deep anxiety to me about this matter."

Superintendent Cummings [concluded in a report that the professors] "seem to feel that they have a mission to protect the young from the errors of their parents."

President Brimhall himself defended the professors—that is, until some students "frankly told him they had quit praying because they learned in school there was no real God to hear them."

Shortly thereafter President Brimhall had a dream.

He saw several of the BYU professors standing around a peculiar machine on the campus. When one of them touched a spring a baited fish hook attached to a long thin wire rose rapidly into the air. . .

Casting his eyes around the sky he [President Brimhall] discovered a flock of snow-white birds circling among the clouds and disporting themselves in the sky, seemingly very happy. Presently one of them, seeing the bait on the hook, darted toward it and grabbed it. Instantly one of the professors on the ground touched a spring in the machine, and the bird was rapidly hauled down to the earth.

On reaching the ground the bird proved to be a BYU student, clad in an ancient Greek costume, and was directed to join a group of other students who had been brought down in a similar manner. Brother Brimhall walked over to them, and noticing that all of them looked very sad, discouraged and downcast, he asked them:

"Why, students, what on earth makes you so sad and downhearted?"

"Alas, we can never fly again!" they replied with a sigh and a sad shake of the head.

Their Greek philosophy had tied them to the earth. They could believe only what they could demonstrate in the laboratory. Their prayers could go no higher than the ceiling. They could see no heaven—no hereafter.

Now deeply embarrassed by the controversy and caught between opposing factions, President Brimhall at first attempted to be conciliatory. He said, "I have been hoping for a year or two past that harmony could be secured by waiting, but the delays have been fraught with increased danger." When an exercise in *administrative diplomacy* suddenly became an *issue of faith*, President Brimhall acted.

SOURCE: Boyd K. Packer, "The Snow-White Birds," 2–3.

"TAKE HOLD OF THAT ROPE"
George Q. Cannon

There were ten of us, of whom I was the youngest, wind-bound in the Bay of San Francisco, and we had been thus delayed for nearly a week near the Golden Gate in consequence of head winds. I dreamed one night that this party of brethren were heaving at the windlass, having a rope attached to it reaching forward to the anchor at the bow of the vessel. We were working with all our might endeavoring to raise the anchor, but seemingly we made but little progress. While thus engaged I thought the Prophet Joseph came from the after part of the vessel dressed in his temple clothes, and tapping me on the shoulder told me to go with him. I went, and he climbed on to the forecastle which was higher than the main deck and on a level with the bulwarks, and there he knelt down, also telling me to kneel down with him. He prayed according to the order of prayer which is revealed. After prayer, he arose upon his feet. "Now," said he, "George, take hold of that rope"—the rope we had been pulling on with all our might. I took hold of it, and with the greatest ease and without the least effort, the anchor was raised. "Now," said he, "let this be a lesson to you; remember that great things can be accomplished through the power of prayer and the exercise of faith in the right way."

SOURCE: George Q. Cannon, in *Journal of Discourses*, 22:289.

"MY HEART CHANGED"
(Related by D. Todd Christofferson)

Not long ago, a friend recounted to me an experience he had while serving as a mission president. He had undergone a surgery that required several weeks of recuperation. During his recovery, he devoted time to searching the scriptures. One afternoon as he pondered the Savior's words in the 27th chapter of 3 Nephi, he drifted off to sleep. He subsequently related:

"I fell into a dream in which I was given a vivid, panoramic view of my life. I was shown my sins, poor choices, the times . . . I had treated people with impatience, plus the omissions of good things I should have said or done. . . . [A] comprehensive . . . [review of] my life was shown to me in just a few minutes, but it seemed much longer. I awoke, startled, and . . . instantly dropped to my knees beside the bed and began to pray, to plead for forgiveness, pouring out the feelings of my heart like I had never done previously.

"Prior to the dream, I didn't know that I [had] such great need to repent. My faults and weaknesses suddenly became so plainly clear to me that the gap between the person I was and the holiness and goodness of God seemed [like] millions of miles. In my prayer that late afternoon, I expressed my deepest gratitude to Heavenly Father and to the Savior with my whole heart for what They had done for me and for the relationships I treasured with my wife and children. While on my knees I also felt God's love and mercy that was so palpable, despite my feeling so unworthy. . . .

"I can say I haven't been the same since that day. . . . My heart changed. . . . What followed is that I developed more empathy toward others, with a greater capacity to love, coupled with a sense of urgency to preach the gospel. . . . I could relate to the messages of faith, hope, and the gift of repentance found in the Book of Mormon [as] never before."

It is important to recognize that this good man's vivid revelation of his sins and shortcomings did not discourage him or lead him to despair. Yes, he felt shock and remorse. He felt keenly his need to repent. He had been humbled, yet he felt gratitude, peace, and hope—real hope—because of Jesus Christ, "the living bread which came down from heaven" (John 6:51).

SOURCE: D. Todd Christofferson, "The Living Bread Which Came Down from Heaven," 37–38.

"WRITE HOME FOR MONEY"
M. F. Cowley

Elder Henry W. Barnett and myself left Salt Lake City, February 24th, 1878, for the South, with instructions to spend some time in Graves County, Kentucky, among the relatives of Elder Samuel R. Turnbow of this city, and from whose nephew B. R. Turnbow, the Elders had received an invitation to visit. If we found no encouraging field of labor there we were to proceed to the State of Virginia. We spent one month in Kentucky, and held a number of public meetings and Gospel conversations. My companion felt impressed that we should go to Virginia, and started for that field about April 1st. Not having a very liberal supply of money we traveled by steamboat instead of rail from Paducah, Ky., to Nashville, Tennessee. From thence we proceeded by rail to Chattanooga, where we found ourselves in a strange city without sufficient means to pay our way to Big Lick, our railroad destination in the State of Virginia. We had enough, however, to pay for lodging a few days, and obtain a little food each day. We had addresses of members of the Church in Kentucky and Virginia, and concluded to write them for means, as a loan, to help us to our field of labor. We did so, but in every instance failed to procure assistance, and in some instances received no response to our letters. In the meantime the little money we had was well nigh exhausted, until we had to get trusted for our lodging, and for food expended sometimes five cents, sometimes ten cents a day each for a few crackers and a little cheese or a bowl of bread and milk.

While in this straightened situation, I dreamed that I was housed up in a room where there was no air, and in struggling for breath I would turn to the North, then to the East, then to the South, but in vain, until I turned my face to the West, when it seemed that an opening was made in the enclosure and I breathed with freedom. Upon awakening I felt very depressed, for it seemed to me that the dream meant that while we had friends North of us in Kentucky, East in Virginia, and South in Georgia, the only hope was to write home for money and this I fought against with a strong resolution. Again, I slept and dreamed that I received two letters from home in the same mail, one was a pale, cream-colored envelope, the other, the old-fashioned deep yellow, and addressed to me in my mother's hand-writing. When I awoke in the morning I was still depressed, for while the dreams were clear to my mind as having a decided importance, it was against my inclination to write home for money, so I held out for several days, and did not tell my companion the dream. In a few days, however, Elder Barnett made a remark to me, which impressed me that it was my duty to write for means, which I did, and when the answer came, there were two letters instead of one. One was contained in a pale, cream-colored envelope, the other a deep yellow, addressed to me in my mother's handwriting, in all particulars just as I had seen it in my dream, and containing means for our assistance.

SOURCE: M. F. Cowley, "Acts of Special Providence in Missionary Experience," 264–65.

"I WAS STANDING UNDER A LARGE TREE"
Philo Dibble

Soon after the death of Joseph and Hyrum, I dreamed I was standing under a large tree in company with others. I looked and saw Brother Joseph coming with a sheet of paper in his hand. The paper was rolled up. Joseph threw the roll into the top of the tree. The roll came tumbling down through the limbs, and all under the tree watched the roll to catch it, and I caught it. This was the end of my dream. I pondered over the dream and was satisfied it had a meaning. The next day I went to the temple about eleven o'clock. Those standing all around me vanished. I saw the martyrdom of Joseph and Hyrum at Carthage. I saw what looked like smoke rising up on the horizon. Then everything came back to me as it was before. I pondered over what I had seen for two days. I was poor and did not know how to accomplish such a work. I thought I would commence it by subscription. I drew up the subscription. I then went to see Brother Brigham and told him that I proposed painting the martyrdom of Joseph and Hyrum at Carthage. Brigham said, "Go ahead and I will assist you." He put his hand into his pocket and gave me two dollars. I then went and bought the canvass. When I came to the place where the tree stood my dream came back to me. I held in my hand the roll that I caught from the tree. I then went ahead at painting some of the scenes through which the saints had passed. I speak of these things to show that the Lord doth nothing except He first shows it to His servants, either in dreams or in visions.*

SOURCE: Philo Dibble, *Reminiscences*.

"I WANT TO KNOW IF I DONE RIGHT"
William Flake

William Flake purchased the Silver Creek Ranch from James Stinson for $12,000 (Lucy has 1,200 in her diary), and three families moved there from the Taylor settlement. . . .

The purchase of Silver Creek Ranch necessitated William's return to Utah for more stock. Knowing of [his wife] Lucy's homesickness, he allowed her and all the children except James to return to Utah with him.

When William had pulled his stock out of the United Order at Taylor, he was accused of being an apostate, a designation which troubled him greatly. On this return trip to Beaver, the company met Erastus Snow a few miles below Brigham City. William counseled with Apostle Snow concerning moving to the new location, relating a dream he had had, in which Brigham Young appeared to him. In his dream he told Brigham about purchasing the ranch after which "President Young ran his hand in his pocket as if to pull out money he said Bro Young I don't want money I want to know if I done right." After relating this dream to Erastus Snow, the Apostle replied that that was all the counsel he needed. William continued to Utah to secure stock while Apostle Snow continued to the new settlement to organize a ward and stake. It was Erastus Snow who gave the settlement its name: "Snow" in honor of his being the

---

*For additional information about the artwork Philo Dibble created as a result of this dream, see R. Devan Jensen, "Philo Dibble's Dream of a 'Gallery in Zion,'" *Journal of Mormon History*, vol. 44, no. 4 (October 2018): 19–39.

Apostle in charge of the Southern Utah-Northern Arizona colonization, and "Flake" to honor its founder.

SOURCE: Chad J. Flake, "From the Diary of Lucy Hannah White Flake," 240–41.

"RETURN TO NAUVOO"
Thomas Grover

During the years from 1840 to . . . 1844, Brother Grover was sent on three missions through the states of Michigan, New York and southern Canada. In June, 1844, while doing missionary service near Kalamazoo, Michigan, he was warned in a dream to return to Nauvoo. He hesitated about the matter until the warning was repeated the third time. Then he awoke his companion, a Brother Wilson, and they got up, made it a matter of prayer and were told to go at once to Nauvoo. They did so, taking the shortest route possible, and arrived at Carthage just after the martyrdom of the Prophet Joseph and his brother Hyrum. Hurrying forward, they overtook the company with the bodies and accompanied them to Nauvoo, where Brother Thomas was requested to assist in the preparation of the bodies for burial. During that service, at the request of Emma Smith, he cut a lock from the Prophet's hair which she divided with him.

SOURCE: Andrew Jenson, *Latter-day Saint Biographical Encyclopedia*, 4:137.

"TRUE LOVE AT FIRST SIGHT"
Jacob Hamblin

It was on a cold, windy day in February (the fifth to be exact), 1849, when she [Lucinda] bundled her infant son in his sweater coat and waited for Jacob and the other three children to return from a visit to his father's place.

She took her thirteen-month-old baby, Lyman Stoddard, in her arms and met Jacob and the children at the fence, shoved the baby under it, and yelled at him to take his "little Mormon brats." There was no need to plead or multiply words; too many angry words had already been uttered. Jacob, in his stoical way, was not surprised. His demeanor seemed unchanged, but his heart was heavy as the wagon rolled away toward his father's house with his four bewildered children. . . .

After several days of travel they were filled with a joyful expectancy by the sight of Council Bluffs in the distance. With the desertion of Lucinda followed by the death of Jacob's mother, his situation had become very precarious. His family needed a mother. . . . . Jacob prayed many times for a solution to his problem, but not until the morning when he entered the settlement did he receive a complete answer. The feeling had been a peculiar one. He knew that soon there would be a mother for his children. Somewhere, not very far away, God would give him a companion and a partner whose value would be above rubies, a woman who would be ready when the time came.

Having entered the outskirts of the settlement, Jacob saw a large, well-built log cabin, neatly fenced, with a rock walk leading to the front door. They wondered why he stared in that direction. They noticed the color mount in Jacobs's face as he continued to gaze toward the house. He hadn't mentioned the dream he had the night before about seeing a log cabin and a widow with two children living there who would become part of his family.

Inside the house was Rachel Judd, a widow and a native of Canada, and two children of her deceased husband by a former marriage, who had migrated to Nauvoo with her parents, who had been among the first to join the Church there. For several days, according to her telling of the story in later years, she had a peculiar feeling come over her. She had a conviction that a man would come to her door that day who would become her future husband. The thought had preyed upon her mind. She had seemed, by instinct, to determine how she would be able to take all her things with her. So sure was she that he would come that she had dressed in her Sunday best and packed her trunk.

The knock on the door didn't seem to surprise her. The first words she heard after she bade the stranger to enter were, "My name is Jacob Hamblin, I was impressed to come to your home and ask you to be my wife." Her reply was, "I am Rachel Judd, and am willing to marry you, but it will be impossible for us to have any children." Jacob, remembering his dream, replied, "My name is Jacob, yours is Rachel, we will have two sons and shall name them Joseph and Benjamin." This proved to be true. In addition, their home was blessed with three daughters, Lois, Rachel Tamar, and Ariminda.

Continuing, Jacob asked, "Are you ready?" She replied, "Yes; wait until I get my things." It was true love at first sight. They were married immediately by the justice of the peace and after at the Endowment house at Salt Lake City.

SOURCE: Pearson H. Corbett, *Jacob Hamblin, the Peacemaker*, 29–30, 31–32.

"BEHOLD, HERE ARE THE PLATES"
Lucy Harris (Related by Lucy Mack Smith)

[Lucy Harris was the wife of Martin Harris, one of the Three Witnesses of the Book of Mormon.]

Accordingly, when Tuesday afternoon arrived, Mrs. Harris made her appearance. As soon as she came in and was well seated, she began to importune my son [Joseph Smith Jr.] as to the truth of what he said concerning the record, declaring that if he really had any gold plates, she *would* see them and she was resolved to help him in publishing them.

He told her that she was mistaken—that she could not see them, as he was not permitted to exhibit them to anyone except those whom the Lord should appoint to testify of them. "And as to assistance," said Joseph, "I always prefer dealing with men, rather than their wives."

This highly displeased Mrs. Harris, for she was a woman who considered herself altogether superior to her husband. "Well, now, Joseph," said she, "are you not telling me a lie? Can you look full in my eye and say before God that you have, in reality, found that record as you pretend?"

He said indifferently, "Why, yes, Mrs. Harris. I would as soon look into your face and say so as not, if you would be at all gratified by it."

"Now, Joseph," said she, "I will tell what I will do. If I can get a witness that you do speak the truth, I will believe it, and I shall want to do something about the translation—and I mean to help you anyway."

This closed the evening's conversation. She went to bed, and in the morning told us a very remarkable dream. She said that a personage had appeared to her the night before and said to her that inasmuch as she had disputed the servant of the Lord, said that his word was not to be believed, and asked him many improper questions, she had done that which was not right in the sight of God. Then he said, "Behold, here are the plates, look upon them and believe."

She then described the record minutely and again said that she had made up her mind as to what she would do; namely, that she had in her possession twenty-eight dollars that her mother had given her just before she died, when she was on her deathbed. Joseph should take that, and if he *would* he might give his note, but he would certainly accept of it on some terms.

This last proposition he acceded to in order to get rid of her importunities.

SOURCE: Lucy Mack Smith, *Revised and Enhanced History*, 152–53.

DREAMS OF INSTRUCTION

"A FIVE-YEAR-OLD DRIVING THE CAR"
Jeffrey R. Holland

Early in our married life my young family and I were laboring through graduate school at a university in New England. Pat was the Relief Society president in our ward, and I was serving in our stake presidency. I was going to school full-time and teaching half-time. We had two small children then, with little money and lots of pressures. . . .

One evening I came home from long hours at school, feeling the proverbial weight of the world on my shoulders. Everything seemed to be especially demanding and discouraging and dark. I wondered if the dawn would ever come. Then, as I walked into our small student apartment, there was an unusual silence in the room.

"What's the trouble?" I asked. "Matthew has something he wants to tell you," Pat said. "Matt, what do you have to tell me?" He was quietly playing with his toys in the corner of the room, trying very hard not to hear me. "Matt," I said a little louder, "do you have something to tell me?"

He stopped playing, but for a moment didn't look up. Then two enormous, tear-filled brown eyes turned toward me, and with the pain only a five-year-old can know, he said, "I didn't mind Mommy tonight, and I spoke back to her." With that he burst into tears, and his entire body shook with grief. A childish indiscretion had been noted, a painful confession had been offered, the growth of a five-year-old was continuing, and loving reconciliation could have been wonderfully underway.

Everything might have been just terrific—except for me. If you can imagine such an idiotic thing, I lost my temper. It wasn't that I lost it with Matt—it was with a hundred and one other things on my mind. But he didn't know that, and I wasn't disciplined enough to admit it. He got the whole load of bricks.

I told him how disappointed I was and how much more I

thought I could have expected from him. I sounded like the parental pygmy I was. Then I did what I had never done before in his life—I told him that he was to go straight to bed and that I would not be in to say his prayers with him or to tell him a bedtime story. Muffling his sobs, he obediently went to his bedside, where he knelt—alone—to say his prayers. Then he stained his little pillow with tears his father should have been wiping away.

If you think the silence upon my arrival was heavy, you should have felt it now. Pat did not say a word. She didn't have to. I felt terrible!

Later, as we knelt by our own bed, my feeble prayer for blessings upon my family fell back on my ears with a horrible, hollow ring. I wanted to get up off my knees right then and go to Matt and ask his forgiveness, but he was long since peacefully asleep.

My own relief was not so soon coming, but finally I fell asleep and began to dream, which I seldom do. I dreamed Matt and I were packing two cars for a move. For some reason his mother and baby sister were not present. As we finished I turned to him and said, "Okay, Matt, you drive one car and I'll drive the other."

This five-year-old very obediently crawled up on the seat and tried to grasp the massive steering wheel. I walked over to the other car and started the motor. As I began to pull away, I looked to see how my son was doing. He was trying—oh, how he was trying. He tried to reach the pedals, but he couldn't. He was also turning knobs and pushing buttons, trying to start the motor. He could scarcely be seen over the dashboard, but there staring out at me again were those same immense, tear-filled, beautiful brown eyes. As I pulled away, he cried out, "Daddy, don't leave me. I don't know how to do it. I'm too little." And I drove away.

A short time later, driving down that desert road in my dream, I suddenly realized in one stark, horrifying moment what I had done. I slammed my car to a stop, threw open the door, and started to run as fast as I could. I left car, keys, belongings, and all—and I ran. The pavement was so hot it burned my feet, and tears blinded my straining effort to see this child somewhere on the horizon. I kept running, praying, pleading to be forgiven and to find my boy safe and secure.

As I rounded a curve, nearly ready to drop from physical and emotional exhaustion, I saw the unfamiliar car I had left Matt to drive. It was pulled carefully off to the side of the road, and he was laughing and playing nearby. An older man was with him, playing and responding to his games. Matt saw me and cried out something like, "Hi, Dad. We're having fun." Obviously he had already forgiven and forgotten my terrible transgression against him.

But I dreaded the older man's gaze, which followed my every move. I tried to say "Thank you," but his eyes were filled with sorrow and disappointment. I muttered an awkward apology and the stranger said simply, "You should not have left him alone to do this difficult thing. It would not have been asked of you."

With that, the dream ended, and I shot upright in bed. *My* pillow was stained, whether with perspiration or tears I do not know. I threw off the covers and ran to the little metal camp cot that was my son's bed. There on my knees and through my tears I cradled him in my arms and spoke to him while he slept. I told him that every dad makes mistakes but that they don't mean to. I told him it wasn't his fault I had had a bad day. I told him that when boys are five or fifteen, dads sometimes forget and think they are fifty. I told him that I wanted him to be a small boy for a long, long time, because all too soon he would grow up and be a man and wouldn't be playing on the floor with his toys when I came home. I told him that I loved him and his mother and his sister more than anything in the world and that whatever challenges we had in life we would face them together. I told him that never again would I withhold my affection or my forgiveness from him, and never, I prayed, would he withhold them from me. I told him I was honored to be his father and that I would try with all my heart to be worthy of such a great responsibility.

SOURCE: Jeffrey R. Holland, "Within the Clasp of Your Arms," 36–38.

"THE TEAPOT"
(Related by Milton R. Hunter)

I do not recall the stake, and so I don't know which stake president to give credit to for this story. . . . He reported that there was a certain lady living in his ward who had joined the Church over in Europe when she was a girl; and like many of the European people she had formed the habit of drinking tea. After she joined the Church of Jesus Christ, like quite a few Mormons (I am sorry to say) she continued the habit of drinking tea. She reared a large family. Her children married. Her husband died, and she became a widow. And then she became a temple worker. Day after day she went to the temple, and no doubt the consciousness of the tea-drinking habit she had bore rather heavily on her mind or on her conscience. One night she had a dream. She dreamed that she died and that she passed on into the other world. There she came into the presence of the Savior, the Prophet Joseph Smith, and many other great and good people who had lived on this earth and whose lives had been such that they were now worthy to become celestial beings. Very sweet, serene, and happy were the feelings that she experienced there. In fact, there were no words to describe how beautiful the conditions were there, until she looked down into her hand and saw her old dirty, black teapot. Then her happiness turned to sorrow and shame. She immediately looked all around in the heavenly realm for some place to hide that teapot, but she couldn't find any place. She had to hang on to it. Then she awoke. Cold drops of perspiration were running down her face. She got out of bed, turned the light on, dressed, and went in the other room. There on her stove sat her old dirty teapot. She picked it up, went down to the back of the lot and threw it into the Jordan River, and she said, "There! I am not going to take you to heaven with me."

SOURCE: Milton R. Hunter, in Conference Report, April 1950, 91–92.

"I WANTED TO CROSS"
Heber C. Kimball

In his journal, Apostle Woodruff records a dream related to him by Heber C. Kimball:

"I dreamed that I was travelling with a companion, and we came to a powerful, rapid stream of water like the Niagara River. The waves were rolling very high and increasing in size. They had been muddy, but were getting clear. As we came to this rushing stream, we did not know how we should get over it. I turned my eyes a few moments from my companion, and when I looked back I saw him on the other side of the river and climbing a steep hill. I did not know how he got there. I wanted to cross, so I called to him as loud as I could to stop and wait for me, but he paid no attention to me, but went on as fast as he could. Then a person came to me and said you have an iron rod in your hand, which I perceived I had. It was several feet long. The angel said to me: 'You must use this rod and feel your way over the river.' Then I awoke.

"I considered my dream and interpreted it as follows: My companion was J. M. Grant, who had suddenly died and left me, and was on the other side of the veil. The waters mean the people. They are increasing in strength and growing better and clearer. The iron rod is the word of God, which I must cling to till I get through life. I consider there are great things awaiting this people."

SOURCE: Matthias Cowley, *Wilford Woodruff*, 376.

"KEEP ABOARD THE SHIP"
Heber C. Kimball

[Brigham Young and other early Church leaders sometimes referred to the Church as "Zion's ship."]

The Zion's ship that was spoken of to-day [October 6, 1854], which runs in Snag harbour, has prospered from the first day it was launched, and every man and woman who stick firmly to that ship will prosper from this time henceforth and for ever. That I know, for I have been on board that ship, and am now sailing upon it.

The first time I went to England, I was on board of Zion's ship, and Joseph came to me while I was sailing, and put into my hand a rod; and I presume, if I have dreamed once of being aboard of that ship, I have dreamed it a hundred times. I have *been in it* in the midst of dangers and in the most dangerous places. I have seen trees and stumps, mountains and rocks, and everything else that could be placed in her course thrown before her to stop her in her course; but she can sail through a mountain or on dry land as well as upon the water. I have this in dreams; and I will say to the brethren, Just so long as you keep aboard of that ship you will prosper. I do not care whether it is in the midst of the Lamanites or among the Jews—whether it is in Italy or in Denmark, in Europe or in America, we will prosper, and I know it. That is my testimony.

SOURCE: Heber C. Kimball, in *Journal of Discourses*, 7:39.

"YOU SHALL NOW HAVE STRENGTH"
Heber C. Kimball

"I was in a great water, swimming, and had swam away, trying to make land, although I saw no land, until I had become weary and tired, when I began to sink; then an angel came to me and placed his hand under my chin, for some time keeping me from sinking, until I had rested and gained strength; he blessed me and said,

'Brother Heber, you shall now have strength to swim ashore.' I again began to swim, and it appeared as though every time I stretched forth my arms and feet, I would move rods at each stroke, and continued doing so until I reached land."

This dream, coming as such dreams generally do, in a season of deep depression, was as a spring of pure water in the desert to the parched lips of the weary traveler. As a promise of success, it was amply verified in the subsequent experience of the father and founder of the British mission.

SOURCE: Orson F. Whitney, *Life of Heber C. Kimball*, 132–33.

"BUILD A DRILL"
John Renouard (Related by Kevin J Worthen)

John [Renouard] started his organization WHOlives shortly after traveling to Africa with his family and seeing the need for clear water. But he didn't know exactly what he needed to do at that point. He went online and saw a brick-making machine that, it turned out, had been developed in an engineering capstone project at BYU. With that in mind, John called the capstone office, was informed that the responsible person was out of town, and then left his number. John described what happened a few weeks later:

In the middle of the night, I had a dream. It was strong enough that it got me out of bed to my kitchen table to write down what I had seen. Intuitively, I knew that it was a drill, but I am not a well driller. I was a finance major, and I lived in Southern California. My water came from a tap. But I knew that this was something that I needed to jot down. That was the first miracle. The next one happened the next day when I got a call from the BYU capstone program asking me if I had a program or a project that they could work on.

John then met with faculty from the engineering program to explain the need that he had observed in Africa. But he did not give them his specific drill ideas. As he put it:

One of the great concepts of capstone projects is that you don't go to the students and tell them, "Go build this," and then give them schematics and everything. You tell them, "This is what we want to do. Now go and do it."

After several months of work by the students, John received a text. As John explained:

"The text said, 'We sent you a CAD drawing. Can you open it?' And I did. When I opened it, I saw that drill, and I recognized it from my dream. It was like, 'There it is! How did they do that?' It was amazing."

SOURCE: Kevin J Worthen, "BYU: A Unique Kind of Education."

"HOW DO YOU DO IT?"
Franklin D. Richards

About this time [about 1846] I had a dream, and about this time also our people were being turned out of the United States to seek a resting place where they could get the farthest from their friends. In my dream I was called upon by a gentleman who said he wanted to talk with me and to introduce me to a committee of men. He took me into a place where there were thirteen men. I can recollect the countenances of quite a number of them today. When I had been introduced to them, the chairman said to me, "Mr. Richards, we want to ask you a certain question. How is it that Mr. Young and you men that labor with him can get your people to do anything you want them to do? If it is to pull up stake and leave their homes and go from state to state, or make any kind of sacrifice or perform any labor, you have no trouble to do it. You don't have to go and preach it up, and labor to get them willing; all you have to do is to let them know that you think it would be well for them to do so and so, and they are in a hurry to get about and do it." Said he, "how do you do it? We would like to know the secret of that operation if you can tell us, for we have to argue a measure before the people and lay before them all the reasons, all the causes and all the probable consequences, and then it is with the utmost difficulties that we can accomplish the matter." I will tell you how in my dream I answered him.

I said to them, "Gentlemen, the way we are enabled to do this is because we make it first appear to the people that what we want them to do is that which is for their greatest good. We have been sent from our country to preach to the people of the world, and we have conferred upon them the blessings of the everlasting Gospel. They have found out that these are the greatest blessings that mortal man can enjoy; and having bestowed upon them in the name of our God these blessings, they feel that we have their interest deeply at heart, and feeling thus they wish us to continue to benefit and bless them. They found that when they rendered obedience to the Gospel it was their privilege to gather to America, the best of all countries, and establish homes, and they did so. They found themselves blessed in things temporal and in things spiritual. When there are offices to fill they want us to fill those offices, because they know that we have labored and have benefitted them so far; and having found out that we first loved and respected them before they loved and respected us they seek unto us for this continued benefit and blessing. That is how, when we signify anything to them they know that it is the best thing that can be done for them."

It was in that way and spirit that I answered their question, having in remembrance that scripture which says that we love God because He first loved us and gave His Only Begotten Son to die for us, and greater love than that hath no man.

That is the spirit and foundation of our work, the principle upon which it has been commenced and carried on so far. I want my brethren and sisters to realize that that is the principle, through all the Church, that is supposed to be employed and should be in every place—a spirit to work and labor for the interest of the people of God.

SOURCE: Franklin D. Richards, in *Collected Discourses, 1886–1898*, 5:176.

"I MUST LOVE MY ENEMIES"
George F. Richards

A few years ago, at the closing of a conference of the St. Johns Stake, we had had a wonderful conference I thought, and I was very happy on retiring. I was sleeping in the home of the president of the stake, Brother Levi Udall, and that night I had a remarkable dream. I have seldom mentioned this to other people, but I do not know why I should not. It seems to me appropriate in talking along this line. I dreamed that I and a group of my own associates found ourselves in a courtyard where, around the outer edge of it, were German soldiers—and Führer Adolph Hitler was there with his group, and they seemed to be sharpening their swords and cleaning their guns, and making preparations for a slaughter of some kind, or an execution. We knew not what, but, evidently we were the objects. But presently a circle was formed and this Führer and his men were all within the circle, and my group and I were circled on the outside, and he was sitting on the inside of the circle with his back to the outside, and when we walked around and I got directly opposite to him, I stepped inside the circle and walked across to where he was sitting, and spoke to him in a manner something like this:

"I am your brother. You are my brother. In our heavenly home we lived together in love and peace. Why can we not so live here on the earth?"

And it seemed to me that I felt in myself, welling up in my soul, a love for that man, and I could feel that he was having the same experience, and presently he arose, and we embraced each other and kissed each other, a kiss of affection.

Then the scene changed so that our group was within the circle, and he and his group were on the outside, and when he came around to where I was standing, he stepped inside the circle and embraced me again, with a kiss of affection.

I think the Lord gave me that dream. Why should I dream of

this man, one of the greatest enemies of mankind, and one of the wickedest, but that the Lord should teach me that I must love my enemies, and I must love the wicked as well as the good?

Now, who is there in this wide world that I could not love under those conditions, if I could only continue to feel as I felt then? I have tried to maintain this feeling and, thank the Lord, I have no enmity toward any person in this world; I can forgive all men, so far as I am concerned, and I am happy in doing so and in the love which I have for my fellow men.

SOURCE: George F. Richards, in Conference Report, October 1946, 139–40.

"THOSE RELATIONSHIPS ARE ENDURING AND UNCHANGING"
Richard G. Scott

When I awoke one night from a most disturbing dream, I ached physically, I was saturated with perspiration, and my heart was pounding. Every sense was sharpened. Although the actual dream was extensive, the key lessons communicated can be summarized by reference to a few specific experiences in the dream.

In it I found myself in a very different and unknown environment. Everything was strange to me. I could not recognize where I was or any of the individuals who surrounded me. I was anxiously seeking my wife, Jeanene. We had been separated, and I wanted very much to find her. Each individual I encountered said that I would not be able to do that. Repeatedly, as I sought in different directions to find her, I was emphatically told to forget her, for she would not be found. I was frustrated at every turn. One said, "She is no longer the same individual. There isn't a Jeanene like you knew."

I thought, "That is impossible. I know her, and I know she will never change."

Then I was told, "You are not the same. There is no individual by the name of Richard Scott, and soon all of the memories you've had of Jeanene, your children, and other loved ones will be eradicated."

Fear entered my heart, accompanied by a horrifying feeling. Then came the thought: "No, that is impossible. Those relationships are enduring and unchanging. As long as we live righteously, they cannot be eliminated. They are eternally fixed."

As more encounters came, I realized that I was surrounded with evil individuals who were completely unhappy, with no purpose save that of frustrating the happiness of others so that they too would become miserable. These wicked ones were striving to manipulate those persons over whom they sought to exercise control. I somehow was conscious that those who believed their lies were being led through treachery and deceit from what they wanted most. They soon began to believe that their individuality, their experience, and their relationships as families and friends were being altered and lost. They became angry, aggressive, and engulfed by feelings of hopelessness.

The pressure became more intense to accept as reality that what I had been no longer existed and that my cherished wife was no longer the same. I resisted those thoughts with every capacity that I could find. I was determined to find her. I knew that there must be a way and was resolute in searching no matter what the cost in time or effort.

It was then that I broke out of that oppressive surrounding and could see that it was an ugly, artificial, contrived environment. So intense were the feelings generated by what I had been told by those bent on destroying my hope to take me captive that I had not realized the forces of opposition that made my efforts appear fruitless could have no power over me unless I yielded through fear or abandonment of my principles. The environment appeared real, yet it had been generated from fear and threat. Although it was simulated, to those who let themselves believe the falsehoods thrust upon them it became reality.

I can now understand that because of my faith in the truths of the gospel plan, I could break through Satan's manipulative, evil environment to see it as it is—not only in the dream, but in real life as well—a confining, controlling, destructive influence that can be overcome by faith in and obedience to truth.

As I awoke, there flooded over me feelings of love and gratitude for our Heavenly Father and His Beloved Son that I do not have the capacity to express. My heart and mind filled with consuming love for Them and inexpressible appreciation for the blessings that are available to every spirit child of Father in Heaven willing to believe and be obedient to the plan of happiness. I cannot convey the unspeakable joy, the feeling of being wrapped in pure love, the absolute assurance that we will never lose our identity or memory of cherished relationships or the benefits of righteous acts as we continue to resist evil and are obedient to truth.

Although I would not welcome another like experience, this dream has taught me how easy it is to take for granted our relationship with our Father in Heaven and His Beloved Son, our Master and Savior. Oh, how blessed are we that They are as They say They are, perfect in every possible capacity and attribute.

Source: Richard G. Scott, *21 Principles*, 77–79.

"HE SAW A LIGHT EMANATING FROM THE BOOK"
(Related by William R. Sloan)

Just recently [1927] I received a letter from one of the missionaries in the Northwestern States mission in which he recounted this experience to me. He said: "President Sloan, we called on a man and left with him a Book of Mormon." . . . During the night, after he had retired and fallen asleep, he had what you may call a dream or a vision, or what you will. He was taken into a valley through which a river of water was running. Trees were on both sides of the stream, and among the trees and on each side of the river were numerous tents of Indians, or tepees, or wigwams, as you wish to call them. The Indians were there in hundreds, going about their daily duties, etc. He saw nothing to this, however, except a large tribe of Indians. Then this part of the dream closed and he was carried over into his own home, into his own bedroom, and lying on a little center table near his bed was a copy of the Book of Mormon. He saw the book lying there and as he beheld the cover of it he saw a light emanating from the book, and it arose about twelve inches above the book. There it stood for a second or two and then gradually ascended clear into the heavens. He connected the two together and the next day he sought the elders. He said: "You did not tell me that the Book of Mormon was a history of the American Indians. Now I know it is. I know it is a record of God's dealings with those people, because he revealed it to me in my dreams last night."

SOURCE: William R. Sloan, in Conference Report, April 1927, 123.

"DO NOT BURY YOUR TESTIMONY IN THE GROUND"
Elizabeth Staheli Walker

Several months ago I read the testimony of my great-grandfather's sister Elizabeth Staheli Walker. As a child, Elizabeth immigrated to America from Switzerland with her family.

After Elizabeth married, she and her husband and children lived in Utah near the Nevada border, where they ran a mail station. Their home was a stopping place for travelers. All day and all night they had to be ready to cook and serve meals for travelers. It was hard, exhausting work, and they had little rest. . . .

One night Elizabeth had a dream. She said: "It seemed I was standing by a narrow wagon road, which led around by the foot of a low rolling hill; halfway up the hill I saw a man looking down and speaking, or seemed to be speaking, to a young man who was kneeling and leaning over a hole in the earth. His arms were stretched out, and it looked as if he was reaching for something from in the hole. I could see the lid of stone that seemed to have been taken off from the hole over which the boy was bending. On the road were many people, but none of them seemed to be at all interested in the two men on the hillside. There was something that came along with the dream that impressed me so strangely that I woke right up; . . . I could not tell my dream to anyone, but I seemed to be satisfied that it meant the angel Moroni [instructed] the boy Joseph at the time he got the plates."

In the spring of 1893, Elizabeth went to Salt Lake City to the dedication of the temple. She described her experience: "In there I saw the same picture [that] I had seen in my dream; I think it was [a] colored-glass window. I feel satisfied that if I saw the Hill Cumorah itself, it would not look more real. I feel satisfied that I was shown in a dream a picture of the angel Moroni giving Joseph Smith the [gold] plates."

Many years after having this dream and several months before she died at nearly age 88, Elizabeth received a powerful impression. She said, "The thought came to me as plain . . . as if someone had said to me, . . . 'Do not bury your testimony in the ground.'

SOURCE: Cheryl A. Esplin, "Filling Our Homes with Light and Truth," 9–10.

"KEEP NO ONE OUT"
Wilford Woodruff

[In 1893,] President [Wilford] Woodruff had another dream wherein Brigham Young said, in essence, to keep no one out of the dedication. If those who wish to attend are minimally worthy and if they have agreed to pray and come fasting, then let them attend the dedication. President Woodruff had assumed the leaders would have to interview and prepare recommends for thousands of people. But after this dream he did precisely what he had been told. Many came. There were twenty-three dedicatory sessions, sometimes three a day, from April 6 on into the latter part of the month. . . . Two sessions were held just for children. More than sixty-five thousand people attended, and the spirit and power of the experience in some ways regenerated the Church. People returned from attending the temple dedication renewed in their faith, in their commitment, and in their love for the Lord Jesus Christ.

SOURCE: Truman G. Madsen, *The Presidents of the Church*, 106.

"AN ENSIGN TO THE NATIONS"
Brigham Young

Before leaving Nauvoo in the winter of 1846, President Brigham Young had a dream in which he saw an angel standing on a cone-shaped hill somewhere in the West pointing to a valley below. When he entered the Salt Lake Valley some 18 months later, he saw just above the location where we are now gathered the same hillside prominence he had seen in vision.

As has often been told from this pulpit, Brother Brigham led a handful of leaders to the summit of that hill and proclaimed it Ensign Peak, a name filled with religious meaning for these modern Israelites. Twenty-five hundred years earlier the prophet Isaiah had declared that in the last days "the mountain of the Lord's house shall be established in the top of the mountains," and there "he shall set up an ensign for the nations."

SOURCE: Jeffrey R. Holland, "An Ensign to the Nations," 111.

"CUT OFF THE DEAD BRANCHES"
Brigham Young

[This dream was originally shared by Brigham Young during a morning meeting on 18 August 1844 in Nauvoo, Illinois, less than two months after Joseph and Hyrum Smith had been killed at Carthage Jail. He shared the dream again while speaking in Pleasant Grove, Utah Territory, on 25 October 1860.]

Some here may recollect a dream I told you in Nauvoo, when

Sidney Rigdon was there, after the death of Joseph. I had a little dream that spoke more than volumes to me.

I had a beautiful tree . . . I thought it was of the sugar maple variety; it was a fine beautiful young thrifty tree. All at once a number of dead limbs came upon it. Some of these dead limbs were about the size of my little finger, and some were larger. . . . I spoke to my friends and said that tree must be trimmed forthwith, or it will certainly be destroyed. And we trimmed it as clean as though it had just Come out of a mould, and the tree flourished and grew beautifully. Those that will not keep the commands of the Lord, and despise his ways, sever them from the tree. I would like to have the people know truth and error for themselves.

SOURCE: *The Complete Discourses of Brigham Young*, 3:1702.

"DON'T BE IN A HURRY"
Brigham Young

[Dated 7 August 1845, this dream was recorded in Brigham Young's Office Journal.]

This morning I dreamed I saw brother Joseph Smith and as I was going about my business he says brother Brigham don't be in a hurry, this was repeated the second and third time, when it came in a degree of sharpness.

SOURCE: *The Complete Discourses of Brigham Young*, 1:96.

"THEY ARE ALL GOOD IN THEIR PLACES"
Brigham Young

Now I am going to tell a dream that I had, which I think is as applicable, to the people to-day—the 21st day of June, 1874, as when I had it. There were so many going to California. . . . It was California, California, California, California. "No," said I, "stay here." After much thought and reflection, and a good deal of praying and anxiety, . . . I had a dream one night, the second year after we came in here. . . . I was going after my goats. When I had gone round the point of the mountain by the Hot Springs, and had got about half a mile on the rise of ground beyond the Spring, whom should I meet but brother Joseph Smith. He had a wagon. . . . Behind the team I saw a great flock of sheep. I heard their bleating, and saw some goats among them. . . . Some of the sheep I should think were three and a half feet high, with large, fine, beautiful white fleeces, and they looked so lovely and pure; others were of moderate size, and pure and white; and in fact there were sheep of all sizes, with fleeces clean, pure and white. Then I saw some that were dark and spotted, of all colors and sizes and kinds, and their fleeces were dirty, and they looked inferior; some of these were a pretty good size, but not as large as some of the large fine clean sheep, and altogether there was a multitude of them of all sizes and kinds, and goats of all colors, sizes and kinds mixed among them. Joseph stopped the wagon, and the sheep kept rushing up until there was an immense herd. I looked in Joseph's eye, and laughed, just as I had many a time when he was alive, about some trifling thing or other, and said I—"Joseph, you have got the darndest flock of sheep I ever saw in my life; what are you going to do with them, what on earth are they for?" Joseph looked cunningly out of his eyes, just as he used to at times, and said he—"They are all good in their places." When I awoke in the morning I did not find any fault with those who wanted to go to California; I said, "If they want to go let them go, and we will do all we can to save them; I have no more fault to find, the sheep and the goats will run together, but Joseph says, "they are all good in their places."

This will apply precisely to what we are doing at the present time. We are trying to unite the people together in the order that the Lord revealed to Enoch, which will be observed and sustained in the latter days in redeeming and building up Zion; this is the very order that will do it, and nothing short of it. We are trying to organize the Latter-day Saints into this order; but I want to tell you, my brethren and sisters, that I have not come here to say that you have got to join this order or we will cut you off the Church, or you must join this order or we will consider you apostates; no such thing, oh no, the Saints are not prepared to see everything at once. They have got to learn little by little, and to receive a little here and a little there. . . . Try and live your religion; get the Spirit of the Lord and keep it; humble yourselves before the Lord and get his Spirit; ask the Father in the name of Jesus to open your minds and let you see things as they are, and you will delight in it.

SOURCE: *The Complete Discourses of Brigham Young*, 5:3035.

"TAKE ONE MORE STEP"
John Young

I recollect a dream that my father had. He dreamed that he was travelling, and that during his journey he came to a tremendous mountain of snow and saw that his pathway was hedged up. But some one said, "Take one more step." My father replied, "But that will be the last." However, he took that step, and then his guide said, "Do you not see that there is room for you to take another?" When he had taken another, his guide told him to take still another in advance; and there was a passage all the way through. So it will be with us. The Lord will not reveal all that we at times wish him to. If a schoolmaster were to undertake to teach a little child algebra, you would call him foolish, would you not? Just so with our Father: he reveals to us as we are prepared to receive, and I hope to continue to learn.

SOURCE: Brigham Young, in *Journal of Discourses*, 5:330.

CHAPTER 10

Dreams of Callings

One of President Thomas S. Monson's oft-quoted promises was, "If we are on the Lord's errand, we are entitled to the Lord's help."[1] At times, part of the "Lord's help" is giving dreams to assist Latter-day Saints in issuing, preparing, or fulfilling callings. In some dreams, people have learned of a future calling and were therefore better prepared to accept when it was offered. Dreams can prepare and encourage us in such a way that we are more willing to sacrifice or consecrate ourselves for the Lord's kingdom.

Several General Authorities have received advance notice through dreams of their impending calls to serve. Preparing leaders through dreams is not limited to our dispensation. The Lord revealed to Aaron and Miriam: "If there be a prophet among you, I the Lord will make myself known unto him in a vision, and will speak unto him in a dream" (Numbers 12:6), and the scriptures include examples from several previous dispensations. Dreams can increase the dreamer's confidence when he or she is called to serve as the Lord's representative. Dreams can also reinforce our resolve to serve and persevere when we might feel inadequate. As such, dreams can provide knowledge sufficient to help us move forward with confidence.

Some dreams included in this chapter were received by those who issue callings in The Church of Jesus Christ of Latter-day Saints. Dreams can guide those with the responsibility to extend callings, wherein the Spirit will instruct leaders regarding who should serve in specific assignments.

Other dreams are shared where a third party will reassure either those who are making a call or those who have been called. Likewise, there are some dreams recorded that have come to parents or other family members about a call received by a loved one.

Just as dreams are given to guide leaders, individuals, and third parties about future callings, dreams can provide reassurance after a calling has been accepted, confirming that the dreamer is serving as the Lord desires. Direction can also be given through dreams regarding how to magnify callings. The Lord can also instruct and increase the faith of his followers through dreams.

In short, our Heavenly Father is very aware of the callings that take place in His Church, and He is willing to facilitate these callings so that they are issued and magnified in a way that He deems appropriate. Dreams can help prepare Church members to serve in the kingdom of God, and they can supply evidence that those who serve in the Church do, indeed, qualify for the Lord's help.

"I JUST HOPED IT WOULDN'T COME TOO SOON"
(Related by Marvin J. Ashton)

A few weeks ago while in Idaho reorganizing a stake presidency, I not only met some outstanding priesthood leaders and set three of them apart as a new stake presidency, but I also met a very special young lady I will not soon forget. The newly called presidency, one of whom was serving as a bishop at the time, asked if I could interview a prospective bishop so if he were cleared he could be installed the following Sunday after conference. The appointment was made. I sat in a private office with a well-groomed, attractive couple.

After a few words of greeting and introductions, I looked at her and said, "Tell me about your husband." She hesitated and finally said, "Elder Ashton, I really don't know him very well." Since this was a most unusual response, I promptly said, "Please tell me about that." She responded with, "We have only been married three weeks."

This young couple, both in their early thirties, he an attorney and she a schoolteacher by profession, were still honeymooning, and their deep, newly found love for each other was most evident. When I said, "I want to talk to the two of you about your husband becoming a bishop," she said, "Some nights ago I had a dream indicating Randy would be a bishop. I just hoped it wouldn't come too soon." She continued with, "Even though we are newlyweds [and incidentally, they told me the reason they had waited until their thirties to marry was because they had spent a long time finding each other] if you are impressed to call Randy to be a bishop, he will be a good one, and I will help him."

SOURCE: Marvin J. Ashton, "Choose the Good Part," 9.

"MY EIGHT-YEAR-OLD DREAMED OF MY CALL"
(Related by Peggy Petersen Barton)

On one occasion in the Northwest, as they [Elder Spencer W. Kimball and Elder Mark E. Petersen] struggled with interviews long into the night, they knelt in prayer at midnight and both independently received the impression that a certain man should be the new [stake] president. Rather than wake the family, they waited until the Sunday morning of stake conference to call on him at his home. His wife was serving breakfast as they entered the room, and the soon-to-be president sat surrounded by his children. Elder Kimball said, "We have come to call you as president of the stake." The man replied, "I knew you were coming. Last night my eight-year-old dreamed of my call and saw you in her dream. When she described two apostles, one short, one tall, I knew it was true."

SOURCE: Peggy Petersen Barton, *Mark E. Petersen*, 96.

"BISHOP OF BEENLEIGH WARD"
Peter Boehme

The years after World War II were difficult in Germany. It was 1948, and fourteen-year-old Peter Boehme added to his family's income by carrying suitcases and bags from the railroad station to travelers' homes. Peter and his family had survived the war, though they lived in Dresden, which had been heavily bombed by the Allied forces.

On this day, he picked up the bags of two men dressed in suits and asked their destination. They explained to Peter that they had traveled from Cottbus to conduct a conference for The Church of Jesus Christ of Latter-day Saints and they had no overnight accommodations arranged. Peter took them home to stay in his family's spare room, and the two men, district president Fritz Lehnig and Otto Sasse, converted the whole family. Peter, his parents, his brother, Lutz, and his two sisters, Ingrid and Helgard, were baptized in a Dresden stream.

Three years later, at age seventeen, Peter fled to West Germany when the tensions between East and West intensified. Wanting to start a new life, he emigrated to Australia and lived for some time in the outback of Queensland before contacting Church members in Brisbane. In 1956 he accepted a call to serve a building mission in that area.

Then he married. He and his wife, Ann, began looking for property where they could build a home. One day, as they headed for the

Gold Coast hinterland, a fierce storm forced them to stop in the town of Beenleigh. Waiting for the weather to clear, or at least improve, they decided to look around at property for a home. Peter and Ann put down a deposit to secure a plot they liked. They intended to go home and pray about whether they should purchase the property.

That night Peter dreamed that he was called as bishop of Beenleigh Ward. In the morning he told Ann of his dream. She teased him that it was probably more an aspiration than an inspiration—after all, only three LDS families lived in Beenleigh. They themselves attended the Eight Mile Plains Ward, about a fifteen-minute drive from Beenleigh.

But the next night, Peter had the same dream again. This time, the dream included a congregation of members and a chapel being built in the area of Beenleigh. The third night, he again dreamed of serving as bishop of the Beenleigh Ward. This time the Beenleigh Ward was so large that members were being moved from that ward to form yet another.

Peter and Ann could no longer make light of the dreams. They obeyed the prompting and agreed to purchase the property. When they applied for a loan, they could show only a few dollars in their account, and the bank manager doubted that the loan would go through. Nevertheless, three hours later, they had received a loan. The land was theirs.

A year later, on 18 December 1978, the Church created the Beenleigh Branch, and Peter Boehme was called to serve as the branch president. There were 29 active members. Five years later, the branch had grown to 245 members, and on 27 November 1983, the Beenleigh Branch was made into a ward. Franz Herman Peter Boehme was called as bishop. The following year, on 14 October 1984, the ward dedicated a newly built chapel.

Church membership in the area continued to grow, and by 1986 the Marsden Ward was formed from the Beenleigh and Eight Mile

Plains First and Second Wards. The new ward met in the Beenleigh Chapel until its own chapel was completed in 1988.

The prophetic dreams of Peter Boehme had been fulfilled in only a little more than ten years.

Source: Heidi S. Swinton, *Pioneer Spirit*, 136–38.

"I HAVE THE SAME PRIVILEGE"
Carl B. Cook

Recently I received a new assignment. I had been serving in the Africa Southeast Area. It was thrilling to serve where the Church is relatively young and being established, and we loved the Saints. Then I was called to return to Church headquarters, and to be honest, I was less than enthusiastic. A change in assignment brought some unknowns.

One night after contemplating the upcoming change, I dreamed about my great-great-grandfather Joseph Skeen. I knew from his journal that when he and his wife, Maria, moved to Nauvoo, he desired to serve, so he sought out the Prophet Joseph Smith and asked how he could help. The Prophet sent him to work on the prairie and told him to do the best he could, so he did. He worked on the Smiths' farm.

I pondered the privilege that Joseph Skeen had in receiving his assignment that way. Suddenly I realized that I have the same privilege, as we all do. All Church callings come from God—through His appointed servants.

I felt a distinct spiritual confirmation that my new assignment was inspired. It is important that we make that connection—that our callings literally come to us from God through our priesthood leaders. After this experience, my attitude changed, and I was filled with a deep desire to serve. I am grateful for the blessing of repentance and for my changed heart. I love my new assignment.

Even if we think that our Church calling was simply our

priesthood leader's idea or that it came to us because no one else would accept it, we will be blessed as we serve. But when we recognize God's hand in our calling and serve with all our hearts, additional power comes into our service, and we become true servants of Jesus Christ.

SOURCE: Carl B. Cook, "Serve," 110–11.

"WE HAVE BEEN LOOKING FOR YOU"
Henry B. Eyring

Having faith in the call from the Lord's servants was crucial in the missionary service of my great-grandfather Henry Eyring.

He was baptized on March 11, 1855, in St. Louis, Missouri. Erastus Snow ordained him to the office of a priest shortly thereafter. The president of the St. Louis Stake, John H. Hart, called him to serve a mission to the Cherokee Nation on October 6. He was ordained an elder on October 11. He left on horseback for the Cherokee Mission on October 24. He was 20 years old and a convert of only seven months. . . .

After Elder Eyring had served for three difficult years and upon the death of the mission president, Henry was nominated and sustained as president of the mission in a meeting held on October 6, 1858. He was surprised and as shocked as a new deacon would be. . . .

The now-President Eyring traveled to the Cherokee, Creek, and Choctaw Nations in 1859. . . .

A year later, Henry was faced with the difficult reality that the political leaders among the people he was serving no longer permitted the Latter-day Saint missionaries to do their work. As he pondered what he should do, he recalled the instruction from his previous mission president indicating that he should prolong his mission until 1859.

In October of that year, Henry wrote to President Brigham

Young for direction, but he did not receive a reply to his question. Henry recorded, "Not being able to hear anything from the Presidency of the Church, I called upon the Lord in prayer, asking him to reveal to me his mind and will in regard to my remaining longer or going up to Zion."

He continued: "The following dream was given to me in answer to my prayer. I dreamt I had arrived in [Salt Lake] City and immediately went to [President Brigham] Young's office, where I found him. I said to him: '[President] Young I have left my mission, have come of my own accord, but if there is anything wrong in this, I am willing to return and finish my mission.' [In the dream the prophet] replied: 'You have stayed long enough, it is all right.'"

Henry wrote in his journal, "Having had dreams before which were literally fulfilled I had faith to believe, that this also would be and consequently commenced at once to prepare for a start."

He arrived in Salt Lake City on August 29, 1860, having walked most of the way. Two days later, he walked into the office of President Brigham Young.

Henry described the experience in these words: "[I] called upon [President] Young, who received [me] very kindly. I said to him, '[President] Young I have come without being sent for, if I have done wrong, I am willing to return and finish my mission.' [Brigham Young] answered: 'It is all right, we have been looking for you.'"

Henry described his joy, saying, "Thus my dream was literally fulfilled."

SOURCE: Henry B. Eyring, "You Are Not Alone in the Work," 81–82.

"GET GOING AND JOIN THE SAINTS"
Brother Hammond (Related by Hugh Nibley)

Brother Hammond joined the Church in Hawaii. Then he came to San Francisco and was one of the first people to settle there.

When the gold rush came, he soon discovered that he could make far more money by selling supplies in the gold fields of Sacramento than he could seeking gold himself. He and Sam Brannan entered into a partnership and got rich. Sam Brannan was the richest man in California.

But the Lord told [Hammond] to go [east] and join the Saints in the valley. Brigham Young wrote to him. He went to Mormon Island and set up and started to sell stuff there. He had a huge covered wagon which he loaded with all sorts of goods, which sold immediately because you couldn't get anything there. He'd make a thousand dollars a day, and that was really something. The gold was very rich too at Mormon Island in the Sacramento River. He said he had a dream one night. The dream told him to get going and join with the Saints. He said, no, I can stay here and make a lot of money. Then think of all the good I can do for the Church. I'll use it to bring the Saints here. The next night he had the same dream, and a great flood of hot lava and filthy water came rushing down the river. The people went on panning gold and paid no attention to it, and it swallowed them up. People were scrambling to escape, and he barely escaped. The third night was too much, so he sold out and came to Utah. He used to say, "Don't ever get the idea that your duty is to get rich to help the Lord. The Lord has all the money he needs. He will take care of that. Don't worry about that. You do what he tells you to do." Of course, if he tells you to get rich, that's a different thing. But we use that as one of the Articles of Faith here, which it isn't. But Sam Brannan was the richest man in California, and he died a broken man.

SOURCE: Hugh Nibley, "Lecture 73," 196–97.

"A DUTY TO PERFORM"
Heber C. Kimball

One night . . . while at Mr. Richard's house, I dreamed that an elderly gentleman came to me and rented me a lot of ground, which

I was anxious to cultivate. I immediately went to work to break it up; and observing young timber on the lot, I cut it down. There was also an old building on the corner of the lot which appeared ready to fall. I took a lever and endeavored to place the building in a proper position, but all my attempts were futile, and it became worse. I then resolved to pull it down, and with the new timber build a good house on a good foundation. While thus engaged, the gentleman of whom I had rented the place came and found great fault with me for destroying his young timber, etc.

This dream was fulfilled in the following manner: After Mr. Richards let me preach in his chapel, I baptized all of his young members, as I had before baptized his daughter. He then reflected upon himself for letting me have the privilege of his chapel; told me that I had ruined his church, and had taken away all his young members. I could not but feel pity for the old gentleman, but I had a duty to perform which outweighed all other considerations.

SOURCE: Orson F. Whitney, *Life of Heber C. Kimball*, 141–42.

"I MUST HAVE HIS ACCEPTANCE"
Spencer W. Kimball

[This experience occurred shortly after Spencer W. Kimball was called to serve as an apostle.]

It was just breaking day this Wednesday, the 14th of July. No peace had yet come, though I had prayed for it almost unceasingly these six days and nights. I had no plan or destination. I only knew I must get out into the open, apart, away. I dressed quietly and without disturbing the family, I slipped out of the house. I turned toward the hills. I had no objective. I wanted only to be alone. I had begun a fast. . . .

My weakness overcame me again. Hot tears came flooding down my cheeks as I made no effort to mop them up. I was accusing myself, and condemning myself, and upbraiding myself. I was praying aloud for special blessings from the Lord. I was telling Him that I had not asked for this position, and that I was incapable of doing the work, that I was as imperfect and weak and human, that I was unworthy of so noble a calling, though I had tried hard and my heart had been right. I knew that I must have been at least partly responsible for offenses and misunderstandings which a few people fancied they had suffered at my hands. I realized that I had been petty and small many times. I did not spare myself. A thousand things passed through my mind. . . .

Never had I prayed before as I now prayed. What I wanted and felt I must have was an assurance that I was acceptable to the Lord. I told Him I neither wanted nor was worthy of a vision or appearance of angels or any special manifestation. I wanted only to the calm peaceful assurance that my offering was accepted. Never before had I been tortured as I was now tortured. And the assurance did not come.

I was getting high and the air was getting thinner and I was reaching some cliffs and jagged rocky points. . . .

As I rounded a promontory I saw immediately above me the peak of the mountain and on the peak a huge cross with its arms silhouetted against the blue sky beyond. It was just an ordinary cross made of two large heavy limbs of a tree, but in my frame of mind, and coming on it so unexpectedly, it seemed a sacred omen. It seemed to promise that here on this cross, on this peak, I might get the answer which I had been praying intermittently for six days and nights and constantly and with all the power at my command these hours of final torture. I threw myself on the ground and wept and prayed and pleaded with the Lord to let me know where I stood. . . .

I mentally beat myself up and chastised myself and accused myself. As the sun came up and moved in the sky I moved with it, lying in the sun, and still I received no relief. I sat up on the cliff and strange thoughts came to: all this anguish and suffering could be ended so easily from this high cliff and then came to my mind the temptations of the Master when he was tempted to cast Himself down—then I was ashamed for having placed myself in a comparable position and trying to be dramatic. . . . I was filled with remorse because I felt I had cheapened the experiences of the Lord, having compared mine with His. Again I challenged myself and told myself that I was only trying to be dramatic and sorry for myself.

Again I lay on the cool earth. The thought came that I might take cold, but what did it matter now. There was one great desire, to get a testimony of my calling, to know that it was not human and inspired by ulterior motives, kindly as they might be. How I prayed! How I suffered! How I wept! How I struggled!

Was it a dream which came to me? I was weary and I think I went to sleep for a little. It seemed that in a dream I saw my grandfather and became conscious of the great work he had done. I cannot say that it was a vision, but I do know that with this new experience came a calm like the dying wind, the quieting wave after the storm has passed. I got up, walked to the rocky point and sat on the same ledge. My tears were dry, my soul was at peace. A calm feeling of assurance came over me, doubt and questionings subdued. It was as though a great burden had been lifted. I sat in tranquil silence surveying the beautiful valley, thanking the Lord for the satisfaction and the reassuring answer to my prayers. Long I meditated here in peaceful quietude, apart, and I felt nearer my Lord than ever at any time in my life. . . .

I felt I knew my way, now, physically and spiritually and knew where I was going.

SOURCE: Edward L. Kimball and Andrew E. Kimball Jr., *Spencer W. Kimball: The Early and Apostolic Years*, 193–95.

"MY FIRST CHOICES WERE WRONG"
Harold B. Lee

"On the Friday night preceding the quarterly conference, I was called to the office of President Rudger Clawson, where I was told by Rudger Clawson and Elder George Albert Smith that I had been chosen by the First Presidency and the Twelve as the new president of Pioneer Stake. I told them I would much prefer working as a counselor to Brother Hyde, and was bluntly told by George Albert Smith that I had been invited to meet with them, not to tell them what should be done, but to find out if I was willing to do what the Lord wanted me to do. There followed a discussion on the selection of my counselors. Again I was told when I asked if they had any suggestions on that, 'We have suggestions, but we are not going to tell you—that is your responsibility. If you are guided by the Spirit of the Lord, you will choose those whom we have in mind.' . . .

"I retired that night, or rather early morning, to a fitful sleep, about three o'clock in the morning, after earnest prayer for guidance. During the few hours I tried to sleep it would seem that I had chosen two counselors and was trying to hold council meetings with them. Disagreements, obstacles, and misunderstandings would arise, and I would awake with a start to realize that my first choices were wrong. This process was repeated with ten or twelve of my brethren until, when morning came, I was certain the Lord had guided me to choose Charles S. Hyde and Paul C. Child as my counselors. When I announced to the Brethren my decision the next morning, they smiled their approval. The men whom they had desired had been selected."

SOURCE: L. Brent Goates, *Harold B. Lee*, 88–89.

DREAMS OF CALLINGS

"YOU WILL BE HEARING FROM ME VERY SOON"
Castle H. Murphy

One night a few weeks before we were called to preside over the temple in Hawaii I had a dream. Then I awoke and called to my wife. I told her that we would soon receive a phone call from President Grant. In the dream which I remember vividly, President Grant came to our home, together with his secretary, Joseph Anderson. As he began to talk with me, people who evidently had learned of his arrival, began to crowd into our living room. As they chatted with the President, Brother Anderson called out that if the President did not leave soon that he would be late for another appointment in the city. President Grant, being a man who respected appointments and promptness, turned to me and said,

"Brother Murphy, I am sorry that we must leave you now, but you will be hearing from me very soon."

Within the week the phone call did come, and we were summoned to Salt Lake City to the office of the President. Upon arrival, before we were seated, President Grant asked,

"How would you like to return to Hawaii and take charge of the Hawaiian Temple?"

Although we had fully expected the phone call because of the vividness of the dream, we were certainly surprised with such a call.

SOURCE: Castle H. Murphy, *Castle of Zion*, 46.

"I HAVE KNOWN FOR WEEKS"
Mark E. Petersen (Related by Peggy Petersen Barton)

One night [Elder Mark E. Petersen] fell into a deep sleep and had a dream. The very existence of the dream made him uncomfortable because he rarely dreamed. The subject of the dream was appalling. He could see the lead headline of the front page of the *Deseret News* with a terrible mistake in it. The headline read

"Lyman R. Richards Dies." How could the copy desk make such an error and reverse the order of Elder Richard R. Lyman's name? He was absolutely certain that regardless of the manpower shortage, he would lose his job because of it. President Grant, President Clark, and President Bowen would nail him to the wall! He woke with a jolt. "I was responsible for the newspaper, and to think of Elder Lyman's name on the front page all scrambled up made me almost sick, even in the dream," he recalled.

At six o'clock on Monday morning Mark hurried to work, and as soon as the first edition was put to bed, he called Henry Smith, the Church Reporter. Had Henry heard of any illness in the Council of the Twelve? How long since he had seen Richard R. Lyman? Why didn't Henry run over to 47 East South Temple just to test the water?

Henry returned with the news that Elder Lyman was fine and in his office. But Mark could not shake the feeling that some terrible accident or swift-moving illness was about to strike down Elder Lyman, and he himself was to replace him in the Twelve. One of Mark's strongest personality traits was his humility. He was totally unimpressed with himself and he had certainly never promoted himself for a church position. But he knew President Grant would call him to the Twelve. . . .

[Elder Petersen recorded:] "Then on a very fateful day, Joseph Anderson came over to the office at *Deseret News* and told me that President Grant wanted the little notice that was in the envelope which he handed me placed in the newspaper. He spelled out exactly how he wanted it used—that it was to be placed in a two-column box at the upper-left hand corner of the page, and that was all. It was a plain announcement, but no news story was to accompany it. When I read it, to my horror I saw that Brother Lyman had been excommunicated from the Church." . . .

Mark began to feel nervous about the second part of his dream in which he took Elder Lyman's place. A few days before April conference he received a telephone call from Joseph Anderson asking him to come to see President Grant—but not the usual "Mark, get over here" at all. . . . [President Grant] sat down and told me that the Brethren had appointed me the new member of the Council of the Twelve. I said, "President Grant, I have known for weeks that this was coming." I told him about my dream. He shook my hand warmly and told me the Lord had given me the right impression.

SOURCE: Peggy Petersen Barton, *Mark E. Petersen*, 85–86.

"I WAS ORDAINED AN APOSTLE"
George F. Richards

I had a most pleasant night's sleep and rest and during the night dreamed that I was ordained an Apostle under the hands of Lorenzo Snow and was told by him that there were other blessings for me . . .

My dream of March 22, [1906], wherein I saw this seemed to have prepared me, in a measure, for this call. [George Franklin Richards was ordained an apostle on April 9, 1906.]

SOURCE: Dennis B. Horne, "*Called of God by Prophecy,*" 42.

"HIS WORDS HAD THRILLED ME"
LeGrand Richards

About the time I was to be released form the Southern States Mission, I had a dream. In it I met President Grant on the street in Salt Lake City and he said, "LeGrand, come into my office, I have a special blessing for you." I went, and he gave me a blessing. When I awoke, I couldn't remember a thing about what he had said, but only how his words had thrilled me. When he laid his hands on my head within the same year and set me apart as the Presiding Bishop of the Church, I knew why the knowledge had been withheld from my memory. It would not have been right for me to know it at that time. I had to wait until the call came and the actual blessing was given.

Source: Lucile Tate, *LeGrand Richards*, 198.

"NOT EVERYONE CAN KEEP BOOKS"
LeGrand Richards

President Trayner called the missionaries in and gave out assignments. . . . Elder Richards would serve as mission secretary. His mind wrestled with the prospects of office routine and confinement. A disappointed but submissive spirit is reflected in his journal entry that day. . . . Reinforcing to his own resolve was a dream which he felt was given to help him in his disappointment:

> In the dream I was keeping books for Father in his lumber and implement business, and I said I was tired of it and wanted to do ordinary work. He agreed to let me seek other employment. I came to Salt Lake and worked with a railroad maintenance crew pushing one of their carts along the track in company with three other men. One said, "What have you been doing?" "Keeping books," I answered. "What did you earn?" he asked. I told him. "You will never earn that on this job," he said. "Anybody can push these carts, but not everyone can keep books."

Not only did the dream comfort Elder Richards, but he came to appreciate his assignment because it taught him the inner workings of a mission and prepared him for his later call as a mission president.

Source: Lucile C. Tate, *LeGrand Richards*, 37–38.

"AN HONORABLE RELEASE"
B. H. Roberts

[Elder Roberts] baptized the converts in the Mississippi River and soon afterwards they left for the West. Young Elder Roberts may have felt a nostalgia to go with them, but reinforcement to stay with his call came "in the form of a very vivid dream which was as real as life itself." He dreamed he was standing in the Centerville School Square at the center of the town "without a proper release." . . . The panorama of his dream was extremely familiar to him:

> I noted, and remembered, the hanging of one of the green shutters of the old school house, which had long been an eyesore to the community; the walk down the sidewalk and the defect in the fences; the houses and the orchards so well remembered until at last I came to the story and a half adobe house where my wife and child were residing. Through the window I saw Emmeline Smith (the wife of President William Smith) and heard her exclaim as she hurriedly left the kitchen of the house, evidently to go in search of my wife. . . . I took advantage of a board which had been broken from the fence surrounding the old homestead which enabled me to make a shortcut to the kitchen door without going on a quarter of a block to the gate entrance. As Mother Smith left the kitchen for her daughter's room in the house, I heard her exclaim, "Well, if it isn't Harry come back." The words produced a peculiar shock in me. Presently my wife, Louisa, came from the further part of the house and met me in the kitchen, putting her arms around my neck and said, "I'm so glad to see you. But oh I do wish you had stayed and finished your mission." By this time I nearly collapsed.

Then came a dream within a dream:

My dream included my retirement and then during the night I seemed to wake up and begin to realize the seriousness of having returned home without an honorable release. I began to speculate upon what kind of an excuse or story I could fix up to tell President Taylor, who was a boyhood hero of mine. What could I tell that battle-scarred hero of a half hundred missions, and what excuse could I offer for having left the post? I resolved I would not make a report to President Taylor, but would undertake to get back to my place in the mission field, and then began contact with innumerable obstacles, having no money, I would have to beat my way back. This I did by stealing rides upon freight trains and getting into all sorts of adventures including hunger, and disgust above all for this unwarranted desertion. And so it went until I began to approach the familiar regions of Omaha, which, of course, is a center of early pioneer reminiscences for the Church.

Winter Quarters, with its cluster of settlements, had been the rallying point of the first Mormon exiles as they launched their westward exodus. Roberts knew, from both reading and talking with participants, the story of the difficult winter of 1846 when many of those camped at Winter Quarters in their hand-built, makeshift lean-to's faced scurvy, cholera and starvation. Today a bronze plaque records the names and ages of six hundred buried near there; more than half of the ages are recorded in months rather than years. It was powerful symbolism to measure Winter Quarters and the costs of discipleship against his homesickness.

I finally noted the moonshine penetrating into the upper chamber to which Elder Palmer and I had been assigned in the Gibbs' home. The thought slowly dawned upon my troubled mind that the experience might not be real, but that I had dreamed the whole thing through. As I lay there I recalled that Elder Palmer ought to be in a bed across the room from me and would be a means of helping me decide whether the experience was a dream or reality. Accordingly I slipped out of bed, crossed the room, and sure enough found Elder Palmer in his bed not only sleeping but snoring. It was the most welcome sound I ever heard! I dropped to my knees at the side of his bed and thanked God I had only been dreaming. And, again, I thanked God for this experience of what would probably happen should I desert my calling and return home without being honorably released. So acute had been my suffering, so real the counterfeit presentments to my mind, that it stood as a permanent lesson through all the years of my missionary service. It was a security against the likelihood of anything happening of that kind in my conscious life; and it never did. It was only necessary to recall the suffering endured in this dream to put such thoughts from my mind thereafter.

SOURCE: Truman G. Madsen, *Defender of the Faith*, 109–11.

"I ALREADY KNOW"
Theodore Tuttle (Related by Lucile C. Tate)

At the time Elder A. Theodore Tuttle left for South America for his first assignment as a Seventy, Brother [Boyd K.] Packer was still a seminary supervisor.

"Before Ted left," he said, "we talked and we prayed together. When we were through praying I said, 'I have the feeling that you and I will stand together to bear witness of the restored gospel on the soil of South America.' Now, that was as improbable as anything, because we had no seminaries there and no reason for me to travel down there.

"After Ted left, I went to work on my doctorate and did what was needed for seminary and institute opening in September. Yet I had the gnawing feeling, 'What does it matter? You are not going to be here.'"

On 30 September 1961 Brother Packer was called as an Assistant to the Twelve. Of the call he said: "There was a spiritual prophecy that preceded it by a few hours. It happened in this way: After the conference announcement I tried to reach Ted in Montevideo and they said he was in Peru. Late that afternoon I got through to him and said, 'I have something to tell you.' He said, 'I already know.' And I said, 'Did somebody call you?' And he said, 'I've learned it otherwise.' Ted had had a dream the night before."

SOURCE: Lucile C. Tate, *Boyd K. Packer*, 282–83.

CHAPTER 11

Dreams of Comfort

Elder Sterling W. Sill of the First Quorum of the Seventy, in the general conference of April 1964, compared a work of English literature to revelation. He recounted that many years ago, the British futurist H. G. Wells wrote an interesting novel entitled *The Time Machine*, in which Wells invented a device that could carry people through time much like an airplane carries us through space. In his fantasy, Wells could travel thousands of years into the past in a few minutes and be an eyewitness to historical events. He could also visit future civilizations that would someday be. Dreams sometimes offer this same time-traveling experience as we visit our past or see a glimpse of our future.

Dreams as time-traveling experiences offer comfort, as dreamers can simulate visiting with those who made their past pleasant, or become a source of strength, as we can preview important future events. As Elder Sill said, "[Dreams can revitalize] . . . life by reabsorbing the original good from the greatest experiences of [our] own past. . . .

DREAMS AS REVELATION

"An even greater source of strength can come from pre-living the important events of our own futures [in our dreams] . . . which is like a giant radar beam searching the skies of future years. . . .

"When in our minds we pre-live our marriage, we help to determine the kind of person that we would like to be when that event arrives. As we pre-live our success, we develop the abilities necessary to bring it about."[1]

Such dreams may provide comfort as they simultaneously alleviate fear and increase faith.

We can see things in our dreams that are more sublime than anything we can see with our mortal eyes, which gives wonderful feelings of comfort, encouragement, joy, and blessed anticipation even amidst terrific trials during stressful times. The Lord can use dreams to encourage us in the most mundane, practical matters to get us through another day, or in the most vital of circumstances to help us through another trial. Some dreams comfort us by confirming our course of action, bringing confirmation that our decisions are correct, and letting us know of His approval of our actions in advance.

In some cases, an inspired dream is given in which there does not seem to be any comfort in the dream itself; but, as the dream is fulfilled, the faith and testimony of the dreamer is strengthened. The dreamer becomes aware of the Lord's love—as well as His great power and omniscience—which can bring comfort.

Dreams may offer general encouragement rather than specific words of instruction, and sometimes feelings, rather than words, impart a message of comfort. "Anciently men communicated with each other by means of pictures. Now we usually use words to express thought, but we still think in pictures" and dream in images.[2] One of the greatest comforts in dreams is that we can experience things that we could not physically experience in mortality.

Dreams can become our personal time machine where sleep acts as a vehicle that returns us to our past or projects us into our future.

DREAMS OF COMFORT

When we awaken, we are sometimes changed by the dreams that we have experienced. Comfort can be received and eternity can be viewed with feelings that are difficult to express.

"AN ASSURANCE THAT ALL WOULD BE WELL"
Melvin J. Ballard (Related by Bryant S. Hinckley)

While Elder Melvin J. Ballard was on his first mission, a son was born to him, whom he did not see until the boy was almost two years old. During his father's absence, this child became desperately ill. They did everything they could, but in spite of their faith, the doctor's help and the care given to the child, it grew steadily worse until they despaired of his life. When Elder Ballard learned of its critical condition, full of sorrow and anxiety, he went alone into the woods to plead with the Lord to save his first born. Under this weight of grief, he fell asleep and in spirit he came home and blessed the child, rebuked the destroyer and when he awoke, he had the assurance that all would be well with his son.

On this particular night, Sister Ballard, the mother of Melvin J., was taking care of the little one. The doctor told her he could do nothing further, that the child would probably pass away before morning. During the night the child took a sudden change for the better and while Mrs. Ballard did not see anything, she felt the unseen presence of Elder Ballard and knew something miraculous had happened. The change took place the very hour he went into the woods to pray.

SOURCE: Bryant S. Hinckley, *The Faith of Our Pioneer Fathers*, 225–26.

"GOD KNOWS WHO I AM"
(Related by David A. Bednar)

Some time ago I spoke with a priesthood leader who was prompted to memorize the names of all of the youth ages 13 to 21 in his stake. Using snapshots of the young men and women, he created flash cards that he reviewed while traveling on business and at other times. This priesthood leader quickly learned all of the names of the youth.

One night the priesthood leader had a dream about one of the young men whom he knew only from a picture. In the dream he saw the young man dressed in a white shirt and wearing a missionary name tag. With a companion seated at his side, the young man was teaching a family. The young man held the Book of Mormon in his hand, and he looked as if he were testifying of the truthfulness of the book. The priesthood leader then awoke from his dream.

At an ensuing priesthood gathering, the leader approached the young man he had seen in his dream and asked to talk with him for a few minutes. After a brief introduction, the leader called the young man by name and said: "I am not a dreamer. I have never had a dream about a single member of this stake, except for you. I am going to tell you about my dream, and then I would like you to help me understand what it means."

The priesthood leader recounted the dream and asked the young man about its meaning. Choking with emotion, the young man simply replied, "It means God knows who I am." The remainder of the conversation between this young man and his priesthood leader was most meaningful, and they agreed to meet and counsel together from time to time during the following months.

SOURCE: David A. Bednar, "The Tender Mercies of the Lord," 100.

"I FELT THE WARMTH OF HIS EMBRACE"
Ezra Taft Benson

In early August Elder [Ezra Taft] Benson learned that Elder Alma Sonne, an Assistant to the Twelve, had been called to succeed him in Europe. The news was unexpected. He had planned to be in Europe for another six months and believed there was much left to do. But he was delighted to be going home. In a moment of rare reflection, he admitted that the previous months had been "a bit rough and rugged, but the Lord has sustained me in a most remarkable way."

But because word of the change came so suddenly, Elder Benson wondered if his performance had been acceptable. Then an unusual experience allayed his fears, and he recorded it in his journal: "Last night, in a dream, I was privileged to spend, what seemed about an hour, with Pres. George Albert Smith in Salt Lake. It was a most impressive and soul-satisfying experience. We talked intimately together about the Great Work in which we are engaged and about my devoted family. I felt the warmth of his embrace as we both shed tears of gratitude for the rich blessings of the Lord. . . . The last day or so I have been wondering if my labors in Europe have been acceptable to the First Pres'y and the Brethren at home and especially to my Heavenly Father. This sweet experience has tended to put my mind completely at ease, for which I am deeply grateful."

Shortly thereafter Elder Harold B. Lee wrote Ezra, "The brethren are united in the feeling that you have performed a glorious mission and a work that could hardly have been accomplished by one of lesser courage and ability . . . and with undaunted faith in the power of the Lord to overcome obstacles."

SOURCE: Sheri L. Dew, *Ezra Taft Benson*, 224.

"I WONDER IF I EVER HAD A PATRIARCHAL BLESSING"
Matthew Cowley (Related by Glen L. Rudd)

On one occasion near the beginning of his mission, [Elder Matthew Cowley] was returning to Judea on horseback and dozed off and had a dream. He saw himself as a little boy sitting on his father's lap. He was scared, but his father put his arms around him and held him. A man with a long beard came over and put his hands on his head. Then he woke up, still on the horse, and the thought came to him, "I wonder if I have ever had a patriarchal blessing?"

So when he got back to Judea, he wrote his mother a letter asking if he had ever had a patriarchal blessing. Two months later (it took a month for the mail to go one way), he received a letter from his mother. She said that when he was five years old, he went with his father down to Mancos, Colorado, and stayed in the home of an old patriarch named Luther Burnham. While visiting, Matthew's father asked the patriarch to give his little boy a patriarchal blessing. Just as in the dream, his mother reported that her husband said Matthew was shivering and scared, so he put his arms around him. The patriarch, who did indeed have a long beard, put his hands on Matthew's head and bestowed upon him his patriarchal blessing. Matthew's mother enclosed the patriarchal blessing with her letter.

For the first time in his life, this wonderful young man read his magnificent patriarchal blessing:

> My beloved son Matthew, I place my hands upon your head and confer upon you a patriarchal blessing. Thou shalt live to be a mighty man in Israel, for thou art a royal seed, the seed of Jacob through Joseph. Thou shalt become a great and mighty man in the eyes of the Lord, and become an ambassador of Christ to the uttermost bounds of the earth. Your understanding shall become great, and your wisdom reach to Heaven. . . . The Lord will give you mighty faith as the brother of Jared, for thou shalt know that he lives and that the Gospel of Jesus Christ is true, even in your youth.

What a wonderful blessing!

SOURCE: Glen L. Rudd, "Memories of Matthew Cowley," 17.

"A HEAVY CHAIN ABOUT HER NECK"
Martha Cragun Cox

Martha was a plural wife and a schoolteacher in St. George in the 1880s, forced to support her children herself because of the federal prosecution of polygamists during that period. In her dream, Martha was bowed down by a heavy chain about her neck from which hung bundles containing the sorrows, disappointments, and resentments that she had allowed to grow and weigh so heavily upon her. Martha was told to place the heavy chain on a rod above the fireplace; then she removed the bundles and examined them one by one. She began to see how embittered she had become and how her resentments had grown far out of proportion to the wrongs she had sustained. She began to realize that the federal marshals, whom she had so bitterly resented, had not done nearly as much harm as they had the power to do; that the mail delivery service that had been imposed on her family to provide, though hard on her young sons, brought them needed income; that those who owed her money were just as poor as she was; and that the 10 percent of her students' tuition kept by the attorney who collected it for her was a small price to pay for relieving her of that burden.

One by one, as she examined them, the bundles began to disappear until she came to the last one, which held her unrelieved sorrow at the loss of her infant. The bundle reminded her of how she often spread out the little baby clothes "on [her] bed on lonely stormy nights when there was no one there to see or hear [her] weep over them." But that bundle also disappeared as she took it from the chain. At last she felt free. When she awoke, she resolved to be truly free. "I made it a rule [from that day on]," she wrote, "to sing a song to the little children on my lap. To the little Indian boy who shared a scolding with [my son] Edward one night and went supperless to his camp, I gave a handsome new shirt to make amends. One day," she noted, "when an Indian woman came to my door with an almost naked child held under her fur robe, I got out the box [of baby clothes] and a feeling of shame came upon me as I gave the little flannel dress and other things to put upon the child, a shame for the tears I had shed over it. I told her to tell the others who had babes to come and get the rest of the things—all but the little shoes—I felt I must keep them. But when I saw the blue feet and legs of one of the little babes I said, 'That bundle must come, all of it, from my chain.'"

SOURCE: Carol Cornwall Madsen, "In the Covenant of Grace," 186–87.

"NEVER TOO LATE OR TOO HARD"
(Related by Henry B. Eyring)

There is . . . temptation to be resisted. It is to yield to the despairing thought that it is too hard and too late to repent. I knew a man once who could have thought that and given up. When he was 12 he was ordained a deacon. Some of his friends tempted him to begin to smoke. He began to feel uncomfortable in church. He left his little town, not finishing high school, to begin a life following construction jobs across the United States. He was a heavy-equipment operator. He married. They had children. The marriage ended in a bitter divorce. He lost his children. He lost an eye in an accident. . . .

One day he told me that in a dream the night before, the sight in his blind eye was restored. He realized that the dream was a glimpse of a future day, walking among loving people in the light of a glorious resurrection. Tears of joy ran down the deeply lined face of that towering, raw-boned man. He spoke to me quietly, with a radiant smile. I don't remember what he said he saw, but I remember that his face shone with happy anticipation as he described the view. With the Lord's help and the miracle of that [Book of Mormon] in the bottom of a trunk, it had not for him been too late nor the way too hard.

SOURCE: Henry B. Eyring, "Do Not Delay," 35.

"I WOULD NOT STRUGGLE FOR THE CHILD"
Heber J. Grant

I have been blessed with only two sons. One of them died at five years of age and the other at seven.

My last son died of a hip disease. I had built great hopes that he would live to spread the gospel at home and abroad and be an honor to me. About an hour before he died I had a dream that his mother, who was dead, came for him, and that she brought with her a messenger, and she told this messenger to take the boy while I was asleep. In the dream I thought I awoke and I seized my son and fought for him and finally succeeded in getting him away from the messenger who had come to take him, and in so doing I dreamed that I stumbled and fell upon him.

I dreamed that I fell upon his sore hip, and the terrible cries and anguish of the child drove me nearly wild. I could not stand it, and I jumped up and ran out of the house so as not to hear his distress. I dreamed that after running out of the house I met Brother Joseph E. Taylor and told him of these things.

He said: "Well, Heber, do you know what I would do if my wife came for one of her children—I would not struggle for that child; I would not oppose her taking that child away. If a mother who had been faithful had passed beyond the veil, she would know of the suffering and anguish her child may have to suffer. She would know whether that child might go through life as a cripple and whether it would be better or wiser for that child to be relieved from the torture of life. And when you stop to think, Brother Grant, that the mother of that boy went down into the shadow of death to give him life, she is the one who ought to have the right to take him or leave him."

I said, "I believe you are right, Brother Taylor, and if she comes again, she shall have the boy without any protest on my part."

After coming to the conclusion, I was waked by my brother, B. F. Grant, who was staying that night with us.

He called me into the room and told me that my child was dying.

I went in the front room and sat down. There was a vacant chair between me and my wife who is now living, and I felt the presence of that boy's deceased mother, sitting in that chair. I did not tell anybody what I felt, but I turned to my living wife and said: "Do you feel anything strange?" She said: "Yes, I feel assured that Heber's mother is sitting between us, waiting to take him away."

Now, I am naturally, I believe, a sympathetic man. I was raised as an only child with all the affection that a mother could lavish upon a boy. I believe that I am naturally affectionate and sympathetic and that I shed tears for my friends—tears of joy for their success and tears of sorrow for their misfortunes. But I sat by the deathbed of my little boy and saw him die, without shedding a tear. My loving wife, my brother, and I upon that occasion experienced a sweet, peaceful, and heavenly influence in my home, as great as I have ever experienced in my life. And no person can tell me that every other Latter-day Saint that has a knowledge of the gospel in his heart and soul, can really mourn for his loved ones; only in the loss of their society in this life.

I never think of my wives and my dear mother, my two boys, my daughter, my departed friends, and beloved associates as being in the graveyard. . . . I think only of the joy they have in meeting with father and mother and loved ones who have been true and faithful to the gospel of the Lord Jesus Christ. My mind reaches out to the wonderful joy and satisfaction and happiness that they are having, and it robs the grave of its sting.

SOURCE: Heber J. Grant, *Gospel Standards*, 364–66.

"WAS THIS NOT A BEAUTIFUL DREAM?"
Alonzo A. Hinckley

While Elder [Alonzo A.] Hinckley was on this mission to the Netherlands his second son was born. His heart was filled with great anxiety concerning the birth of this boy. When he received word from his wife that all was well, he wrote as follows:

"November 18, 1897. I have never received better news that I have received from you this morning. I am so happy and relieved of anxiety that I actually am beside myself. I cannot keep from laughing when I meet any one, and tell them of my good fortune. I am the most thankful man in Holland; and I tell you, it did not take me long to get on my knees and pour out my heart in gratitude to God for his mercies unto us.

"I have had such a lovely dream. I have been with you all—seen you, my dear wife, and the little newcomer, and all those kind ones who have surrounded you. I saw you made comfortable and happy. It seemed that I was in a hurry to get off again for Holland. But I first thanked all, with my heart so full of love that I gathered you all in my arms and embraced you, and then took one more peek in the door at Rose (his wife) and the children, and then landed back in Holland. Was this not a beautiful dream for one in my mood?"

In that far off land he knew the very day and hour that his son was born and his heart was filled to overflowing with joy.

SOURCE: Bryant S. Hinckley, *The Faith of Our Pioneer Fathers*, 234.

"A ROD TO GUIDE THE SHIP"
Heber C. Kimball

"While crossing the sea, . . . I dreamed that the Prophet Joseph came to me while I was standing upon the forecastle of the ship, and said, 'Brother Heber, here is a rod (putting it into my hands), with which you are to guide the ship. While you hold this rod you shall prosper, and there shall be no obstacles through before you but what you shall have the power to overcome, and the hand of God shall be with you.' After this I discovered every kind of obstruction was placed before the ship to stop its progress; but the bow being sharp, the obstacles were compelled to move out on either side; and when the ship would come to a mountain, it would plow its course straight through, as though it was in water. This rod which Joseph gave me was about three and a half feet in length. His appearance was just as natural as I ever beheld him in the flesh. He blessed me and disappeared."

It is a singular fact that during fifty years, the period covered by the history of Mormon emigration from the nations abroad, not a ship-load of Latter-day Saints, not a vessel bearing the Elders of Israel to or from foreign shores, has even been lost at sea. Even rough captains and sailors have learned to regard this with feelings akin to reverential awe, and to accept as a good omen, an assurance of a safe and prosperous voyage, the presence of Mormon Elders or emigrants among their ship's passengers.

In such a light, Heber's dream of Joseph and the rod wherewith he was to "guide the ship," takes on added interest and significance.

SOURCE: Orson F. Whitney, *The Life of Heber C. Kimball*, 115.

"I HAVE FELT CONTENTED ABOUT YOU"
Heber C. Kimball

His [Heber C. Kimball's] next letter is dated Kirtland, November 16, 1839; but being too feeble to sit up, Brother Dean Gould wrote the most of it for him. He says: . . .

"My dear Vilate, you know what we are called to do; we will press forward to the mark which is laid before us at the expense of all things. I was thankful to God to hear of your health, for I believe it is He who has raised you and the children up, for when I was in the town of Winchester, at Father Murray's, I had such a travail of soul for you as I never had before. I would go into the woods four and five times a day to call on the Father in the name of Jesus for you. I saw you in a dream in a sickly state, almost dead; I clasped my hands on each side of your face and raised you upon your feet. And since that I have felt contented about you and the children; but once in a while, being among our kindred, it brings home back to me, and I feel a little homesick. They are all pleading with me to stay till warm weather, on account of my poor health. A little fatigue brings me down again."

Source: *A Woman's View*, 136.

"FATHER, I'M SO GLAD TO SEE YOU"
Spencer W. Kimball

At about Christmas time 1956 Spencer W. Kimball's throat began to bother him again. The earlier hoarseness, which had disappeared after a blessing in 1950, recurred. He woke one morning with blood in the back of his throat and a weakening voice. Dr. Cowan, alarmed by the inflamed vocal cords, urged him to see Dr. Hayes Martin in New York, the best in the world for throat cancer. Spencer was scheduled to visit the New York Stake in February and he hoped to consult with the specialist then.

His fear of cancer, stilled for years, troubled him again. At night he lay sleepless as his mind wandered restlessly back to his boyhood in Arizona. He followed his life forward until it came to the disquieting vision of his sister Helen's death from cancer. He had watched "the octopus literally eat away her face" and now imagined the "horrors and deprivations" he might expect if he had cancer in his throat.

After these thoughts, however, as he later recalled, "I came to myself." He thought of the thirteen years of service he had given and his children all married and settled. He began to face possible death without self-pity. He wrote, musing: "So what? You have had a long and abundant life. You have had bliss, been granted privileges and opportunities far beyond your deserts. Suppose your time has come! What if your mortality does give way to immortality, is it so bad?"

A calmness fell on him and through his mind passed vividly "a hallowed experience when about a year ago my own beloved father, Andrew Kimball, came to me" in a dream. In the dream it had seemed he was in a room, tying a ribbon onto a child's braided hair, when his father appeared. "I dropped the child's hair and called loudly, 'Father, Father, oh, Father.' His smile was radiant as in life. It warmed me. I was pulsating with gladness. . . . Then he drew away further and I followed him across the room still calling so happily: 'Father, Father, I'm so glad to see you, Father, oh, Father.' It was very real. I seemed fearful that he would leave me. At the far side of the room I was still near him and reaching toward him and calling him when. . . Father faded out of the picture. I awakened." He had lain in bed, reliving the dream, not wanting it to end. Now a year later, enveloped again in the feeling of his father's love for him, "somehow a new peace filled me and my fear of death began to leave me."

SOURCE: Edward L. Kimball and Andrew E. Kimball Jr., *Spencer W. Kimball*, 301–2.

"DELIVERANCE IS AT HAND"
Elizabeth Horrocks Jackson Kingsford

A few days after the death of my husband, the male members of the company had become reduced in number by death; and those who remained were so weak and emaciated by sickness that on reaching the camping place at night, there were not sufficient men with strength enough to raise the poles and pitch the tents. The result was that we camped out with nothing but the vault of heaven for a roof and the stars for companions. The snow lay several inches deep upon the ground. The night was bitterly cold. I sat down on a rock with one child in my lap and one on each side of me. In that condition I remained until morning. . . .

It will be readily perceived that under such adverse circumstances I had become despondent. I was six or seven thousand miles from my native land, in a wild rocky mountain country, in a destitute condition, the ground covered with snow, the waters covered with ice, and I with three fatherless children with scarcely anything to protect them from the merciless storms. When I retired to bed that night, being the 27th of October, I had a stunning revelation. In my dream, my husband stood by me, and said, "Cheer up, Elizabeth, deliverance is at hand." The dream was fulfilled for the next day (October 28, 1856) Joseph A. Young, Daniel Jones, and Abel Garr galloped unexpectedly into camp, amid tears and cheers and smiles and laughter of the emigrants. These three men were the first of the most advanced relief company sent out from Salt Lake City to meet the belated emigrants.

Source: Andrew Jenson, *Latter-day Saint Biographical Encyclopedia*, 2:530–31.

"MOTHER CAN STILL BE WITH YOU"
Harold B. Lee (Related by L. Brent Goates)

L. Brent Goates relates this experience after the death of President Harold B. Lee's daughter Maurine Wilkins:

"Life had to go on and the shocked family in Provo needed loving administration. Aunt Helen never left the family those first two weeks. The bags she had packed for a two-week vacation, which was aborted at the news of Maurine's death, served Helen well as she stayed to take care of her sister's grief-stricken family. That first night she slept with Maurine's daughter, twelve-year-old Marlee, to comfort her. This little flaxen-haired girl had a dream so vivid that she awakened, gripped her aunt by the arm, and said: 'Aunt Helen, I've had such a funny dream! I dreamed we were sitting in the family room with Mother—you and me and Jane [her cousin]. Mother was sewing a button on Jay's shirt. [Jay was her younger brother.] We were all talking while Mother sewed. Jay came in and said he was sad because Mother was gone, and I said, "No she's not gone—see, she's right here—can't you see her?" Jay couldn't understand what I was saying, and I asked you and Jane if you could see her, and you just smiled. None of you could see her, but I could—I knew she was there. Isn't that funny, Aunt Helen?'

"Aunt Helen, conditioned by the wise teachings received in her childhood home, replied: 'No, Martsy dear, that's not just a funny dream. I think it's Heavenly Father's way of letting you know that even though your mommy has been taken from you, she can still be with you when you need her. You won't always be able to see her as you did in your dream, but she'll be close by and you'll feel her presence. Remember your dream, Martsy, when you're sad and lonesome for her, and it will help to make you feel better.' Reassured, Marlee went back to sleep."

SOURCE: L. Brent Goates, *Harold B. Lee*, 353–54.

"WALKING OUT OF THE FOG"
(Related by Harold B. Lee)

I saw and heard such a miracle recently when a man who had been incorrigible much of his life, now reaching up to his middle-age years, spoke by his own request at the funeral services of his elderly mother. His father and mother, obedient to the Lord's instruction, had persisted in teaching their children, including this son, who vigorously and rudely resisted their efforts. Despite this opposition, the father continued in his role as a faithful father should; he not only taught, but every Sunday he fasted and prayed, especially for this wayward son. The father was shown in a dream, as though to reassure him, his unruly son walking in a dense fog. In the dream he saw this son walk out of the fog into bright sunlight, cleansed by genuine repentance. We have seen that boy now a changed man and enjoying some of the Lord's choicest blessings in the Church because of his faithful parents who didn't fail him.

SOURCE: Harold B. Lee, in Conference Report, April 1965, 14.

"I SEE YOU HAVE RECEIVED YOUR SIGHT"
(Related by David O. McKay)

A number of years ago President Francis M. Lyman and President B. H. Roberts had attended a quarterly conference at Loa, Wayne County, Utah. In those days traveling was by team and whitetop. The brethren had started early that morning to catch the train at Sigurd—fifty or sixty miles distant. They stopped for breakfast at Koosharem. While they were eating, a very singular incident occurred. A young man, seeing the whitetop, knowing the elders were in the house, dismounted from his horse, entered, and eagerly asked: "How long are you brethren going to stay here?"

"Just long enough to finish our breakfast. Why?" queried Elder Lyman.

"Because I should like to bring my uncle here and have you administer to him."

Before the brethren had finished their breakfast, there entered the living room of the house a man who was led in his physical blindness by his wife and this young, outstanding rancher. As the elders entered the living room, Brother Lyman, in his bighearted way, putting his hand on the man's knee, said: "Well, so you want to be administered to, do you?"

"No, I do not," was the surprising reply.

"Well, then," said President Lyman, "why are you here?"

"Because my wife and my nephew put me in the wagon and brought me here," was his frank statement.

"How long has it been since you lost your sight?" asked President Lyman. The man told him. And Brother Lyman said: "Well, you believe the Lord can heal you, do you not?"

The man answered, "Well, I think he can. I don't know if he will."

There seemed to be an absolute absence of faith so far as the man was concerned.

"Do you belong to the Church?" asked President Lyman.

"No, I do not," was the reply.

"Well, if the Lord heals you, you would be glad to acknowledge his power, should you not?"

"Yes, if he did, I think I should."

Let me tell you at this point now what seemed to me in that instance to be most significant, and then I will finish the story. That young man had seen in a dream or vision the night before two men who had administered to his uncle, and the latter had received his sight through that administration. That is what prompted him to dismount from his horse, and make the request.

President Lyman and President Roberts performed the administration. The man, his wife, and nephew returned to their home. Presidents Lyman and Roberts resumed their journey to Salt Lake City.

Two or three months later, President Lyman was attending a conference in Blackfoot, Idaho. Among those who greeted him, walking unaided, was this man to whom they had administered. "Do you remember me?" the man asked.

President Lyman said, "Yes, and I see you have received your sight."

"Yes, I have," said the man; "I can read a newspaper as well as you can."

During the brief interview that followed, President Lyman remarked: "I remember our conversation—how do you account for your having received your sight?"

"Well," said the skeptic, "I believe that the medicine I was taking had just begun to work."

There was a miracle, but its effect in converting the man to the power of God was nil.

To me a most important phase of the story is the pre-vision of that young rancher, for I know that pre-vision is an actual fact in life, and it was through his faith that the man had been blessed.

SOURCE: David O. McKay, *Gospel Ideals*, 515–16.

"WHAT DOES THAT LIGHT MEAN?"
Marriner W. Merrill (Related by Heber J. Grant)

Brother Merrill told me, he had a dream in which he saw my brother in all kinds of wicked company in many different states, and he saw that a light surrounded him. In the dream, he said: "What does that light mean?" And a voice answered: "That is the influence that a faithful, God-fearing and God-serving father can have over a son to keep him from going astray, and to eventually bring him back to the truth."

Years later when my brother did come back and joined the Church, as I related here last conference, he fulfilled Brother Merrill's dream, because Brother Merrill said that he saw him laboring all over the Church, bringing wayward boys to a knowledge of the truth, and he did labor from Canada to Mexico in that service.

SOURCE: Heber J. Grant, in Conference Report, October 1944, 7.

"THEY ARE HEAVY TEARS"
Mrs. P———. (Related by Wreno Bowers)

The following dream was told to me one day by Mrs. P———, shortly after her child daughter had died. The little woman's story made such an impression on me that I wrote it down from memory as soon as I had time. Here it is:

After my little girl, Ethel, died I was very lonely and I cried most of the time. She had been my only companion after her father's death and it seemed almost impossible to face the long years without her. Everywhere that I looked; everywhere that I went, I saw some of her clothes or some of her playthings which brought back memories and tears. Every few hours of the night I awoke, crying. Indeed, I cried so much that my head began to ache as well as my heart.

Then one night I had a dream. I dreamed that I was in a strange land, where the trees were all green and the flowers were of many colors. Avenues of gold ran through the forest leading to a beautiful city. Everywhere, among the green tree foliage, birds were flashing their gorgeous plumage and singing wonderful songs.

As I walked toward the city, marveling at the beauty of the place, I met a group of children—running, laughing, singing with glee. Their little faces shone like the brightness of the sunbeams and their eyes sparkled with joy. They waved their hands at me as they passed and sang songs of the greatness of God.

As I turned toward the city again my heart sank and a great sadness came over me. I saw coming, far behind the other children, a lone child carrying a vase on her head. She walked with a weary tread and her face drooped with sorrow. When she drew nearer I recognized my own child—my own little Ethel!

Going to her I asked: "Why do you carry that heavy vase, Ethel? Why don't you leave it and run and play with the other little girls and be happy?"

She lifted her face to mine and a ray of happiness lighted up her face as she replied: "These are your tears I'm carrying, mama, and they are heavy tears. And I can't leave them, I have to carry them wherever I go. If you would not cry so much, mama, then I could play with the other little girls and be happy. You should not cry, you should rejoice, for some day we will be together again and live in that beautiful city with Jesus our Lord."

For a moment a silence fell on the room, then Mrs. P——— concluded: "This was only a dream, but to me it was a reality. I saw my little girl, as plainly as in life, and heard her speak. Her words were impressed upon my mind so that I cannot forget. Since then I have tried always to be cheerful; to look at the brighter side of life and look forward to the time when there will be no tears and all will be happy in the presence of God."

SOURCE: Wreno Bowers, "The Vase of Tears," 332.

"A DREAM FRAUGHT WITH DARKNESS"
Boyd K. Packer

Boyd [K. Packer] went aboard ship with other servicemen for the long voyage to Seattle and his mustering out at Fort Lewis. En route he thought of Verna, the sister who had been so good to him since babyhood. He dreamed about her, a dream fraught with darkness. He determined to visit her in Portland, just a bus ride away.

He found her very ill from crippling arthritis. She asked for a blessing, and in faith Boyd and her bishop blessed her. Soon after, her doctor discovered that she had a large tumor they had not known was there. Surgery was performed and her health improved.

SOURCE: Lucile C. Tate, *Boyd K. Packer*, 68.

"SISTER SPAFFORD IS IN TROUBLE"
Boyd K. Packer

On Sunday morning September 19, 1977, I awakened in the early hours of the morning greatly troubled over a dream that concerned Sister Spafford. My wife also awakened and asked why I was so restless. "Sister Spafford is in trouble," I told her. "She needs a blessing." When morning came I called her. She was deeply troubled indeed. I told her I had a blessing for her. She wept and said it came as an answer to her fervent prayer the night long. She had not been well. There had been tests. The day before the doctor told her the results. They were frightening—ominous indeed. There was a tumor and other complications. [The blessing] was most unusual. Her life was not over. Her days were to be prolonged for a most important purpose. Promises, special promises were given, among them that her mind would be sharp and alert as long as she lived. There would be no diminution of her mental capabilities, and other promises not to be mentioned here, were given. All of them now have been fulfilled, and she has accomplished those things so dear to her. When further tests were made that next week, the tumor was not there.

SOURCE: Boyd K. Packer, *That All May Be Edified*, 119.

"IT WILL BE A MIRACLE"
Electa Peck (Related by Newel Knight, as told to Andrew Jenson)

On the second of January 1831, the Church held its third conference at Fayette, on which occasion the Saints were first instructed as a people to begin the gathering of Israel [see Doctrine and Covenants 38:17–20]. . . . In the early part of April [we] started for our destination [Kirtland, Ohio]. . . .

"We had proceeded but a few days on our journey when I was subpoenaed as a witness, and had to go to Colesville. . . . The whole company declined traveling until I should return.

"Soon after I left, my aunt, Electa Peck, fell and broke her shoulder in a most shocking manner; a surgeon was called upon to relieve her sufferings, which were very great. My aunt dreamed that I had returned and laid my hands upon her, prayed for her, and she was made whole and pursued her journey with the company. She related this dream to the surgeon, who replied, 'If you are able to travel in many weeks, it will be a miracle, and I will be a Mormon, too.'

"I arrived at the place where the company had stopped, late in the evening; but on learning of the accident, I went to see my aunt, and immediately upon entering the room, she said, 'O, Brother Newel, if you will lay your hands upon me, I shall be well and able to go on the journey with you.' I stepped up to the bed and, in the name of the Lord Jesus Christ, rebuked the pain with which she was suffering and commanded her to be made whole; and it was done, for the next morning, she arose, dressed herself, and pursued the journey with us."

SOURCE: Andrew Jenson, *The Contributor*, 375.

"A PROMISE OF DELIVERANCE"
Parley P. Pratt

[The following event occurred while Parley P. Pratt was being held in jail in Richmond, Missouri during the spring of 1839 with other Latter-day Saint prisoners, including King Follett.]

Under these circumstances, and half way between hope and despair, I spent several days in fasting and prayer, during which one deep and all-absorbing inquiry, one only thought, seemed to hold possession of my mind. It seemed to me that if there was a God in Heaven who ever spake to man on earth I would know from Him the truth of this one question. It was not how long shall I suffer; it was not when or by what means I should be delivered; but it was simply this: Shall I ever, at any time, however distant it may be, or whatever I may suffer first; shall I ever be free again in this life, and enjoy the society of my dear wife and children, and walk abroad at liberty, dwell in society and preach the gospel, as I have done in bygone years?

Let me be sure of this and I care not what I suffer. To circumnavigate the globe, to traverse the deserts of Arabia, to wander amid the wild scenes of the Rocky Mountains to accomplish so desirable an object, would seem like a mere trifle if I could only be sure at last. After some days of prayer and fasting, and seeking the Lord on the subject, I retired to my bed in my lonely chamber at an early hour, and while the other prisoners and the guard were chatting and beguiling the lonesome hours in the upper apartment of the prison, I lay in silence, seeking and expecting an answer to my prayer, when suddenly I seemed carried away in the spirit, and no longer sensible to outward objects with which I was surrounded. A heaven of peace and calmness pervaded my bosom; a personage from the world of spirits stood before me with a smile of compassion in every look, and pity mingled with the tenderest love and sympathy in every expression of the countenance. A soft hand seemed placed within my own, and a glowing cheek was laid in tenderness and warmth upon mine. A well known voice saluted me, which I readily recognized as that of the wife of my youth, who had for nearly two years been sweetly sleeping where the wicked cease from troubling and the weary are at rest. I was made to realize that she was sent to commune with me, and answer my question.

Knowing this, I said to her in a most earnest and inquiring tone: Shall I ever be at liberty again in this life and enjoy the society of my family and the Saints, and preach the gospel as I have done? She answered definitely and unhesitatingly: "YES!" I then recollected that I had agreed to be satisfied with the knowledge of *that* one fact, but now I wanted more.

Said I: Can you tell me how, or by what means, or when I shall escape?' She replied, "THAT THING IS NOT MADE KNOWN TO ME YET." I instantly felt that I had gone beyond my agreement and my faith in asking this last question, and that I must be contented at present with the answer to the first.

Her gentle spirit then saluted me and withdrew. I came to myself. The doleful noise of the guards, and the wrangling and angry words of the old apostate again grated on my ears, but Heaven and hope were in my soul.

Next morning I related the whole circumstance of my vision to my two fellow prisoners, who rejoiced exceedingly. This may seem to some like an idle dream, or a romance of the imagination, but to me it was and always will be a reality, both as it regards what I then experienced and the fulfillment afterwards.

SOURCE: Parley P. Pratt, *Autobiography of Parley P. Pratt*, 204–5.

"WHAT HAVE YOU DONE WITH MY NAME?"
George Albert Smith

A number of years ago I was seriously ill. . . . One day, under these conditions, I lost consciousness of my surroundings and thought I had passed to the Other Side. I found myself standing with my back to a large and beautiful lake, facing a great forest of trees. There was no one in sight, and there was no boat upon the lake or any other visible means to indicate how I might have arrived there. I realized, or seemed to realize, that I had finished my work in mortality and had gone home. I began to look around, to see if I could not find someone. There was no evidence of anyone's living there, just those great, beautiful trees in front of me and the wonderful lake behind me.

I began to explore, and soon I found a trail through the woods which seemed to have been used very little, and which was almost obscured by grass. I followed this trail, and after I had walked for some time and had traveled a considerable distance through the forest, I saw a man coming towards me. I became aware that he was a very large man, and I hurried my steps to reach him, because I recognized him as my grandfather. . . . I remember how happy I was to see him coming. I had been given his name and had always been proud of it.

When Grandfather came within a few feet of me, he stopped. His stopping was an invitation for me to stop. Then . . . he looked at me very earnestly and said: "I would like to know what you have done with my name."

Everything I had ever done passed before me as though it were a flying picture on a screen—everything I had done. Quickly this vivid retrospect came down to the very time I was standing there. My whole life had passed before me. I smiled and looked at my grandfather and said: "I have never done anything with your name of which you need be ashamed."

He stepped forward and took me in his arms, and as he did so, I became conscious again of my earthly surroundings. My pillow was as wet as though water had been poured on it—wet with tears of gratitude that I could answer unashamed.

SOURCE: George Albert Smith, "Your Good Name," 139.

"A GREAT WORK YET TO DO"
Joseph F. Smith (Related by Susan Arrington Madsen)

Joseph F. was still missing his father, Hyrum, when he experienced yet another great sorrow. His mother's health was very bad, and she died just four years after their arrival in the Salt Lake Valley. When his father was killed, Joseph F. was five years old. Now when his mother died, he was thirteen. He was still so young! How would he survive? Who would take care of him? He felt alone and frightened.

But the Lord had plans for Joseph F. Smith. There was a great work for him yet to do. To comfort him, the Lord blessed him with a beautiful dream soon after his mother died. He dreamed that, when his life was over, his beloved mother and father, the Prophet Joseph Smith, and President Brigham Young met him in heaven. They put their arms around him, and he could feel how much they loved him. It made him feel so peaceful inside.

Joseph F. later said, "When I awoke that morning, I was a man. There was not anything in the world that I feared. I promised myself that I would so live that both Mother and Father would be proud of me." Now he had the courage to do whatever the Lord would ask of him.

A year and a half later, the Lord called Joseph F. on a mission to preach the gospel to the people of the Hawaiian Islands. He was fifteen years old, an unusually young age for a missionary.

SOURCE: Susan Arrington Madsen, *The Lord Needed a Prophet*, 96.

"I AM CLEAN"
Joseph F. Smith

I did have a dream one time. To me it was a literal thing; it was a reality.

I was very much oppressed, once, on a mission. I was almost naked and entirely friendless, except the friendship of a poor, benighted, degraded people. I felt as if I was so debased in my condition of poverty, lack of intelligence and knowledge, just a boy, that I hardly dared look a white man in the face.

While in that condition I dreamed that I was on a journey, and I was impressed that I ought to hurry—hurry with all my might, for fear I might be too late. I rushed on my way as fast as I possibly could, and I was only conscious of having just a little bundle, a handkerchief with a small bundle wrapped in it. I did not realize just what it was, when I was hurrying as fast as I could; but finally I came to a wonderful mansion, if it could be called a mansion. It seemed too large, too great to have been made by hand, but I thought I knew that was my destination. As I passed towards it, as fast as I could, I saw a notice, "Bath." I turned aside quickly and went into the bath and washed myself clean. I opened up this little bundle that I had, and there was a pair of white, clean garments, a thing I had not seen for a long time, because the people I was with did not think very much of making things exceedingly clean. But my garments were clean, and I put them on. Then I rushed to what appeared to be a great opening, or door. I knocked and the door opened, and the man who stood there was the Prophet Joseph Smith. He looked at me a little reprovingly, and the first word he said: "Joseph, you are late." Yet I took confidence and said:

"Yes, but I am clean—I am clean!"

He clasped my hand and drew me in, then closed the great door. I felt his hand just as tangible as I ever felt the hand of man. I knew him, and when I entered I saw my father, and Brigham, and Heber, and Willard, and other good men that I had known, standing in a row. I looked as if it were across this valley, and it seemed to be filled with a vast multitude of people, but on the stage were all the people that I had known. My mother was there, and she sat with a child in her lap; and I could name over as many as I remember of their names, who sat there, who seemed to be among the chosen, among the exalted.

The Prophet said to me, "Joseph," then pointing to my mother, he said: "Bring me that child."

I went to my mother and picked up the child, and thought it was a fine baby boy. I carried it to the Prophet, and as I handed it to him I purposely thrust my hands up against his breast. I felt the warmth; I was alone on a mat, away up in the mountains of Hawaii; no one was with me. But in this vision I pressed my hand up against the Prophet, and I saw a smile cross his countenance. I handed him the child and stepped back. President Young stepped around two steps, my father one step, and they formed a triangle. Then Joseph blessed that baby, and when he finished blessing it they stepped back in line; that is, Brigham and father stepped back in line. Joseph handed me the baby, wanted me to come and take the baby again; and this time I was determined to test whether this was a dream or a reality. I wanted to know what it meant. So I purposely thrust myself up against the Prophet. I felt the warmth of his stomach. He smiled at me, as if he comprehended my purpose. He delivered the child to me and I returned it to my mother, laid it on her lap.

When I awoke that morning I was a man, although only a boy. There was not anything in the world that I feared. I could meet any man or woman or child and look them in the face, feeling in my soul that I was a man every whit. That vision, that manifestation and witness that I enjoyed at that time has made me what I am, if I am anything that is good, or clean, or upright before the Lord, if there is anything good in me. That has helped me out in every trial and through every difficulty.

SOURCE: Joseph F. Smith, *Gospel Doctrine*, 541–43.

"I HAD A CHANCE TO THANK HER"
Reed Smoot

I do not know why it is, but from the opening session of this conference, I have thought of my mother, perhaps more times, from that moment until this, than any other time since she was called to the beyond. I had a chance, last night in my dreams, to thank her—her boy thanked her—for the teachings that she gave and instilled in my heart when I was but a boy. It seems that I can hear her voice ringing out now; it seemed in my dreams but last night that I could hear her pleadings to me, and her sound counsel and wise advice. I remember so well that she used to impress upon me that no person, whether he be baptized into the Church or not, can retain a testimony that God lives, without he asks of Father in heaven, in humility and prayer, to give him, and help him maintain that testimony and the love of the work. She used to tell me that if I did not have a testimony, then, that Jesus is the Christ, the way to get it was to pray to God constantly and in earnestness, and she promised me—my mother promised me,—that the Lord God would give it to me in due time, if I kept myself unspotted from the sins of the world. That promise came true, not perhaps in the way that I intended it should come; not in the way that I expected it must come, to satisfy my soul, but it came in God's own way, and there is nothing that I appreciate so much in all the world, and I shall never cease asking my God to help me as long as I live, to maintain that testimony and be true to God's work and cause here upon this earth.

SOURCE: Reed Smoot, in Conference Report, October 1922, 100.

"HE IS WORTHY; LET HIM BE CLOTHED"
Lorenzo Snow

While the Saints were crossing the plains, they stopped at Mount Pisgah, in Iowa Territory, to replenish their supplies. While they were there Lorenzo Snow became so critically ill that his family thought he was delirious, and therefore they couldn't trust what he was saying. But he was conscious and aware of his circumstances, and he had faith that he would emerge from his illness.

During this period he had a dream in which he experienced the most acute suffering that the heart can conceive. "I was led," he reported, "into the full and perfect conviction that I was entirely a hopeless case in reference to salvation, that eternities upon eternities must pass, and still I saw my case would remain the same. I saw the whole world rejoicing in all the powers and glories of salvation without the slightest beam of hope on my part, but doomed to separation"—and here we see his conviction about how crucial the family is—"from my friends and family, all I love most here, to eternity upon eternity. I shudder, even now, at the remembrance of the torments and agony of my feelings. No tongue can describe them, or imagination conceive. Those who were attending me at that time describe me as being in a condition of [death]. . . . My body was cool and my eyes and countenance denoted extreme suffering."

Then came the contrast. His exquisite pain of spirit was followed by what he calls "rapturous enjoyment." He said, "My spirit seemed to have left this world and [I was] introduced into that of Kolob. I heard a voice calling me by name saying, 'He is worthy, he is worthy, take away his filthy garments.' My clothes were then taken off piece by piece, and a voice said, 'Let him be clothed, let him be clothed.' Immediately I found a celestial body gradually growing upon me until at length I found myself crowned with all its glory and power. The ecstasy of joy I now experienced no man can tell. Pen cannot describe it. I conversed familiarly with Joseph, Father

Smith, and others, and mingled in the society of the Holy One. I saw my family all saved, and observed the dispensations of God with mankind until at last a perfect redemption was effected. . . My spirit must have remained, I should judge, for days, enjoying the scenes of eternal happiness."

SOURCE: Truman G. Madsen, *Presidents of the Church*, 123–24.

"WE ARE HERE FOR A SHORT TIME ONLY"
John Taylor

When I was in Paris, France, about thirty years ago, I had a dream that troubled me very much, in which I saw my first wife—as the deceased here is his [Bro. Cannon's] first wife—lying sick at the point of death. And it so affected me that I awoke, being troubled in my feelings. I fell asleep again, and again the same scene presented itself to me when I again awoke and experienced the same feelings of sorrow, and after some time slept again, and it was repeated a third time. I knew then that my wife was very sick, lying at the point of death.

I got up and fervently prayed the Lord to spare her life until, at least, I should have another opportunity of meeting her in the flesh. He heard my prayer. I took a note of the circumstance at the time, and learned afterwards that such had been the case exactly as it had been shown to me. On the following morning I remember meeting a gentleman who was a Protestant minister, and he observed that my countenance looked sorrowful, and he enquired the cause. I told him that my wife was lying at the point of death, and he asked me if I had received a letter? I told him no; but related to him how it had been shown to me. But, I said, I got up and prayed the Lord to spare her life, and I feel consoled in knowing that she will be healed.

SOURCE: John Taylor, in *Journal of Discourses*, 22:354.

"HAVE YOU THE AUTHORITY TO SAY NO?"
(Related by Edward J. Wood)

I remember once a woman on the Islands—to show you how the Lord goes before and with us, his elders and servants, and after us, on those Islands—a lady had a very sick child, and when they are sick they have faith in the power of the Priesthood to restore. We had only been there a few weeks. Nobody knew us there, did not know that we had arrived. A man came up to the house where we were holding service. He did not understand us; he had to speak through an interpreter; and he said to me, "There is a lady, on the other Island with a sick child. She wants you three men to go to her, and heal her child." It was right on the verge of the war there. The first edict made by the king under the German government was that a "Mormon" missionary who preached was to be fined $100 for the first sermon, and for the second he was to be banished from the Island. They made that edict, and we thought we were in trouble till this man said, that that woman had asked that we three men go unto her and lay our hands upon her child and the child should recover. We went out to a palm tree and talked to the Lord as I am talking to you, wanting the inspiration of his Spirit. Soon we decided we would go. After going across a strait some three miles in a little canoe, expecting almost every moment that the canoe would be overturned, we arrived. The woman was standing in front of her house. She had her handkerchief to her eyes, and said, "I am glad that you have come. It is all right. Here is my child." And under the sheet was the body of the child. We lifted that up and saw the child, and we said, "the child is already dead," and we covered it up again; and she hastily said, "No, it is not dead at all. You do what I saw you do last night in my dream, and he will be well." We asked the Lord, "suppose we administer to this child, and it does not get well, and they will say you are all evil spirits. They are a superstitious people." We had no faith that the child would recover. But the unprecedented faith of this native woman inspired us to do it. And she said, "Have you authority to do what I saw you do? You anointed that child with oil; you laid your hands upon his head." Yes, we had that authority. And then I thought of that passage that "my servants must go forth, and my authority shall be with them, and none shall stay them." I said, "Yes, we have that authority." Said she, "have you the authority to refuse?" I said, "no." We anointed the child, laid our hands upon it, covered it up, and went away. The cyclone came on, the social condition of the natives was upset; we never heard of the woman and child for a long while. I didn't expect to hear from it, until about a year after when I saw a number of natives under trees, with long knives. I saw them running along beneath the trees in their half-clad condition. Then I thought again that none should stay the preaching of this gospel So I buoyed myself up as best I could, and marched on. I saw the natives surrounding me on all sides, and as I came to a house in that tropical forest, they commenced to get closer to me, when all at once a woman marched out, and said, "How do you do, Brother Wood?" I rather sank back, and said, "I don't know you." "O yes, you do," and she turned, and called a child about nine years of age. She stood the child upon the trunk of a tree, and then she bore this testimony to the great crowd of natives: "This child is a living testimony of the great power of the gospel, and the power and authority held by Brother Wood and his associates. They administered to this child over two years ago. I have never seen them since, but I know they have the power of God with them, and all of you must listen to their message. I am the daughter of the high chief of the island, and you can come to my house and have everything you want."

SOURCE: Edward J. Wood, in Conference Report, October 1920, 126–27.

"GET THE SPIRIT OF THE LORD AND KEEP IT"
Wilford Woodruff (Related by Marion G. Romney)

Now, it is very important, my brethren, that we each live so that we can have this spirit of the Lord. Its importance did not cease with the death of the Prophet Joseph Smith. In 1879, two years after the Prophet Brigham Young had died, President Wilford Woodruff was down in the mountains of Arizona traveling with Lot Smith. On one occasion, he had a vision or a dream in which he saw Brigham Young and Orson Hyde, and he asked Brigham Young if he would not come with him to Arizona and speak to the people. Brigham Young answered that he had done his talking in the flesh and that work was now left for Elder Woodruff and others to do. In his diary, President Woodruff quotes President Young as saying: "Tell the people to get the spirit of the Lord and keep it with them."

SOURCE: Marion G. Romney, in Conference Report, April 1944, 140.

"ALL THIS I SAW IN THE NIGHT VISION"
Brigham Young (Related by Dean C. Jessee)

Ten days later from Manchester where [Brigham Young] and Parley P. Pratt were working on the publication of the hymn book, Brigham found time to address his family in a letter. A highlight of the letter is his recounting of "a visit" he had made to them in a dream the night before:

"To my Dearest Mary. I now take my pen to wright a fue words to you. I have ben verry desirus to here from you. I get a little knews ecasenely [occasionally] by the Br[ether]in that recive letters from there wifes. Grately to my sa[t]esfaction last night I paid you a visit in that contry. I first saw Elizabeth. I shoke her by the hand. Enquired whare you was. She said you was about the house. Still I thaught we ware out of dores, but you soon came along whare I was.

I shok you hartley by the hand and kist you two or three times and said to you whare is my Dear Children. You and Elizabeth boath spoke and said the ware at [s]chool and are all well. I says is Violate at [s]chol? Yeas you boath said. You then replied the children feele verry well suited with there situation and was verry fond of there Books. I wanted to see Violate and my little Jode Boy or Joseph and Mary and Brigham but did not. All this I saw in the night vision."[3]

SOURCE: Dean C. Jessee, "Brigham Young's Family," 6.

"KEEP THE SPIRIT OF THE LORD"
Brigham Young (Related by Ronald K. Esplin)

Moving the Saints across Iowa had required more time and resources than Brigham Young had ever imagined. For a time it seemed as if the whole Church was mired, both literally and metaphorically, hub-deep in the spring prairie mud. The experience overwhelmed him, drained him, and forced him to confront his own (and all human) limitations. He had long known that without the overseeing hand of God the Saints had neither safety nor promise, but now, after exhausting his own physical and emotional reserves to little avail, he understood more than ever the need for God's intervention. And he longed for Joseph to counsel him and to reassure the people.

Illness seized him during the night of 16 February 1847 and the pre-dawn hours of 17 February, a sickness so severe that he "fainted away, apparently dead for several moments." . . . [He later said]: "All that I know, is what my wife told me about it since." She reported that his first words upon being revived were that he "had been where Joseph & Hyrum was" and that "it is hard coming back to life again."

Revived and returned to his bed, Brigham Young fell asleep and dreamed, and when he awoke, he called for writing materials. "In my dream I went to see Joseph," he wrote. He found him sitting by a large window looking "perfectly natural." Brigham took him by the hand, kissed his cheeks, and asked him why they could not be together as before. Joseph arose from his chair and "looked at me with an ernest and plesent countenance, spoak in his usual way it is all right. I then said to him I due not like to be a way from you. it is wright he replied we can not be together yet, we shall be by en by[.] but you will have to do things with out me a while and then we shall be together again." Brigham then addressed Joseph as his mentor in the priesthood, one who knew the Saints better than he did. "The Bretheren [especially Brother Brigham!] have grate anxiety to understand the law of adoption or sealing principls and . . . if you have a word of councel for me I should be glad to receive it." The counsel was very simple: "be sure to tel[l] the people to keep the spiret of the Lord." . . .

The interview over, Brigham turned and saw Joseph standing in the light "but where I had to go was as midnight darkness." Because Joseph insisted, Brigham "went back in the darkness" and awoke. . . . As he described the experience not long afterward, "I have been with Joseph and Hyrum; it is hard to come back to life again." President Young affirmed that he knew this experience was "from the Lord through Joseph."

Source: Ronald K. Esplin, "Discipleship: Brigham Young and Joseph Smith," 263–64.

CHAPTER 12

Dreams of Death

Like birth, death is a necessary and essential part of the plan of salvation (see Moses 6:59–62)—which Jacob and Alma both called the "great plan of happiness" (2 Nephi 9:6; Alma 42:8). Facing death can be one of the most fearful experiences of mortality. For the righteous, though, death can be sweet and need not be feared (see Alma 27:28). Indeed, the Lord revealed to Joseph Smith that "those that die in me shall not taste of death, for it shall be sweet unto them" (Doctrine and Covenants 42:46). On the other hand, for people who die not in Christ, death can be a bitter experience (see Doctrine and Covenants 42:47), and the thought of an approaching death can create foreboding, trepidation, and fear. Dreams regarding death can serve as a powerful reminder that this life is the time for us to prepare to meet God (see Alma 12:24; 34:32).

This chapter shares dreams about the experience of death. There are many different kinds of dreams about death. Someone near the end of his or her life may receive the spiritual gift of a comforting dream. Other people may receive dreams foreshadowing their own deaths or the death of others. Some dreams are given shortly before a loved one or acquaintance is called by death, especially if that death seems particularly difficult or untimely. Some people have received dreams that include counsel and guidance encouraging them to repent and turn their lives over to Christ. Other dreams regarding death are given to comfort, uplift, and support those who face a pending death. Dreams of understanding can also be given to comfort the living who grieve the death of loved ones and associates.

Even if death is not imminent, our Heavenly Father can send comfort through dreams that testify to the fact that our existence will not end with our last breath. These dreams testify that the sting of death is swallowed up in the victory of Christ's Atonement (see 1 Corinthians 15:55; Mosiah 16:7–8; Alma 22:14). Dreams associated with death can cause us to reflect on the core principles of the plan of salvation. They are a testimony that God loves and succors his children.

"SLEEP UNTIL THE EVENTIDE"
Barbara Smith Amussen (Related by Ezra Taft Benson)

[Barbara Smith Amussen] knew the exact time she was to depart mortal life. Her husband, a Danish convert and Utah's first pioneer jeweler and watchmaker, Carl Christian Amussen, appeared to her in either a dream or a vision. She admitted, "I'm not sure which, but it was so real it seemed that he was right in the room. He said he had come to tell me that my time in mortal life was ending and that on the following Thursday [it was then Friday], I would be expected to leave mortal life."

Her oldest daughter, Mabel, said, "Oh, Mother, you've been worrying about something. You've not been feeling well."

Her mother replied, "Everything's fine. I feel wonderful. There's nothing to worry about. I just know I'll be leaving next Thursday." Then she added, "Mabel, when the time comes, I'd like to pass away in your home in the upper room where I used to sit and tell the boys Book of Mormon and Church history stories when they were little fellows."

As the time drew near, she attended fast meeting in her ward. The bishop told us she stood and talked as though she were going on a long journey. "She was bidding us all goodbye," said the bishop, "expressing her love for us and the joy that had been hers working in the temple, which was just a few yards away from the chapel." And then she bore a fervent testimony.

The bishop was so impressed that, following her testimony, he arose and announced the closing song, although the ward members had not been together quite an hour.

As the days passed, she went to the bank, drew out her small savings, paid all her bills, and went to Bishop Hall's mortuary and picked out her casket. Then she had the water and the power turned off in her home and went down to Mabel's. The day before she passed away, her son came to visit her. They sat by the bed and held hands as they talked.

On the day of her passing, Mabel came into the room where her mother was reclining on the bed. Her mother said, "Mabel, I feel a little bit drowsy. I feel I will go to sleep. Do not disturb me if I sleep until the eventide."

Those were her last words, and she peacefully passed away.

SOURCE: Ezra Taft Benson, *Come unto Christ*, 21–22.

"MY DEAR FRIEND LOST NOTHING"
Feramorz L. Young (Related by Heber J. Grant)

[Please see "Working with the Wayward Boys and Girls," pp. 242–43, for more information about Feramorz L. Young.]

A woman came to Sister Young, [Feramorz L. Young's] mother,

with photographs of one of this lady's near and dear friends, a very beautiful woman, and said: . . .

"This girl friend of mine was one of the noblest, finest, choicest kind of girls and young women that ever lived. She has come to me in this city of Salt Lake on three separate occasions at night in dreams, and has given me this information: the date of her birth, the date of her death, and. . . she has told me that your son, Feramorz L. Young, has converted her . . . 'I want you to go to Mrs. Young and give her this information and vouch for my honesty, virtue, integrity and upright life, and have the work done for me.' . . .

This woman who visited Mrs. Young said: . . . "The last time this friend of mine came—which was the third time—she said, 'There is nobody in Salt Lake City who knows me and can vouch for me except you. You are the only individual that I know in Salt Lake City.'" She said further to Mrs. Young: "I can furnish you any references you may wish regarding my character, from the place where I formerly lived. The last time this young woman came to me she said, 'You might just as well go to Mrs. Young and give her this information, because I am going to come, and come, and come, until you do it.'" And the woman continued, "I just cannot bear to have her come again; it is so uncanny." . . .

I am convinced that my dear friend lost nothing by dying in his youth.

SOURCE: Heber J. Grant, "Comforting Manifestations," 190.

"A MAN CAME INTO THE ROOM"
Oscar McConkie

Oscar was promised in his patriarchal blessing that he would dream dreams and see visions. This privilege was accorded him even from the days of his youth. In this manner he was frequently warned of the deaths of friends and relatives. When his uncle Andrew Somerville was sick, he dreamed that he went to see him, and as he stood in the room looking at him, a man came into the room. He did not come through the door nor leave by it but passed through the wall. "I observed him closely," Oscar recalled, "both his appearance, features, and manners," though he had never seen him before. The man walked straight to his uncle's bedside and studied him, shook his head, and with a very grave look on his face turned and left the room with no acknowledgment of Oscar's presence.

It was Oscar's habit to share such experiences with his mother. From his descriptions Emma recognized that the man he had seen was her father. She asked her son the meaning of the dream and was told that her brother was going to die. She got up, put on her shawl, and went immediately to Andrew's bedside. When she returned, she said he seemed much better and that the doctor had said he would be fine. Two days later he passed away.

From such experiences Oscar learned much about the workings of the Spirit. For instance, he said that in the dream when the father saw that his son would die, his face became very grave and the lines on it deepened, not because he was going to die but because his work was not finished and because he had not been as faithful as he should have been. This alone, he was able to determine, was the source of his sorrow.

SOURCE: Joseph Fielding McConkie, *The Bruce R. McConkie Story*, 36–37.

"HIS FAMILY WERE PREPARING A HAPPY REUNION"
David O. McKay

[Elder Mark E. Petersen] felt that his health problem was providential, for it allowed him to hear President McKay explain a little more about the reason for his overseas assignment. President McKay told him that he had been ill and thought he was dying. Then he dreamed that he had gone to the other side and that all his family there were preparing a happy reunion for him. But just as he reached his arms toward his waiting relatives, a voice said to him that his time had not come, for he had work still to do. President McKay felt a deep conviction that it was Mark Petersen who must go abroad. Mark was humbled by the story and vowed to give all his energy for the work of the Lord.

SOURCE: Peggy Petersen Barton, *Mark E. Petersen*, 128.

"YOU OUGHT NOT TO HAVE LEFT ME"
George Miller

On the morning of the 28th of June, 1844, I had a dream, or vision, in an upper room in the house of a Mr. Saunders, where I then lodged with Brother Thomas Edwards. It took place after sunrise. I was lying on my bed, and suddenly Joseph Smith appeared to me, saying, "God bless you, Brother Miller. The mob broke in upon us in Carthage jail and killed Brother Hyrum and myself. I was delivered up by the brethren as a lamb for the slaughter. You ought not to have left me; if you had stayed with me, I should not have been given up." I answered, "But you sent me." "I know I did, but you ought not to have gone"; and then approaching me he said, "God bless you for ever and ever," making as though he was about to embrace me, and, as I was in the act of extending my arms to return the embrace, the vision fled, and I found myself standing on the floor in the midst of the room. Brother Edwards, roused from his slumbers, was calling me, "What is the matter, Brother Miller; whom are you talking to?" I requested him to rise and dress himself, so that we might take a morning walk, as was our custom.

Whilst on our walk I related to Brother Edwards my vision, and told him my mission was fulfilled, for my firm belief was that Joseph was dead. Brother Edwards told me that I had preached too much, and that my mind was somewhat deranged, and that I must not think of going home until our present appointments were fulfilled—the last a week hence—and as to the rumors of trouble at

Nauvoo, he did not believe a word of them. I told him that if I stayed he would have to do the preaching.

SOURCE: Mark L. McConkie, *Remembering Joseph*, 986–87.

"I RECEIVED MY COMMISSION TO PREACH THE GOSPEL"

Andrew C. Nelson (Related by Spencer J. Condie)

[Andrew C. Nelson, grandfather of President Russell M. Nelson, reported,] "On the night of April 6th, 1891, I had a strange dream or vision in which I saw and conversed with my father who died January 27, 1891."

"When father came to the bed, he first said: 'Well, my son, being you were not there . . . when I died, so that I did not get to see you, and as I had a few spare minutes. . . .'

"'What have you been doing since you died, father?' . . .

"'My son, I have been traveling together with Apostle Erastus Snow ever since I died; that is, since three days after I died; then I received my commission to preach the Gospel. You can not imagine, my son, how many spirits there are in the Spirit world that have not yet received the Gospel; but many are receiving it, and a great work is being accomplished. Many are anxiously looking forth to their friends, who are still living, to administer for them in the Temples. I have been very busy in preaching the Gospel of Jesus Christ.'

"'Will all the spirits believe you, father, when you teach them the Gospel?' 'No, they will not.'

"'How are you and mother, the boys, Emillie and the girls getting along?' 'I am well, father, and when I last heard from Redmond the folks there were well.'

'Father, can you see us at all times, and do you know what we are doing?' 'No, my son, I can not. I have something else to do. I can not go when and where I please. There is just as much, and much more, order here in the Spirit world than in the other world. I have been assigned work and that must be performed.'

"'We intend to go to the Temple and get sealed to you as soon as my school is closed. I have talked with the girls about it and they want to be sealed to you.' 'That, my son, is partly what I came to see you about. We will yet make a family and live throughout Eternity.'

"'How do you feel at all times, father?' 'I feel splendid, and enjoy my labors; still, I must admit that at times I get a little lonesome to see my family; but it is only a short time till we will again see each other.'

"'O, father, how glad I am that you died in full faith in the Gospel, and in full fellowship in the Church.' 'Well, my son, your father always did know since he joined the Church that the Gospel was true, and you know that I always taught it to you, when you were a small boy. I got a little stubborn, but who is there of us that has not been a little cross and naughty at times. The short time that I was cross does not amount to 15 minutes in comparison to Eternity. I was punished for it. But it is all right. My son, you take care that you do not get that way.'

"'Father, is it natural to die? Or does it seem natural? Was there not a time when your spirit was in such a pain that it could not realize what was going on or taking place?' 'No, my son, there was not such a time. It is just as natural to die, as it is to be born, or for you to pass out of that door (here he pointed at the door). When I had told the folks that I could not last long, it turned dark and I could not see anything for a few minutes. Then, the first thing I could see was a number of spirits in the Spirit world. Then, I told the folks that I must go. The paper you gave me, my son, is dated wrong, but it makes no particular difference; correct records are kept here.'

"'Father, is the principle and doctrine of the Resurrection as taught us true?' 'True. Yes, my son, as true as can be. You can not avoid being Resurrected. It is just as natural for all to be Resurrected as it is to be born and die again. No one can avoid being

Resurrected. There are many spirits in the Spirit world who would to God that there would be no Resurrection.'

"'Father, is the Gospel as taught by this Church true?' 'My son, do you see that picture' (pointing to a picture of the First Presidency of the Church hanging on the wall)? 'Yes, I see it.' 'Well, just as sure as you see that picture, just so sure is the Gospel true. The Gospel of Jesus Christ has within it the power of saving every man and woman that will obey it, and in no other way can they ever obtain a salvation in the Kingdom of God. My son, always cling to the Gospel. Be humble, be prayerful, be submissive to the Priesthood, be true, be faithful to the covenants you have made with God. Never do anything that will displease God. O, what a blessing is the Gospel! My son, be a good boy.'

"'Good bye.'

"I then saw him leave the room. He was neatly dressed in a suit of light gray clothes, which I had never seen him wear when alive."

SOURCE: Spencer J. Condie, *Russell M. Nelson*, 9–11.

"TED WILL NOT BE WITH US MUCH LONGER"
Boyd K. Packer

Sometime before the fatal illness of his friend A. Theodore Tuttle was diagnosed, Elder Packer had a dream. He never spoke of it in detail, but he told Sister Packer, "Ted will not be with us much longer." She asked if something had been said. He responded, "No. Just that." She understood.

And so it was. Great blessings were given Elder Tuttle, and many prayers were offered in his behalf. But he pleaded with the Lord to give them, instead, to poor Saints in South America. Those who were close to Brother Tuttle knew at the time he died that his prayers had been, would be, answered as he wished.

SOURCE: Lucile C. Tate, *Boyd K. Packer*, 287.

DREAMS AS REVELATION

"YOUR TURN NEXT"
John Rowberry

The following was related by Heber J. Grant:

I was out in Tooele at a quarterly stake conference. The patriarch of the stake, Brother John Rowberry, had told me many years before of having had a dream (as I remember it, thirty years before), in which he was on a great vessel, and every once in a while somebody fell overboard, and he finally fell overboard himself. When he struggled through the water he came out into the most beautiful country that he had ever seen, and he met Brother Orson Pratt there. He asked Brother Pratt: "Where am I?" and Brother Pratt said: "You are in heaven, Brother Rowberry."

Brother Pratt happened to be out in Tooele at that particular time, visiting the various wards in that stake. Brother Rowberry told him of this dream, praying to the Lord that Brother Pratt would not ask him who the man was that he met in his dream. He did not want to tell him that he, Brother Pratt, had to die first. Brother Pratt said: "I will pray about it and if I get the interpretation I will give it to you."

Just before leaving (he was there several weeks), Brother Pratt said:

"Well, I prayed about your dream, Brother Rowberry, and I got the interpretation. The people on that vessel represented the people of the world. You said that the majority of the people who fell overboard you did not know. If you will write down a list of those you did know in the order in which they fell overboard I promise you that they shall die in that exact order, and I promise you that when you shall go to heaven you shall meet the identical man that you met in your dream, and when you meet him tell him that the dream was from the Lord and the interpretation was also from the Lord through Brother Orson Pratt."

And Brother Rowberry said: "Brother Pratt, I will tell him."

While I was still in Tooele as president of the stake, I received a telegram to the effect that Brother Orson Pratt was in a very serious condition of health and requested that we hold a prayer meeting in both Grantsville and Tooele for his recovery. We did so, and as we were going into the prayer circle room in Tooele, Brother Rowberry said to me: "Heber, do you remember my dream?"

I told him, "Yes."

He said: "Well, it is Brother Pratt's turn next." And indeed, that proved to be Brother Pratt's last illness.

Some years later I was out in Tooele at a stake conference at which Brother Rowberry was one of the speakers. He was in very good health, although he was an aged man at the time. He spoke with a great deal of power and vigor and expressed his gratitude for the gospel. After the meeting he said: "Brother Grant, do you remember my dream?"

I said, "Yes."

He said: "The people have died in the exact order in which they fell off the vessel. They are all gone, and it is my turn next and I am the happiest man in all Tooele County. I am anxious to meet Brother Pratt and to meet your father and other men and women I have loved with all my heart. By the way, I will tell your father, Brother Grant, that you are doing very well as an apostle." The next time I went to Tooele he had passed on.

SOURCE: Heber J. Grant, *Gospel Standards*, 297–99.

"WANTED ON THE OTHER SIDE"
Edwin S. Sheets (Related by William A. Morton)

I can scarcely realize that Bishop Sheets is dead. A little more than a week ago he and I were working in the office together. We did not think at that time that in a few days one of us would be taken. His death is a great loss to the Church, to the community, and especially to his family. Yet I am one of those who acknowledges the hand of God in it. Had it been the will of the Lord that he should have remained with us longer, it would have been a very easy thing for Him to have answered the earnest, fervent prayers that were offered up for his recovery; for no man was more worthy of having prayers answered in his behalf than was Bishop Sheets. The fact that the Lord did not grant us the desire of our heart—the prolongation of our brother's life—when he could have done so so easily, is evidence to me that the bishop had filled his earthly mission.

One morning last summer he told me a dream he had dreamed the night before, and which seemed to have made a deep impression on his mind. He said he dreamed that he was wanted on the other side of the veil, that there was a certain work for him to do there. I asked him what his feelings were concerning death, and he answered that he had as little dread of it as he had of going into the other room. This because of the godly, righteous, sober life he had lived.

SOURCE: William A. Morton, "Bishop Edwin S. Sheets as I Knew Him," 405–6.

"WORKING WITH THE WAYWARD BOYS AND GIRLS"
Horace G. Whitney (Related by Heber J. Grant)

Feramorz L. Young had been in the East and had been graduated with honors from the Troy Polytechnic Institute, then went on a mission to Mexico, where he died and was buried in the Gulf of Mexico. . . . One of my nearest and dearest friends in boyhood was Horace G. Whitney. Horace had a dream after Fera died in which the two had a conversation. Horace asked him what he was doing, and received this reply: "I am here working, Horace, with the wayward boys and girls of the Church, who are drifting away from it, and I am trying to turn their hearts back to the truth. That is my calling, and it is of far greater importance than it would have been for me to remain upon the earth. I have a great influence with them."

I remember relating this to one of my wayward brothers who subsequently joined the Church after being out of it for very many years, and he said: "Well, if there was a boy on earth whom I respected when he was alive that boy was Fera Young."

I do not think that Fera Young in his life ever listened to an unclean story. If anyone started to tell such a story he would excuse himself and walk away. I never heard an unchaste word uttered by him. If there ever was a clean, sweet, absolutely pure young man upon the earth, he was that young man.

When he died his mother said she could not remember a word or thought or act of his life that would bring her the least sorrow or uneasiness. There is many a mother perhaps who might say such a thing of her son, but usually if the man who without exception was the most intimate friend of that son from his boyhood up to the time of his death should tell everything he knew of him the mother could not say that. My mother could not say that of me, if others told her what I did as a youngster, but I could say it of Feramorz Young.

SOURCE: Heber J. Grant, "Comforting Manifestations," 190.

"AN AGED MAN WITH A BEAVER HAT"
Wilford Woodruff

When I was a boy eleven years old, I had a very interesting dream, part of which was fulfilled to the very letter. In this dream I saw a great gulf, a place where all the world had to enter at death, before doing which they had to drop their worldly goods. I saw an aged man with a beaver hat and a broadcloth suit. The man looked very sorrowful. I saw him come with something on his back, which he had to drop among the general pile before he could enter the gulf. I was then but a boy. A few years after this my father and mother removed to Farmington, and there I saw that man. I knew him the moment I saw him. His name was Chauncy Deming. In a few years afterwards he was taken sick and died. I attended his funeral. He was what you may call a miser, worth hundreds of thousands of dollars. When the coffin was being lowered into the grave my dream came to me, and that night his son-in-law found one hundred thousand dollars in a cellar belonging to the old man. I name this merely to show that in this dream I had manifested to me certain things that were true. I think of all the inhabitants of the world having to leave their goods when they come to the grave.

SOURCE: Wilford Woodruff, in *Journal of Discourses*, 22:332.

"SARAH EMMA DIED"
Wilford Woodruff

[November] 28th [1839] I spent the day at Mr Tiltons & the night, & had a dream while upon my bed. And in my Dream I saw Mrs Woodruff & notwithstanding we rejoiced much at having an interview with each other yet our embraces were mixed with sorrow for after conversing a while about her domestic affairs I asked whare *Sarah Emma* was (our ownly Child). She Says weeping <and kissing me> She is dead. We sorrowed a moment & I awoke. Phebe Also said she had not received my letters.

Is this dream true? Time must determin. This dream was a warning of what was to come. *Sarah Emma* Died 17th of July AD 1840.

SOURCE: *Wilford Woodruff's Journal*, 1:255.

"THEY ALL APPEARED TO BE IN A HURRY"
Wilford Woodruff

[September] 20th [1846] Sunday I met with the Saints in the Bowery. Was Called upon to Address the meeting. I gave An account of my mission to the East. I spoke of my dream I dreamed of dying & going to the place of the departed spirits. I saw Brother

Joseph & Hyram Smith & many of the Saints who had died. They all appeared to be in a Hurry. I thought Strange to find them in A Hurry And I enquired the Cause. They informed me that the time was set for Christ to Come as the great Bridegroom to the Earth to meet the Bride the Lambs wife & they had not had time to prepare as those of other dispensations & Had to be in a Hurry in order to get ready. And when I awoke I was overwhelmed with a peculiar sensation at the view of the work the Latter Day Saints Had to perform in order to prepair the Bride for to meet the Bridegroom.

SOURCE: *Wilford Woodruff's Journal*, 3:578–79.

"TO TEACH US A PRINCIPLE"
Wilford Woodruff

When I was in the city of London on one occasion, with Brother George A. Smith, I dreamed that my wife came to me and told me that our first child had died. I believed my dream, and in the morning while at breakfast, I felt somewhat sad. Brother George A. noticed this and I told him my dream. Next morning's post brought me a letter from my wife, conveying the intelligence of the death of my child. It may be asked what use there was in such a thing. I don't know that there was much use in it except to prepare my mind for the news of the death of my child. But what I wanted to say in regard to these matters is, that the Lord does communicate some things of importance to the children of men by means of visions and dreams as well as by the records of divine truth. And what is it all for? It is to teach us a principle. We may never see anything take place exactly as we see it in a dream or a vision, yet it is intended to teach us a principle.

SOURCE: *The Discourses of Wilford Woodruff*, 286.

CHAPTER 13

Dreams of Opposition

From the first moments of Joseph Smith's prayer that brought forth the First Vision to the end of his life, he battled Satan and his hosts. Though Joseph never recorded dreaming of Satan or his followers, he had many contests with the adversary and witnessed the devil's power manifest from time to time, especially with the coming forth of the Book of Mormon.[1] Joseph taught that "the nearer a person approaches the Lord, a greater power will be manifested by the adversary to prevent the accomplishment of His purposes."[2] Elder Erastus Snow, of the Quorum of the Twelve Apostles, explained:

"So far as this generation is concerned it has been since the Prophet Joseph came forth and declared his belief in revelations, visions and angels that the powers of darkness have operated by external and supernatural manifestations, and as the power of God increased with the people and extended throughout the earth and was felt by other nations besides this, the Evil One manifested his power among men to a greater extent."[3]

Though many Latter-day Saints may be near to approaching the Lord, the power manifest by the adversary appears seldom to be manifest in their dreams.

In our research, we found few instances of Satan or his followers appearing in dreams. Latter-day Saints have seldom reported evil spirits as part of their dreams. There are many instances of dreams that supplied optimism, peace, comfort, and inspiration, but far fewer dreams of opposition. Joseph Smith explained why this may be the case. "Wicked spirits," he said, "have their bounds, limits, and laws by which they are governed or controlled."[4] There may be bounds which Satan and his followers cannot cross involving our dreams.

In dreams of opposition that have been recorded, Satan and his followers generally appear as themselves. They are not disguised. Though satanic spirits make great effort to deceive people while they are awake, in the dreams in this chapter, the dreamers were not deceived. Throughout the history of The Church of Jesus Christ of Latter-day Saints, there have been many times when Latter-day Saints have fallen victim to revelations that did not come from God, but dreamers can apparently recognize when something is not of the Spirit. In 1913, the First Presidency clarified the correct order of revelation in the Church:

"From the days of Hiram Page . . . at different periods there have been manifestations from delusive spirits to members of the Church. . . . When visions, dreams, tongues, prophecy, impressions or any extraordinary gift or inspiration, conveys something out of harmony with the accepted revelations of the Church or contrary to the decisions of its constituted authorities, Latter-day Saints may know that it is not of God, no matter how plausible it may appear. . . Lord's church is a 'house of order.' It is not governed by individual gifts or manifestations, but by the order and power of the Holy

Priesthood as sustained by the voice and vote of the Church in its appointed conferences."[5]

Even those who are sincere can be misled and misguided into interpreting satanic promptings as being revelations from God; but, in the case of dreams, Latter-day Saints were not deceived. As Joseph Smith taught, "All beings who have bodies, have power over those who have not. The devil has no power over us only as we permit him."[6] Those who have bodies can control those without mortal tabernacles, and that power appears to be manifest not only in consciousness but also in slumber.

In our dreams, as in our conscious hours, "Satan cannot seduce us by his enticements unless we in our hearts consent and yield."[7] The Prophet Joseph Smith instructed that "some revelations are of God: some revelations are of man: and some revelations are of the devil."[8] Our responsibility and opportunity is to listen closely to the whisperings of the Spirit so that we can correctly identify revelatory sources.

"THE DEVIL APPEARED TO ME"
J. Golden Kimball

After making [a] declaration in the Logan tabernacle, that I would never doff my hat and be servile to any man because of his money, that night I had a dream. I am not a dreamer; I believe in dreams when they come true, and I haven't any use for them until they do. It was very vivid. I haven't forgotten it, and it has been nearly forty years since it occurred. I have not repeated it but a few times. The devil appeared to me at the northeast corner of the Temple block. I was not very well acquainted with the devil. . . man I saw, and I seemed to know he was Satan, was of great personality in appearance, in height and bigness; he was dark and swarthy and seemed to be a real man. When he looked at me with those black eyes they pierced me to the soul.... I trembled from head to heels with fear. He repeated what I had said at the Logan tabernacle. The Spirit of God came on me and thrilled me from crown to toe. I told him I would not bow to man. I then became frightened [in my dream] and ran like a coward. I was arrested and put in jail for four years. I saw myself come out of jail. My clothes were threadbare. I was thinner than I am now, if such a thing can be possible: but I was free. In four years from that time our creditors stripped us to the skin, and that dream came true. I do not want any more dreams of that kind.

SOURCE: J. Golden Kimball, in Conference Report, October 1931, 56–57.

"A LOOK OF BAFFLED RAGE"
Thomas A. Shreeve

I dreamed that I was back in Sydney, [Australia,] sick in bed. Brother May was at a table in the room, and we were conversing. Across the room, to the right of my bed, was an open door, which I could see without lifting my head from the pillow.

While I lay there listening to the words of Brother May, a personage clothed in a white robe entered the room. He appeared to be a young man, and had a very pleasing countenance.

This personage passed around the bed and stood near the table. Brother May rose and offered the visitant a chair, and then withdrew. The young man seated himself at the table and opened a book. He said:

"Are you ready to report the Sydney Branch?"

"Yes, sir," I responded.

"Then proceed."

I gave him an account of all our doings in Sydney, beginning with our first effort of reorganizing, and closing with my last act previous to sailing—for all these things seemed plain to my mind. The recital seemed to occupy me several minutes, and I continued to speak freely. He wrote in the book rapidly, and never once interrupted me. I felt that he was taking every word I uttered. When I stopped, he asked:

"Have you anything more to say?"

"No, sir," I answered.

Then he turned the leaves back, and seemed to read from the beginning. He said:

"Very well. Now where are you going?"

"To New Zealand."

He recorded my answer in the book, and then signed his name—I could not see the words of his name, but I felt that he was writing his own signature. He closed the book and walked around to the right side of the bed, shook hands with me, and said:

"Good-by; I will be there before you."

He passed from the room, and then I saw the figure of a little child standing at the foot of the bed. I looked closely and recognized my little brother Teddy, who had been drowned nearly twenty years before. I seemed to know that he had come from the spirit world, and in my anxiety I sprang from the bed, and, resting one knee upon the floor, gazed intently at him. He stepped near me, and I took one little arm in my hand. Although a spirit, he seemed palpable to my touch. I said:

"I think you are my little brother Teddy; but it is so long since I saw you that I had almost forgotten how you looked."

Then the thought came into my mind that I must ask him some question. I said:

"Teddy, have you seen our Heavenly Father yet?"

He answered in the sweet voice of a child:

"No—but I shall see Him."

I noticed that he was trembling, and that from his eyes there went a glance of fear to the open door. I asked again:

"Have you brought any message to me?"

DREAMS OF OPPOSITION

To this question he answered, "Yes," shaking at the time more violently with fear; but he turned his glance from the door and his eyes looked straight into mine, and he came nestling into my arms. He lifted the fore finger of his right hand toward my face and said:

"Only be true!"

He turned his head, still with that frightened glance, at the open door, and this time I also looked. And I saw an evil spirit standing just outside and shaking its fist at the little one, and bearing on its face a demoniacal scowl. Its whole bearing and gesture implied the words, "Don't you dare to give that message!"

When I saw this, I said to Teddy:

"Have no fear—I know how to drive him away."

For even in my dream I seemed to understand what power the evil one possessed and how he could be rebuked. And I seemed now to have got back my faith and the power of my calling. I strode to the door and stood close to the wicked spirit. I raised my arm to the square, with my hand open and the palm extended toward him, saying at the same time:

"In the name of the Lord Jesus Christ of Nazareth, the Son of the living God, I command you to be gone."

He looked at me with a hateful glare, but slowly walked three or four steps down the stairway which was there. Then he stopped, folded his arms, and, looking at me defiantly, cried:

"I will not go! I will not go! I will not go!"

I said:

"You will go."

And then I followed him down, again standing close to him. Again I brought my arm to the square and repeated my solemn adjuration. He walked down the stairs and took refuge in a corner. This time he assumed a most resolute mien. His face expressed intense malice and hatred. He cried:

"I will not go—you shall not drive me away!"

For the last time I invoked that supreme name of our Lord Jesus, and then the demon—shaking his hands at me still in a threatening manner, fled with a look of baffled rage on his hideous countenance.

Source: George Q. Cannon, Thomas A. Shreeve, and Orson F. Whitney, *Helpful Visions*.

"SAW THE DEVIL WITH A LOOKING GLASS"
John Young

It is our privilege, for you and me to live, from this day, so that our consciences will be void of offense towards God and man; it is in our power to do so, then why don't we? What is the matter? I will tell you what the difficulties and troubles are, by relating brother John Young's dream. He dreamed that he saw the devil with a looking glass in his hand, and the devil held it to the faces of the people, and it revealed to them everybody's faults but their own.

The difficulty is, neglecting to watch over ourselves. Just as soon as our eyes are turned away from watching ourselves, to see whether we do right, we begin to see faults in our neighbors; this is the great difficulty, and our minds become more and more blinded until we become entirely darkened. So long as I do the thing the Lord requires of me, and do not stop to inquire what I shall tell to my neighbor as his duty, and pay very close attention to my individual person, that my words are right, that my actions are right before God, that my reflections are right, and that my desires are according to the holy Gospel, I have not much time to look at the faults of my neighbors.

Source: Brigham Young, in *Journal of Discourses*, 3:195.

CHAPTER 14

Dreams of Prophecy

Dreams can sometimes be prophetic. Church President John Taylor once declared, "You cannot prevent these manifestations: they are associated with the Gospel."[1] Indeed, all who have a testimony of Jesus Christ have the spirit of prophecy—"for the testimony of Jesus is the spirit of prophecy" (Revelation 19:10). Many early Latter-day Saints embraced this manifestation of the gift of prophecy. Their prophetic dreams were included in journals, letters, magazines, and sermons. The same Spirit that inspired those early Saints continues today to inspire the dreams of Church leaders and laymen alike. Several General Authorities have testified that prophetic dreams do occur. J. Golden Kimball said in general conference that he believed in dreams that came true.[2] Moreover, President Harold B. Lee agreed, almost verbatim, when he testified: "I am a great believer in dreams that have come true."[3]

This chapter shares dreams that gave the dreamers an ability to know of things to come. As Elder Orson Pratt described, "I do not know what the Lord will hereafter do with this people; I have not myself a sufficiency of the spirit of prophecy to understand all the events of the future; and I doubt very much, whether there is an individual in this Church that does know; but we do know, as far as the things of the future are revealed; and we may know many things by dreams and visions."[4]

Prophetic dreams come in the Lord's time, but prayer can be an impetus or preparatory action. Some prophetic dreams require action on the part of the dreamer for fulfillment of the dream. Other dreams may be fulfilled without the dreamer playing an active role.

Prophetic dreams can remind us that our Heavenly Father is very much aware of each of His children. He knows the details of our lives and is cognizant of the decisions we make. From glimpses of the future that they can provide, dreams can sometimes become an important influence on decision-making and faithfulness, and as President Thomas S. Monson taught, "decisions determine destiny."[5]

"NUGGETS OF TARNISHED GOLD"
Melvin J. Ballard

On Wednesday, March 4, 1917, on his way to Helena, Montana, Elder [Melvin J.] Ballard had an impressive dream. He dreamed that he was crossing a great desert, when he came upon the remains of a Pony Express rider. As he looked around, he discovered some leather pouches, kicked them, and they broke open and out fell nuggets of tarnished gold. He picked up some of them and rubbed them together with his hands until they became brilliant.

The meaning of the dream was made known when, during that year, he discovered more than one hundred Mormon boys who had drifted away from the teachings of the Church. As he talked to them, they became interested, so he hired a hall and began to round them up. He visited them often, and at the close of the year he had established a number of branches of the Church. One of these boys later became a president of the Northwestern States Mission.

SOURCE: Bryant S. Hinckley, *The Faith of Our Pioneer Fathers*, 225.

"GO BACK TO SLEEP"
(Related by Ronald C. Barker)

President Doxey called a stake fast and prayer to seek the Lord's help [with unprecedented growth in the stake], and two days later, the owner of the original site called and said it was available for purchase.

By then, plans were underway to divide the stake and President Doxey assigned me to acquire property for a new stake house. After careful study and prayer, we selected a four-acre site owned by two families in Hunter Sixth Ward. The bishop arranged for me to meet with each family. The first generously agreed to contribute the two acres. When I met the other couple, the husband, a convert of about a year, began: "I know why you've called us in."

He had had a dream the previous night that he had been called to come to this same office. All of the same people were there. I had explained that his neighbor had agreed to contribute two acres for a stake house and invited him to do the same. He woke his wife, told her the dream, fell asleep again, dreamed the same dream a second time, again woke his wife and told her the dream, fell asleep a third time, dreamed the same dream a third time and, for a third time, woke his wife. With feeling, she said, "Tell him the Church can have the two acres and go back to sleep!"

A new stake center has now been built on this ideal site.

SOURCE: Ronald C. Barker, "To Build Chapels for the Saints," 49–50.

"A HIVE OF BEES"
Charles Card (Related by Heber S. Allen)

I remember that, about fifteen years ago, President [Charles] Card related a dream he had. He said that when he first went to Canada everything looked forbidding, and only a few of our people accompanied him to that country the first season. He dreamed he saw a hive of bees, or at least a few bees, and more continued to come, until the hive they had entered became too full, and they swarmed and went out, and other colonies were formed. Now, that dream has been fulfilled, I have lived to see it. The beginning in the country was a very small one, but the Saints have kept "swarming," and new settlements have formed, until they became so numerous that the stake had to be divided and a new one created. While we have had a great many difficulties to contend with, which are incidental to the establishment of homes in a new country, the hand of the Lord has been over the people.

SOURCE: Heber S. Allen, in Conference Report, October 1903, 31.

"A HOME WITH FRUIT TREES"
Gene R. Cook

When we returned home from living in South America, our family had grown from six persons to eight, and we decided to sell our small home. First we tried selling it on our own and then with two different real estate companies.

These were difficult times economically. Mortgage rates were up around 20 percent, and almost no homes were selling. To sell our home and buy another one seemed just this side of impossible. Some people came to see it, but for a year and a half no one made a concrete offer of any kind.

Neither realtor brought anyone to see the house, even though we cleaned it from top to bottom to make it more appealing. We re-carpeted, painted, and so on. We prayed off and on about the sale of the home and about finding another one. Nothing seemed to fall into place.

During this time we found a house to buy in our own ward, and then a house in another one. We actually made an offer on both houses contingent on the sale of our own. However, neither realtor would take our home on a trade, and because it didn't sell, the deals on the other two houses fell through. We felt as if all the doors had closed.

About six months later we began feeling strong impressions that we should have another child. Yet we said to ourselves, "How can that be when there's really no place to put a baby except in our chest of drawers?" Although we felt awfully crowded in our home, we decided in faith to have another child.

We wanted a larger house not just because of our growing family. We also wanted a place where we could grow crops and fruit trees and have some running space for teenage children, a place where they could bring their friends. We seriously began to consider moving to another town.

A few months later, my wife and I were driving through another area of the city, and I told her of a strong impression I had had the day before that we should stop worrying about moving to another town, buying a new home, or building a new home. I told her about a dream I had had in which we were living in a large older home with a garden and mature fruit trees, and I felt strongly that it would be given to us in time. These impressions seemed to quiet my wife's heart.

Six months later we again listed our home with the realtors, and this time we began to pray intently, knowing we were just six weeks away from the delivery of our new baby. We and our children prayed morning, noon, and night in our family prayers and in our personal prayers that the Lord would show us a house that we should buy, and that he would bring someone to buy our home. The difficulty with selling our home centered in the fact that we had paid it off before going to South America, and thus there was no mortgage to be assumed. Also, we wanted to be cashed out of the home, and in those days, when almost no one could get a loan, that seemed nearly impossible. Anyone who had that kind of cash would put it into a lot nicer home than ours. Nevertheless, we went on praying intently for two or three weeks.

About this time a home in a beautiful area of our city came to our attention. It had been for sale privately for a couple of years, and it had a big yard and fruit trees. We went over and looked at it two or three times within a few days. After praying about it, we felt strongly that it was the house we should buy, although we felt uneasy about doing so without having sold our old one. But after more prayer, we determined to buy it in faith.

We began bargaining with the owners. Originally they agreed to take our home in on the deal, then later agreed to take just a lot that we owned. Now we were really committed, and our whole family began to pray even more fervently that before the baby came, the Lord would bring someone to buy our old home.

The Lord seems to like close calls. To our delight, just before our new son was born, some Church members moving from California came to see our house. The wife, especially, was impressed with it. They made an offer on the home and paid us *in cash*, which was almost unbelievable.

We felt that the Lord had directly intervened because of the faith of our children, and in fact the whole family, in helping us find a home with fruit trees, a level lot (which in our city on a hill is hard to come by), ample bedrooms, and all the space we wanted inside and out. It would provide work for the children and enough land that we could be self-sustaining, with plenty of room for the new baby.

SOURCE: Gene R. Cook, *Raising Up a Family to the Lord*, 88–90.

"EVERY DETAIL WAS FULFILLED TO THE LETTER"
William Daybell

Leaving my home in Charleston, Wasatch County, Utah, in the spring of 1885, I was assigned to the Middle Tennessee Conference. With Elder Jesse N. Perkins I was further directed to labor in Warren County, and in August, 1886, we were traveling in the vicinity of the Cumberland mountains. The weather was very hot, do as we would, the people would not listen to us, and the result was that we seemed to accomplish very little good; and further, we were constantly denied food and shelter. Under these circumstances we became discouraged and determined to leave the neighborhood for other parts. We had learned to ask the Lord when in trouble, so one night we sought him in fervent prayer believing that he would direct us aright. We petitioned him to lead us to the doors of the honest in heart and to a people among whom we might do some good. We obtained lodgings that night; and during my slumbers, I had a dream in which I clearly saw what to do upon the morrow. This is the dream:

I thought we arose in the morning, and directed our way from the head of the Stones River in a northerly direction, up a certain ridge, in that vicinity. Arriving at the top of the mountain, we passed a school house in which school was in session. As we passed, the children came to the door and evinced surprise at seeing us, but remained very quiet while we went on our way. Going a half mile further on, we came to a house near which, as we approached, we could see two women peeling apples, while two men stood by a well busy in getting the women a drink. On nearing the place, I thought we were asked to come in. They brought us two chairs, and asked us to be seated, we accepting the invitation. One of the men gave us to drink, and the women gave us apples. They wished to know who we were, and upon being told by me seemed much surprised. One of the men said he would like to hear us preach our doctrine, and I told him we would be pleased to speak if they would secure their school house for our service, whereupon the other man said that he was a trustee of the district and furthermore owned an interest in the house and the land upon which it stood, and declared that we could preach there as long as we desired. I then thought we gave out an appointment for a meeting at ten o'clock the following Sunday morning, and we were invited to stay with them.

At this juncture, I awoke, and told my dream to my companion both of us feeling reconciled. After breakfast, in the morning, we proceeded on our way in a northerly direction, taking care to follow the scenes of my dream, as near as we knew how. During that day's travel everything came to pass as I had seen it in my dream: the school house, the children, the people at the well—every detail was fulfilled to the letter. The school house was offered, the appointment made, the people at the house entertained us, and became our friends. Further than this, we opened up a prosperous field of labor, and it was only a day's journey from where every avenue seemed closed and we could do nothing.

SOURCE: William Daybell, "Missionary Experiences: A Dream Fulfilled," 686–87.

"MUSIC IN THE NIGHT"
Crawford Gates

[Crawford Gates] set to work on a musical background for the "Christ scene" of the [Hill Cumorah] pageant. Seventeen attempts later, he was ready to concede failure. To Brother Harold I. Hansen, he confided, "Harold, I need a blessing."

An appointment was arranged with Elder Harold B. Lee, then of the Quorum of the Twelve. "I remember five or six things from my blessing," he said. "One stands out in mind: 'You will hear music in the night.'"

He made another attempt at the score.

Brother Gates said he rarely dreams, and when he does, the dreams make no sense. This time it was different. He dreamed of being in a recording session in the Salt Lake Tabernacle. He heard the choir and orchestra performing his music. Some months later, the scene was played out as he had dreamed it. To him it was a confirmation that the composition was acceptable to the Lord. And it was a fulfillment of Elder Lee's blessing.

SOURCE: R. Scott Lloyd, "Crawford Gates, composer," 11.

"TAKE THAT NARROW PATH"
James LeSueur

During the fall of 1898, while laboring in Harrogate, York, England, my companion and I had difficulty in getting a foothold. Time and time again, we tried to reach the aristocracy as well as the poorer classes, but they all seemed to have no desires to cast aside their vanity and listen to the servants of the Lord. In the midst of these discouragements, we were very earnest in our pleadings for heavenly aid. One night, before retiring, we pleaded with the Lord to make known unto us some honest souls who might listen to our message. That same night "in a dream or vision of the night," I beheld myself walking to my tracting field, when a voice seemed to say to me: "Take that narrow path, and it will lead you to a small house by the side of the railroad." I obeyed and gained admittance into a signalman's cabin. He seemed to welcome me, and from my conversation with him, learned he was a religious-minded man, having studied the claims of many sects, but embraced none, as he had found none right. I received the impression that he had plenty of time to read our literature and converse; that while it was not the custom of the company to allow visitors at a signal office, yet I would be allowed. All this I learned in my dream.

Next day, on my way to distribute tracts, for the first time I noticed a footpath, similar to that of my dream. I could see no little house, but, taking the path for four or five hundred yards, I beheld a small signal-cabin in a ravine, built by the railroad company. A sign-board in front of me read about as follows: "Any one found trespassing along this track, and at the signalman's cabin, will be prosecuted and fined not less than ten pounds and not more than forty pounds. By order—"

The notice in my dream was to go into the cabin, so over the fence I went, and to the shanty. There I explained to the signalman my mission, and in a two or three hours' conversation with him, found that he was seeking to know the truth, having read the claims of many faiths, joining none, as he had not yet found the truth. He had abundance of time to read and converse between trains. In the next two or three months, I visited often, leaving him Church literature and conversing on our most holy faith. The signal-cabin was the resting-place of track repairers, inspectors and railway employees in general. Sometimes the cabin was crowded with people and nearly every time, a few called in. With these workmen, and the signal-man and his wife, I had many talks on the Gospel and loaned books, gave away tracts, and was invited into a few of the homes of the people. In this way, my prayer was answered, my dream fulfilled to the smallest particular, and time may tell the amount of good done by the Lord opening up the way to that little signal station.

SOURCE: James W. LeSueur, "Letters from Missionaries," 679–80.

"A GIANT PUZZLE"
Jim Magleby

When the actual work commenced in March 1976 on the São Paulo Brazil temple, Elder James E. Faust and others continued to feel the Lord's influence in its construction. Ross Jensen came from Salt Lake City to supervise the construction, and he and Elder Faust quickly determined that although marble was inexpensive, plentiful, and beautiful, the pollution in São Paulo would be so corrosive that the building ought to have a facade of cast stone instead. As a result, Jim Magleby was sent to Brazil from Buehner Stone in Salt Lake City to cast the stone for the temple, which, he explained in an interview, "is like a giant puzzle. We must make 3,000 panels of 400 different sizes and shapes which, after they are finished, must fit perfectly on specific places over the exterior temple walls. Our tolerance on the size of each panel is four hundredths of an inch."

Brother Magleby had cast the stone for the Los Angeles and Washington, D.C., temples, but found the work in Brazil to be particularly primitive and challenging. He was sustained, however, by a dream he had years earlier in which he found himself working on a very important building where the workmen under him could not understand him and he couldn't understand them. Believing his current assignment to be a fulfillment of that dream, he set up shop in a little shack on the temple grounds and taught Brazilian laborers how to cast stone.

As the work progressed toward the spire of the temple, Brother Magleby was having difficulty figuring out how to reverse a pattern to be used on the tower. In frustration, he tried to convince himself that a minor defect where no one could see it would not make any real difference, but one night he received the inspiration he needed to correct the flaw, as well as a strong witness that this was to be the House of the Lord and that even minor flaws were unacceptable.

SOURCE: James P. Bell, *In the Strength of the Lord*, 110–11

"WHEN DID I EVER REVEAL ANYTHING IN A DREAM AND IT FAILED TO COME TO PASS?"
Parley P. Pratt

In July, 1836, while lodging at the house of brother Joseph Fielding, the voice of the Lord came unto me in a dream, saying: "*Parley!*" And I answered: "Here am I;" for I was in a vision of the Spirit and knew that it was the Lord who spake unto me. And he said: "When did I ever reveal anything unto you in a dream and it failed to come to pass?" And I answered: "Never, Lord." "Well, then," He continued, "go unto this people and cry unto them with a mighty voice that they repent, lest I smite them with a curse and they die; for, notwithstanding the present fruitfulness of the earth, there shall be a famine in the land; and not only a famine for bread, but a famine for the Word of the Lord; for I will call my servants out from their midst and send them to the nations afar off."

Having heard these words I took courage, and I continued to lift up my voice in the congregations, both in town and country, testifying of the gospel and warning the people of things to come. Many repented and were baptized, while many hardened their hearts and were filled with a contentious and lying spirit. But the Saints were filled with faith, joy, and love; and they met together oft, and had great union and peace, and were happy in the society of each other.

SOURCE: Parley P. Pratt, *Autobiography of Parley P. Pratt*, 134.

"I WANT YOU TO BAPTIZE ME"
B. H. Roberts

[Brigham H. Roberts, who later served as a General Authority, received this dream in 1881 while serving in Tennessee as a missionary in the Southern States Mission.]

"In the dream I found myself coming over the winding path from the turnpike toward the residence. There were four in the company of Elders approaching the homestead and as we came to the gateway of the woodslot, entering into the before described mound two of the number passed on and one came through the gate with me to the Huddleston home. It seemed we had been away for some time and received a very hearty welcome to the quarters where we had before stayed. Shortly after the dinner was announced, being served out of doors on the lawn, I noted the absence of Mrs. Vaughn but said nothing of the absence. Presently, however, observing that I had finished my dinner before the rest at the table I good-naturedly said I would excuse them for not getting through as soon as I and arose and walked out under the young trees on the lawn. Presently in my dream I saw Mrs. Vaughn standing in the doorway of one of these cabins on the lawn and as I drew nearer I noticed she was crying. She made an effort to stop the tears and extended her hand to me, as I drew close, saying, 'I am so glad that you have returned. I was afraid you never would come back and I want you to baptize me.' This was a matter of surprise because directly we had heard nothing of her interest in joining the Church. With this the dream closed."

The elders had talked seriously about moving to a new area, but Roberts awoke from this dream, shook his companion and said decisively, "We are not going to leave this neighborhood. We will stay and see what comes of it." But later at the conference, either because his memory or his enthusiasm had dimmed, Roberts asked for a transfer. President Morgan not only ignored the request but assigned two additional elders to the area. Thus Elders Snow and Hammond returned with Elders Roberts and Ford to the Moccasin District.

The young elder did not remember his dream until he "lived through it," for on return the exact sequence of events he had dreamed unfolded, "wonderful, definite fulfillment." The gate leading to the plantation, the departure of Ford and Snow, a dinner spread out under the trees, the absence of Mrs. Vaughn, his approach, and the exact words she spoke: "I was afraid you would never come back and I want you to baptize me." She continued on, however: "Richard [her doctor-husband] is opposed to my being baptized and is making things disagreeable for me. What is to be done?" Roberts then approached the doctor and told him that neither he nor his missionary successors would undertake to baptize his wife without his explicit permission (a firm Church policy reflecting the sense of the patriarchal tradition and a father's rights). That forthright statement gave the doctor "much pleasure." A few days later he came to the elders and gave his full consent. A beautiful clear spring of water, twenty feet at its deepest, became the baptismal font for Mrs. Vaughn and eight other converts. Soon Dr. Vaughn himself was baptized, and before long he and his wife visited the temple in Salt Lake City, "drinking in by nature the spirit of the New Dispensation." They became stalwarts, lasting lights in the Moccasin District of Wilson County, Tennessee.

For Roberts this dream experience showed that "the future can be exactly revealed to the mind of man." And if, therefore, it is an axiom of higher criticism—as it is of most forms of scientific naturalism—that prophecy is impossible, he had firsthand compelling evidence to the contrary. "With a shock the young elder remembered his dream," he later wrote. Hence, "the first Isaiah can do all that is attributed to the second Isaiah."

SOURCE: Truman G. Madsen, *Defender of the Faith*, 131–32.

"THE SMALLNESS OF MY PRIZE"
Lorenzo Snow

Here I may relate a dream, which, though simple in itself, presented a theme for meditation under our peculiar circumstances. I thought I was in company with some friends, descending a gentle slope of beautiful green, till we came to the bank of a large body of water. Here were two skiffs; and as I embarked in the one, my friends followed in the other. We moved slowly over the face of this widespreading bay, without wind or any exertion on our part. As we were on a fishing excursion, we were delighted to behold large and beautiful fish on the surface of the water, all around, to a vast distance. We beheld many persons spreading their nets and lines, but they all seemed to be all stationary, whereas we were in continual motion. While passing one of them, I discovered a fish had got upon my hook, and I thought it might perhaps disturb this man's feelings to have it caught, as it were, out of his hands, nevertheless, we moved along, and came to the shore. I then drew in my line, and was not a little surprised and mortified at the smallness of my prize. I thought it very strange, that among such a vast multitude of noble, superior looking fish, I should have made so small a haul. But all my disappointments vanished when I came to discover that its qualities were of a very extraordinary character.

While encircled by many persons of noble bearing and considerable intelligence, a prospect seemed opening for the employment of some among them, in the work of the ministry. But the Lord judgeth not as man judgeth. The first native of these valleys that I ordained to preach the Gospel was one who swayed no extended influence, and boasted no great natural abilities; but he sought the Lord with fasting and prayer; and the Spirit began to rest upon him mightily, showing him in the dreams of night, the glorious reality of the work with which he had become associated.

SOURCE: Eliza R. Snow, *Biography and Family Record of Lorenzo Snow*, 172–73.

"A TEMPLE OF GRANITE"
Wilford Woodruff

When in the western country, many years ago, before we came to the Rocky Mountains, I had a dream. I dreamed of being in these mountains, and of seeing a large fine looking temple erected in one of these valleys which was built of cut granite stone, I saw that temple dedicated, and I attended the dedicatory services, and I saw a good many men that are living to-day in the midst of this people. And I saw them called of God and sent forth unto the United States and to Babylon, or what is called the Christian world, to bind up the law and seal up the testimony against the nations of the earth, because they had rejected the testimony of Jesus, and of the establishment of the kingdom of God upon the earth. When the foundation of that temple was laid I thought of my dream and a great many times since. And whenever President Young held a council of the brethren of the Twelve and talked of building the temple of adobe or brick, which was done I would say to myself, "No, you will never do it;" because I had seen it in my dream built of some other material. I mention these things to show you that things are manifested to the Latter-day Saints sometimes which we do not know anything about, only as they are given by the Spirit of God.

SOURCE: Wilford Woodruff, in *Journal of Discourses*, 21:299–300.

"UNCLE OZEM WOODRUFF"
Wilford Woodruff

After this scene [an earlier dream] had passed before me I was placed in a great temple. It was called the kingdom of God. The first man who came to me was Uncle Ozem Woodruff and his wife whom I helped into the temple.

In process of time, after embracing the gospel, and while on my first mission to Tennessee, I told Brother Patten of my dream, who told me that in a few years I would meet that man and baptize him. That was fulfilled to the very letter, for I afterwards baptized my uncle and his wife and some of the children; also my own father and stepmother and stepsister; and a Methodist priest or classleader—in fact, I baptized everybody in my father's house. I merely mention this to show that dreams sometimes do come to pass in life.

SOURCE: *Discourses of Wilford Woodruff*, 284.

Notes

Foreword

1. Parley P. Pratt, *Key to the Science of Theology*, 122–25.

Introduction

1. Edward L. Kimball, ed., *Teachings of Spencer W. Kimball*, 455.
2. Lehi's dream is found in 1 Nephi 8–11. Abraham Lincoln received and related that dream a few weeks before his assassination in April 1865. According to Ward Hill Lamon, a self-appointed bodyguard and friend, Lincoln related his dream as follows: "I kept on until I arrived at the East Room, which I entered. There I met with a sickening surprise. Before me was a catafalque [a bier used to support a coffin], on which rested a corpse wrapped in funeral vestments. Around it were stationed soldiers who were acting as guards; and there was a throng of people, gazing mournfully upon the corpse, whose face was covered, others weeping pitifully. 'Who is dead in the White House?' I demanded of one of the soldiers, 'The President,' was his answer, 'he was killed by an assassin.'" See Ward Hill Lamon, *Recollections of Abraham Lincoln*, 115–16.

Chapter 1: Revelation in the Form of Dreams

1. Some early Church members occasionally and mistakenly referred to Moroni's visit as a dream. Martin Harris, who later became one of the Three Witnesses to the Book of Mormon, stated, "While Joseph Smith laid upon his bed he had a remarkable dream." Oliver Cowdery, along with Peter Whitmer, was reported in the *Ohio Star* in December of 1830 as stating, "Joseph had three times been visited in a dream by the spirit of the Almighty," and Joseph Smith Sr., the prophet's father, during an 1830 interview referred to Moroni's visits as "a very singular dream." See Parley P. Pratt, "Beware of Imposters," Letter from Amherst, Ohio, 26 November 1830. Also Dale Morgan, *Early Mormonism*; Photocopy of letter, Photocopy in folder 8, box 149, H. Michael Marquardt Papers, J. Willard Marriott Library, University of Utah; John Clark Gleanings, "Martin Harris Interview," 226; "The Golden Bible," *Ohio Star*, 9 December 1830; Madeline R. McQuown Papers, Marriott Library University of Utah, in folder 4, box 46; Vogel, *Early Mormon Documents*, 1:458; reprint from Fayette Lapham's original work from 1830, "Interview with the Father of Joseph Smith, the Mormon Prophet."
2. Henry B. Eyring, "CES Satellite Training Broadcast," August 4, 2004; see also Sarah Jane Weaver, "Expectations," 7.

NOTES

3. Henry B. Eyring, "CES Satellite Training Broadcast."
4. Henry B. Eyring, "CES Satellite Training Broadcast."
5. Henry B. Eyring, "CES Satellite Training Broadcast."
6. See Richard L. Bushman, "Joseph Smith's Many Histories," 6.
7. Richard T. Hughes, "Joseph Smith as an American Restorationist," 34.
8. Dallin H. Oaks, "Joseph Smith in a Personal World," 153.
9. Jan Shipps, "Joseph Smith and the Making of a Global Religion," 303. Jan Shipps is Professor Emerita of History and Religious Studies at Indiana University–Purdue University at Indianapolis.
10. "History, 1838–1856, vol. E-1," 1921; spelling and grammar modernized; available at https://www.josephsmithpapers.org/paper-summary/history-1838-1856-volume-e-1-1-july-1843-30-april-1844/293; accessed 6 February 2019.
11. See Terryl L. Givens, "Joseph Smith: Prophecy, Process, and Plentitude," 56–57.
12. David L. Paulsen, "Joseph Smith Challenges the Theological World," 177.
13. See Richard L. Bushman, *Joseph Smith and the Beginnings of Mormonism*, 79.
14. Bushman, *Joseph Smith and the Beginnings of Mormonism*, 79.
15. Erastus Snow, in *Journal of Discourses*, 19:133.
16. "Letter to Isaac Galland, 22 March 1839," 54; available at https://www.josephsmithpapers.org/paper-summary/letter-to-isaac-galland-22-march-1839/4; accessed 6 February 2019.
17. The Book of Mormon contains many references to Lehi's inspired dreams: 1 Nephi 1:16; 2:1–3; 3:2; 8:2, 4, 36; 10:2; 15:21. Korihor, an anti-Christ, preached against revelatory dreams in Alma 30:28; Omer is warned in a dream to depart out of the land in Ether 9:3. See chapter 3.
18. "Brigham Young Remarks, 15 August 1847," in *The Complete Discourses of Brigham Young*, 1:240.
19. James E. Talmage, *Articles of Faith*, 226–27.
20. Spencer W. Kimball, "Preparing for Service in the Church," 47.
21. Robert D. Hales, "Personal Revelation," 88.
22. Hugh B. Brown, in Conference Report, October 1961, 95.
23. Marion G. Romney, in Conference Report, April 1978, 76.
24. Gerald N. Lund, *Hearing the Voice of the Lord*, 11.
25. Margaret McConkie Pope, *This Chosen Generation*, 50–51.
26. Bruce R. McConkie, quoted in Robert L. Millet, *The Power of the Word*, 7.
27. James E. Talmage, *Articles of Faith*, 226, 227.
28. Errol R. Fish, *Promptings of the Spirit*, 77.
29. Charles W. Penrose, in *Journal of Discourses*, 23:159.
30. Henry W. Naisbitt, in *Journal of Discourses*, 21:111.
31. Edward L. Kimball and Andrew E. Kimball Jr., *Spencer W. Kimball*, 228–29.
32. Wilford Woodruff, *The Discourses of Wilford Woodruff*, 283.
33. Boyd K. Packer, "The Book of Mormon," 8.
34. Orson F. Whitney, in Conference Report, April 1910, 60–61.
35. Harold B. Lee, *The Teachings of Harold B. Lee*, 417.
36. Franklin D. Richards, in *Collected Discourses*, 3:145.
37. Charles W. Penrose, in Conference Report, October 1922, 25.
38. Richard G. Scott, "How to Obtain Revelation," 46.
39. Richard G. Scott, "How to Obtain Revelation," 46.

Chapter 2: Inspiration, Indigestion, or Imagination

1. Gerald N. Lund, *Hearing the Voice of the Lord*, 39.
2. Gerald N. Lund, *Hearing the Voice of the Lord*, 75.
3. "Discourse, between circa 26 June and circa 4 August 1839–A," 72; spelling and grammar modernized; available at https://www.josephsmithpapers.org/paper-summary/discourse-between-circa-26-june-and-circa-4-august-1839-a-as-reported-by-willard-richards/10; accessed 6 February 2019.

NOTES

4. Mack David, Al Hoffman, and Jerry Livingston, "A Dream Is a Wish Your Heart Makes."
5. David O. McKay, "The Most Important Thing in Life."
6. Joseph F. Smith, in Conference Report, April 1900, 41.
7. Brigham Young, in *Journal of Discourses*, 14:113; paragraphing altered.
8. Levi Hancock, in *They Knew the Prophet*, 19.
9. Boyd K. Packer, "The Candle of the Lord," 56.
10. Charles W. Penrose, in Conference Report, October 1922, 26.
11. Harold B. Lee, *Stand Ye In Holy Places*, 142.
12. George Reynolds and Janne M. Sjodahl, *Commentary on the Book of Mormon*, 1:24.
13. Wilford Woodruff, *Discourses of Wilford Woodruff*, 283; paragraphing altered.
14. Gerald N. Lund, "The Voice of the Lord."
15. Robert D. Hales, "The Holy Ghost," 106.
16. George Albert Smith, in Conference Report, October 1945, 118–19.
17. Dallin H. Oaks, "Revelation."
18. Charles W. Penrose, in Conference Report, April 1913, 60.
19. "Brigham Young Remarks, 7 October 1854," in *The Complete Discourses of Brigham Young*, 2:844.
20. Boyd K. Packer, "The Quest for Spiritual Knowledge," 4.
21. See Brigham Young, in *Journal of Discourses*, 3:155.
22. Joseph Fielding McConkie and Craig J. Ostler, *Revelations of the Restoration*, 656–57.
23. See James E. Talmage, *Articles of Faith*, 232.
24. Harold B. Lee, *Stand Ye In Holy Places*, 136–38.
25. Wilford Woodruff, in *Journal of Discourses*, 22:333.
26. Henry B. Eyring, "Gifts of the Spirit for Hard Times," 23–24.
27. Boyd K. Packer, "The Candle of the Lord," 53.
28. Dallin H. Oaks, "Revelation."
29. Boyd K. Packer, "Prayers and Answers," 21.
30. Brigham Young, quoted in "History, 1838–1856, volume D-1," 1526; available at https://www.josephsmithpapers.org/paper-summary/history-1838-1856-volume-d-1-1-august-1842-1-july-1843/169; accessed 6 February 2019.
31. See Spencer W. Kimball, *Faith Precedes the Miracle*, 24.
32. Boyd K. Packer, "Revelation in a Changing World," 14.
33. Thomas S. Monson, *Favorite Quotations*, 104.
34. Charles W. Penrose, in Conference Report, October 1922, 26.
35. See James E. Faust, "The Voice of the Spirit."
36. Joseph F. Smith, Anthon H. Lund, and Charles W. Penrose, "A Warning Voice," 1149.
37. See Leland Ryken, *How to Read the Bible as Literature*, 171.
38. See Donald W. Richardson, *The Revelation of Jesus Christ*, 16.
39. *Teachings of Spencer W. Kimball*, 457.
40. Thomas G. Alexander, *Things in Heaven and Earth*, 39.
41. W. Jeffrey Marsh, "Dealing with Personal Injustices," 117.
42. Orson F. Whitney, *Life of Heber C. Kimball*, 101–2.
43. Anthony Uzodimma Obinna, "Voice from Nigeria," 30. As the article's introduction notes, Brother Obinna "and his wife, Fidelia Njoku Obinna, [were] the first black members of the Church in West Africa. Brother Obinna was the first branch president and Sister Obinna the Relief Society president of the first native branch of the Church established in black Africa." See "Years of Waiting in Nigeria" in chapter 6.
44. Richard G. Scott, "Finding Happiness."
45. Henry B. Eyring, CES Satellite Training Broadcast, 4 August 2003; punctuation added for clarity.
46. Richard G. Scott, CES Satellite Training Broadcast, 4 August 2003.
47. "Discourse, between circa 26 June and circa 2 July 1839," 21; spelling and grammar modernized; available at https://www.josephsmithpapers.org/paper-summary/discourse-between-circa-26-june-and-circa-2-july-1839-as-reported-by-willard-richards/7; 6 February 2019.

NOTES

48. Parley P. Pratt, *Key to the Science of Theology*, 101.
49. See Ezra Taft Benson, *Come unto Christ*, 20.
50. Charles W. Penrose, in Conference Report, October 1922, 26.
51. "History, 1838–1856, vol. E-1," 1975; available at https://www.josephsmithpapers.org/paper-summary/history-1838-1856-volume-e-1-1-july-1843-30-april-1844/347; accessed 6 February 2019.
52. Parley P. Pratt, *Key to the Science of Theology*, 121.
53. Orson F. Whitney, *Through Memory's Halls*, 82–83. See "I was asleep at my post" by Orson F. Whitney in chapter 5.
54. Joseph Fielding Smith, *Life of Joseph F. Smith*, 446–47.
55. Richard G. Scott, "To Learn and to Teach More Effectively."
56. Joseph F. Smith, in Conference Report, April 1900, 40.
57. Joseph F. Smith, in Conference Report, April 1900, 40–41.
58. Joseph F. Smith, *Gospel Doctrine*, 7.

Chapter 3: Scriptural Dreams

1. A majority of scripturally-recorded dreams are associated with just four people: Joseph (five dreams) and Daniel (three dreams) in the Old Testament, Lehi (three dreams) in the Book of Mormon, and Joseph (four dreams) in the New Testament. Most prophets and faithful Saints do not have any revelatory dreams associated with them.
2. Differentiating between visions and dreams in the scriptures is not always straightforward. In Daniel 8:1–26, for example, Daniel declares that he saw a vision (vv. 1, 2, 13, 15–17, and 26), but he also notes that as a heavenly messenger "was speaking with me, I was in a deep sleep on my face toward the ground" (v. 18) implying that at least part of his experience was received in a dream. A similar situation occurs in Daniel 10:4–21. Daniel refers to receiving a vision (in vv. 7, 8, 14, and 16) but reports that "when I heard the voice of his words, then was I in a deep sleep on my face" (v. 9).

Chapter 4: Dreams in Joseph Smith's Family

1. Richard Lloyd Anderson, *Joseph Smith's New England Heritage*, 88.
2. See Anderson, *Joseph Smith's New England Heritage*, 23–24; Solomon Mack died in August of 1820, so he did not live to see the Book of Mormon published or the LDS Church organized. There is no record indicating that he heard of Joseph Smith Jr.'s "First Vision."
3. See Lucy Mack Smith, *Revised and Enhanced History of Joseph Smith by His Mother*, 17–18.
4. See Bushman, *Joseph Smith and the Beginnings of Mormonism*, 17.
5. See Lucy Mack Smith, *Revised and Enhanced History of Joseph Smith by His Mother*, 58–60.
6. Lucy Mack Smith, *Lucy's Book*, 277–80.
7. Lucy Mack Smith, *Lucy's Book*, 296–97.
8. Larry C. Porter and Susan Easton Black, *The Prophet Joseph*, 12.
9. See Richard Lloyd Anderson, "Heritage of a Prophet," 15–19.
10. Mark L. McConkie, *The Father of the Prophet*, 4.
11. Several of Joseph Smith Jr.'s dreams are included in this chapter. Spelling and punctuation match transcriptions on the Joseph Smith Papers website (https://josephsmithpapers.org). Additional references to Joseph Smith Jr.'s dreams can be found on the Joseph Smith Papers website: (1) "Letter to Emma Smith, 16 August 1842," 173–74; (2) "Journal, December 1842–June 1844; Book 1, 21 December 1842–10 March 1843," 7; (3) "Journal, December 1842–June 1844; Book 1, 21 December 1842–10 March 1843," [136–37]; (4) "Journal, December 1842–June 1844; Book 1, 21 December 1842–10 March 1843," [141–43]; (5) "Journal, December 1842–June 1844; Book 2, 10 March 1843–14 July 1843," 3–4; (6) "Journal, December 1842–June 1844; Book 2, 10 March 1843–14 July 1843," 10; (7) "Instruction, 2 April 1843, as Reported by William Clayton," 71–72; (8) "Journal, December 1842–June 1844; Book 2, 10 March 1843–14 July 1843," [208]; (9) "History, 1838–1856, volume E-1 [1 July 1843–30 April 1844]," 1725; (10) "Journal, December 1842–June 1844; Book 3, 15 July 1843–29 February 1844," [224]; and (11) "Appendix 4: William Clayton, Daily Account of Joseph Smith's Activities, 14–22 June 1844," [1]. An

NOTES

additional reference to Joseph Smith Jr.'s dreams is available at the Church History Library (Phebe Carter Woodruff to Wilford Woodruff, June 16, 1844, in "Letters from Bathsheba W. Smith [wife], 1842–1844," MS 1322); https://churchhistorycatalog.lds.org.

12. "Jesse Smith was particularly opposed to organized religion. He was the only one of the [four] living sons of Asael and Mary Smith who did not accept the restored gospel" (Lucy Mack Smith, *Revised and Enhanced History of Joseph Smith by His Mother*, 61n1).

13. Joseph Smith's journal entry for Thursday, June 13, 1844, recorded by Willard Richard, states: "P. M. attended meeting in 70's Hall J. G. [George J.] Adams preached— after which I made some observations—" ("Journal, December 1842–June 1844; Book 4, 1 March–22 June 1844," [155]; spelling and grammar modernized; available at https://www.josephsmithpapers.org/paper-summary/journal-december-1842-june-1844-book-4-1-march-22-june-1844/157; accessed 6 February 2019). Concerning the public recitation of this and the following dream, a note (n459 in the previous citation) states: "Miles Romney later reported that JS related two dreams he had the night before. In the first, JS saw two snakes 'so fast locked together that either of them had no power.' In his dream, JS learned that the snakes represented Robert D. Foster and Chauncey L. Higbee, who wanted to 'destroy' JS but had no power to do so. In the second, JS dreamed that William and Wilson Law placed him in a deep pit and then later called for his help. JS was able to pull himself up enough to see a snake strangling Wilson Law and a bear tearing William Law to pieces. At that moment, JS's guardian angel appeared, pulled him out of the pit and led him away from the Laws. (Miles Romney Report, [1]–[2]; see also Jones, 'Martyrdom of Joseph and Hyrum Smith,' 6–7.)" This is a transcribed copy of Miles Romney's report.

14. The account of this dream immediately follows the previous dream in Miles Romney's report.

Chapter 6: Dreams of Missionary Work and Conversion

1. Orson Pratt, in *Journal of Discourses*, 6:271–72.
2. Orson Pratt, in *Journal of Discourses*, 18:19, 22.
3. Orson Pratt, in *Journal of Discourses*, 25:144–45.

Chapter 7: Dreams of Family History and Temple Work

1. This is the only prophecy that appears in all four of the LDS Standard Works: Malachi 4:5–6, 3 Nephi 25:5–6, Doctrine and Covenants 2:1–3, and Joseph Smith–History 1:38–39. The last two references were given by Moroni to the Prophet Joseph Smith in September 1823, and it is instructive to identify and ponder the slight changes in wording and emphasis.
2. John Taylor, in *Journal of Discourses*, 19:155.
3. Franklin D. Richards, *Millennial Star*, 430.
4. Sterling W. Sill, "Father's Day," 165.
5. James E. Faust, "Dear Are the Sheep That Have Wandered," 67.
6. Alex Haley is the author of *Roots*, a book about his genealogy that was made into a TV miniseries in the 1970s.

Chapter 8: Dreams of Warning

1. *Merriam-Webster's Collegiate Dictionary*, s.v. "exhort."
2. George Q. Cannon, in *Journal of Discourses*, 19:230–31.
3. George Q. Cannon, in *Journal of Discourses*, 19:231.
4. Joseph Young, in *Journal of Discourses*, 9:232.
5. Joseph F. Smith, *Gospel Doctrine*, 436.

Chapter 9: Dreams of Instruction

1. Wilford Woodruff, in *Journal of Discourses*, 22:333.
2. Parley P. Pratt, *Key to the Science of Theology*, 120.
3. Harold B. Lee, "Divine Revelation."
4. Heber C. Kimball, in *Journal of Discourses*, 7:41.

NOTES

Chapter 10: Dreams of Callings
1. Thomas S. Monson, "Your Eternal Voyage," 46.

Chapter 11: Dreams of Comfort
1. Sterling W. Sill, in Conference Report, April 1964, 11–12.
2. Sterling W. Sill, in Conference Report, April 1964, 13.
3. Regarding this dream, Dean Jessee's article includes this footnote (on pp. 15–16): "On 11 June 1840 Brigham recorded the account of his dream in his diary: 'Thursday 11. Went to visit a garden. It was raney and unplesant. Came home. I was rejoiced because I had a comfortable home. After Br. P. P. Pratt and myself talked some[e] time about the nesesity of the Elders having the power of God with them. I fell asleep and dremed a dreme. I first dremed of being at home in the Stat[e]s. I first saw Elizabeth. I asked her whare her mother was. She said she was about the house. She soon came in. I shook hands [with] her hart[i]ly as I had don with Elizabeth. I imbraced her in my arms and kissed [her] 2 or 3 times and asked hir whare my dear children was. She and Elizabeth boath ansard [answered] and said they ware at [s]chool and they ware well and enjoyed the [s]chool and loved there Books. My wife ways we feele well buy you must provide for you own families for the Church are not able to doe [it] for them' (Diary of Brigham Young)."

Chapter 13: Dreams of Opposition
1. See Orson F. Whitney, *Life of Heber C. Kimball*, 258–59.
2. Orson F. Whitney, *Life of Heber C. Kimball*, 132.
3. Erastus Snow, in *Journal of Discourses*, 19:133.
4. "History, 1838–1856, vol. C-1," 1307; available at https://www.josephsmithpapers.org/paper-summary/history-1838-1856-volume-c-1-2-november-1838-31-july-1842/481; accessed 6 February 2019.
5. Joseph F. Smith, Anthon H. Lund, and Charles W. Penrose, "A Warning Voice," 1148–49.
6. "Discourse, [5 January 1841], as Reported by Unknown Scribe-A," 1; available at https://www.josephsmithpapers.org/paper-summary/discourse-5-january-1841-as-reported-by-unknown-scribe-a/1; accessed 6 February 2019.
7. *Teachings of Presidents of the Church: Joseph Smith*, 213; quoted by William P. McIntire, reporting a discourse given by Joseph Smith in early 1841 in Nauvoo, Illinois; William Patterson McIntire, Notebook 1840–45, Church Archives.
8. "Revelation, circa Early 1830," Historical Introduction; available at https://www.josephsmithpapers.org/paper-summary/revelation-circa-early-1830/2#historical-intro; accessed 6 February 2019.

Chapter 14: Dreams of Prophecy
1. John Taylor, in *Journal of Discourses*, 25:180.
2. J. Golden Kimball, in Conference Report, October 1931, 57.
3. Harold B. Lee, in Conference Report, April 1973, 127.
4. Orson Pratt, in *Journal of Discourses*, 3:15.
5. See Thomas S. Monson, "Decisions Determine Destiny."

Works Cited

Adams, Kellene Ricks. "A Dream Come True in Hong Kong." *Ensign*, June 1996.
Alexander, Thomas G. *Things in Heaven and Earth: The Life and Times of Wilford Woodruff.* 1991.
Anderson, Richard Lloyd. "Heritage of a Prophet." *Ensign*, February 1971.
———. *Joseph Smith's New England Heritage: Influences of Grandfathers Solomon Mack and Asael Smith.* 2003.
Andrus, Hyrum L. "Little Known Friends of the Prophet Joseph Smith." *1963 Seminar on the Prophet Joseph Smith: Friends of the Prophet Joseph Smith*, 1963. L. Tom Perry Special Collections, Harold B. Lee Library, Brigham Young University, Provo, UT.
Andrus, Hyrum L. and Helen May Andrus, comps. *They Knew the Prophet.* 1974.
Ashton, Marvin J. "Choose the Good Part." *Ensign*, May 1984.
Ballantyne, Richard. "With the Remnants at Nauvoo." *Improvement Era*, February 1901.
Ballard, M. Russell. "Duties, Rewards, and Risks." *Ensign*, November 1989.
Barker, Ronald C. "To Build Chapels for the Saints." *Ensign*, February 1981.
Barton, Peggy Petersen. *Mark E. Petersen: A Biography.* 1985.
Batey, Carol. As told to Brad Wilcox. "Finding My Black Ancestors." *Ensign*, June 1987.
Bednar, David A. "The Tender Mercies of the Lord." *Ensign*, May 2005.
Bell, James P. *In the Strength of the Lord: The Life and Teachings of James E. Faust.* 1999.
Benson, Ezra Taft. *Come unto Christ.* 1983.
Bowen, Hubert E. "Record Providentially Obtained." *Improvement Era*, January 1941.
Bowers, Wreno. "The Vase of Tears." *Improvement Era*, February 1924.
Bushman, Richard L. *Joseph Smith and the Beginnings of Mormonism.* 1984.
———. "Joseph Smith's Many Histories." *BYU Studies Quarterly*, Vol. 44, no. 4, art. 3 (2005).
Cannon, George Q., Thomas A. Shreeve, and Orson F. Whitney. *Helpful Visions: Faith-Promoting Series, No. 14.* 1887.
Christensen, Joe J. "Good Memories Are Real Blessings." *Ensign*, November 1989.
Christofferson, D. Todd. "The Living Bread Which Came Down from Heaven." *Ensign*, November 2017.
"The Church in Spain and Gibraltar." *The Friend*, May 1975.
Clarke, J. Richard. "Love Extends beyond Convenience." *Ensign*, November 1981.
Condie, Spencer J. *Russell M. Nelson: Father, Surgeon, Apostle.* 2003.
Conference Report. October 1897–present.
Cook, Carl B. "Serve." *Ensign*, November 2016.

WORKS CITED

Cook, Gene R. *Raising Up a Family to the Lord*. 1993.
Corbett, Pearson H. *Jacob Hamblin, the Peacemaker*. 1952.
Covey, Steven R. *Six Events: The Restoration Model for Solving Life's Problems*. 2004.
Cowley, M. F. "Acts of Special Providence in Missionary Experience." *Improvement Era*, February 1899.
Cowley, Matthias F., comp. *Wilford Woodruff: History of His Life and Labors*. 1964.
David, Mack, Al Hoffman, and Jerry Livingston. "A Dream Is a Wish Your Heart Makes." In *Cinderella* (motion picture). 1950.
Daybell, William. "Missionary Experiences: A Dream Fulfilled." *Improvement Era*, July 1899.
Dew, Sheri L. *Ezra Taft Benson: A Biography*. 1987.
Dibb, Ann M. "I Believe in Being Honest and True." *Ensign*, May 2011.
Dibble, Philo. *Reminiscences*. MS 15447, Church History Library, Salt Lake City, UT.
Dunn, Emile C. and Evelyn H. Dunn. Oral history. Interview by R. Lanier Britsch (1978). The James Moyle Oral History Program, OH 499, Church History Library, Salt Lake City, UT.
Esplin, Cheryl A. "Filling Our Homes with Light and Truth." *Ensign*, May 2015.
Esplin, Ronald K. "Discipleship: Brigham Young and Joseph Smith." In *Joseph Smith: The Prophet, the Man*. Susan Easton Black and Charles D. Tate Jr., eds. 1993.
Eyre, Linda and Richard. *Teaching Children Charity*. 1986.
Eyring, Henry B. "CES Satellite Training Broadcast," 4 August 2004.
———. "Do Not Delay." *Ensign*, November 1999.
———. "Gifts of the Spirit for Hard Times." *Ensign*, June 2007.
———. "Hearts Bound Together." *Ensign*, May 2005.
———. "A Priceless Heritage of Hope." *Ensign*, May 2014.
———. "You Are Not Alone in the Work." *Ensign*, November 2015.
Faust, James E. "Dear Are the Sheep That Have Wandered." *Ensign*, May 2003.
———. "The Voice of the Spirit." Church Educational System fireside for young adults, 5 September 1993. Available at https://speeches.byu.edu.
Featherstone, Vaughn J. *Commitment*. 1982.
Fidel, Steve. "A temple to be built in Ghana." *Church News*, February 21, 1998.
Fish, Errol R. *Promptings of the Spirit*. 1990.
Flake, Chad J. "From the Diary of Lucy Hannah White Flake." In *Supporting Saints: Life Stories of Nineteenth-Century Mormons*. Donald Q. Cannon and David J. Whittaker, eds. 1985.
Fonoimoana, Carl. "Opapo: The Power of His Faith." *Ensign*, July 1981.
Givens, Terryl L. "Joseph Smith: Prophecy, Process, and Plentitude." *BYU Studies Quarterly*, Vol. 44, no. 4, art. 8 (2005).
Gleanings, John Clark. "Martin Harris Interview," *Testimonies of Book of Mormon Witnesses*. 1842.
Goates, L. Brent. *Harold B. Lee: Prophet and Seer*. 1985.
"The Golden Bible." *Ohio Star* (Ravenna, Ohio), 9 December 1830.
Grant, Heber J. "Comforting Manifestations." *Improvement Era*, February 1931.
———. *Gospel Standards: Selections from the Sermons and Writings of Heber J. Grant*, comp. G. Homer Durham. 1969.
Hales, Robert D. "The Holy Ghost." *Ensign*, May 2016.
———. "Personal Revelation: The Teachings and Examples of the Prophets." *Ensign*, November 2007.
Hamblin, Jacob. *Jacob Hamblin: A Narrative of His Personal Experience*. 1909.
Hardy, David L. "Warned in a Dream." *Ensign*, June 1985.
Hawkins, Chad S. *The First 100 Temples*. 2000.
Heidenreich, John F. "An Acorn Becomes an Oak." John F. Heidenreich Papers, L. Tom Perry Special Collections, Harold B. Lee Library, Brigham Young University, Provo, UT.
Hinckley, Bryant S. *The Faith of Our Pioneer Fathers*. 1956.
Hinckley, Gordon B. "Pres. Hinckley addresses 'My fellow servants' in priesthood fireside." *Church News*, May 24, 1997.
Holland, Jeffrey R. "An Ensign to the Nations." *Ensign*, May 2011.
———. "Within the Clasp of Your Arms." *Ensign*, May 1983.

WORKS CITED

Holzapfel, Jeni Broberg and Richard Neitzel Holzapfel, eds. *A Woman's View: Helen Mar Whitney's Reminiscences of Early Church History.* 1997.

Horne, Dennis B. *"Called of God by Prophecy": Spiritual Experience, Doctrine, and Testimony from Church Leaders Reveal How God Chooses His Servants.* 2001.

Hughes, Richard T. "Joseph Smith as an American Restorationist." *BYU Studies Quarterly*, Vol. 44, no. 4, art. 5 (2005).

Hunter, Milton R. "The Miracle of Missionary Work." *Ensign*, July 1972.

Jensen, Nephi. Nephi Jensen Journal. L. Tom Perry Special Collections, Harold B. Library, Brigham Young University, Provo, UT.

Jenson, Andrew. *The Contributor*, vol. 12, no. 10 (August 1891).

———. *Latter-day Saint Biographical Encyclopedia.* 1901–1936. 4 vols.

Jessee, Dean C. "Brigham Young's Family: Part I, 1824–1845." *BYU Studies* 18:3 (1978).

Jones, Dan. "The Martrydom of Joseph Smith and His Brother Hyrum." *BYU Studies*, vol. 24, no. 1 (1984).

The Joseph Smith Papers. "Appendix 4: William Clayton, Daily Account of Joseph Smith's Activities, 14–22 June 1844." Available at https://www.josephsmithpapers.org.

———. "Discourse, between circa 26 June and circa 2 July 1839, as reported by Willard Richards." Available at https://www.josephsmithpapers.org.

———. "Discourse, between circa 26 June and circa 4 August 1839–A, as Reported by Willard Richards." Available at https://www.josephsmithpapers.org.

———. "Discourse, [5 January 1841], as Reported by Unknown Scribe-A." Available at https://www.josephsmithpapers.org.

———. "History, 1838–1856, vol. C-1 [2 November 1838–31 July 1842]." Available at https://www.josephsmithpapers.org.

———. "History, 1838–1856, volume D-1 [1 August 1842–1 July 1843]." Available at https://www.josephsmithpapers.org.

———. "History, 1838–1856, vol. E-1 [1 July 1843–30 April 1844]." Available at https://www.josephsmithpapers.org.

———. "History, 1838–1856, volume F-1 [1 May 1844–8 August 1844]." Available at https://www.josephsmithpapers.org.

———. "Instruction, 2 April 1843, as Reported by William Clayton." Available at https://www.josephsmithpapers.org.

———. "Journal, December 1842–June 1844; Book 1, 21 December 1842–10 March 1843." Available at https://www.josephsmithpapers.org.

———. "Journal, December 1842–June 1844; Book 2, 10 March 1843–14 July 1843." Available at https://www.josephsmithpapers.org.

———. "Journal, December 1842–June 1844; Book 3, 15 July 1843–29 February 1844." Available at https://www.josephsmithpapers.org.

———. "Journal, December 1842–June 1844; Book 4, 1 March–22 June 1844." Available at https://www.josephsmithpapers.org.

———. "Letter to Emma Smith, 16 August 1842." Available at https://www.josephsmithpapers.org.

———. "Letter to Isaac Galland, 22 March 1839." Available at https://www.josephsmithpapers.org.

———. "Revelation, circa Early 1830." Available at https://www.josephsmithpapers.org.

Journal of Discourses. 26 vols. London: Latter-day Saints' Book Depot, 1854–86.

Kikuchi, Yoshihiko. "Daughter of God." *Ensign*, May 1988.

Kimball, Edward L., ed. *Teachings of Spencer W. Kimball.* 1995.

Kimball, Edward L. and Andrew E., Jr. *Spencer W. Kimball: The Early and Apostolic Years.* 2006.

———. *Spencer W. Kimball: Twelfth President of the Church of Jesus Christ of Latter-day Saints.* 1977.

Kimball, Spencer W. "The Cause Is Just and Worthy." *Ensign*, May 1974.

———. *Faith Precedes the Miracle.* 1974.

———. "Preparing for Service in the Church." *Ensign*, May 1979.

WORKS CITED

———. *Teachings of Spencer W. Kimball: Twelfth President of the Church of Jesus Christ of Latter-day Saints*. Edward L. Kimball, ed. 1982.
Kohlberg, W. J. "Editor's Table: Messages from the Missions." *Improvement Era*, May 1906.
Lamon, Ward Hill. *Recollections of Abraham Lincoln 1847–1865*. 1895.
Laney, I. C. "Struggles of an 1847 Pioneer." *Improvement Era*, July 1927.
LeBaron, E. Dale. "Revelation on the Priesthood: The Dawning of a New Day in Africa." In *Doctrines for Exaltation: The 1989 Sperry Symposium on the Doctrine and Covenants*. Susan Easton Black, ed. 1989.
Lee, Harold B. "Divine Revelation." BYU devotional, October 15, 1952. In *Miscellaneous Speeches*. 1952. L. Tom Perry Special Collections, Harold B. Lee Library, Brigham Young University, Provo, Utah
———. "Follow the Leadership of the Church." *Ensign*, July 1973.
———. *Stand Ye in Holy Places*. 1974.
———. *The Teachings of Harold B. Lee*. Clyde J. Williams, ed.. 1996.
LeSueur, James W. "For a Wise Purpose." *Improvement Era*, June 1946.
———. "Letters from Missionaries: The Way Cleared." *Improvement Era*, July 1900.
Lloyd, R. Scott. "Crawford Gates, composer." *Church News*, August 2, 2003.
———. "Longtime dream to sing with choir." *Church News*, 27 March 2004.
Lund, C. N. Jr., comp. "Conversion and Testimony of the Late President C. N. Lund." *Improvement Era*, November 1921.
Lund, Gerald N. *Hearing the Voice of the Lord: Principles and Patterns of Personal Revelation*. 2007.
———. "The Voice of the Lord." Brigham Young University devotional, 2 December 1997. Available at https://speeches.byu.edu.
"Madeline's Dream." *The Friend*, November 1971.
Madsen, Carol Cornwall. "In the Covenant of Grace." In *LDS Women's Treasury: Insights and Inspiration for Today's Woman*. 1997.
Madsen, Susan Arrington. *The Lord Needed a Prophet*. 1990.
Madsen, Truman G. *Defender of the Faith: The B. H. Roberts Story*. 1980.
———. *The Presidents of the Church: Insights into Their Lives and Teachings*. 2004.
Marsh, W. Jeffrey. "Dealing with Personal Injustices: Lessons from the Prophet Joseph Smith." *The Religious Educator* 4, no. 3 (2003).
McConkie, Joseph Fielding. *The Bruce R. McConkie Story: Reflections of a Son*. 2003.
McConkie, Joseph Fielding and Craig J. Ostler. *Revelations of the Restoration: A Commentary on the Doctrine and Covenants and Other Modern Revelations*. 2000.
McConkie, Mark L. *The Father of the Prophet: Stories and Insights from the Life of Joseph Smith, Sr.* 1993.
———. *Remembering Joseph: Personal Recollections of Those Who Knew the Prophet Joseph Smith*. 2003.
McKay, David O. *Cherished Experiences from the Writings of David O. McKay*. Clare Middlemiss, comp. 1970.
———. *Gospel Ideals: Selections from the Discourses of David O. McKay*. 1953.
———. "The Most Important Thing in Life—a Building Character," February 1, 1952. In David O. McKay, Scrapbook No. 19, not paginated, LDS Church Archives.
Merriam-Webster's Collegiate Dictionary, Eleventh Edition. 2005.
Millet, Robert L. *The Power of the Word: Saving Doctrines of the Book of Mormon*. 1994.
Monson, Thomas S. "Decisions Determine Destiny." Brigham Young University devotional, November 6, 2005. Available at https://speeches.byu.edu.
———. *Favorite Quotations from the Collection of Thomas S. Monson*. 1985.
———. "Your Eternal Voyage." *Ensign*, May 2000.
Morgan, Dale. *Early Mormonism: Correspondence and a New History*. 1986.
Morrison, Alexander B. *Feed My Sheep: Leadership Ideas for Latter-day Shepherds*. 1992.
Morton, William A. "Bishop Edwin S. Sheets as I Knew Him." *Improvement Era*, March 1919.
Moyle, James H. "Looking Back Sixty Years in the Southern States Mission." *Improvement Era*, May 1941.

WORKS CITED

Murphy, Castle H. *Castle of Zion—Hawaii: Autobiography and Episodes from Life of Castle H. Murphy, Missionary to Hawaii.* 1963.
Nibley, Hugh. "Lecture 73." In *Teachings of the Book of Mormon, Semester 3.* 2004.
Oaks, Dallin H. "All Men Everywhere." *Ensign*, May 2006.
———. "Joseph Smith in a Personal World." *BYU Studies Quarterly*, Vol. 44, no. 4, art. 14 (2005).
———. "Revelation." Brigham Young University devotional, 29 September 1981. Available at https://speeches.byu.edu.
Obinna, Anthony Uzodimma. "Voice from Nigeria." *Ensign*, December 1980.
Packer, Boyd K. "The Book of Mormon: Another Testament of Jesus Christ—Plain and Precious Things." *Ensign*, May 2005.
———. "The Candle of the Lord." *Ensign*, January 1983.
———. "Prayers and Answers." *Ensign*, November 1979.
———. "The Quest for Spiritual Knowledge." *New Era*, January 2007.
———. "Revelation in a Changing World." *Ensign*, November 1989.
———. "The Snow-White Birds." Brigham Young University devotional, August 29, 1995. Available at speeches.byu.edu.
———. *That All May Be Edified: Talks, Sermons & Commentary by Boyd K. Packer.* 1982.
Palmer, Annie D. "How Elsa Came from Germany." *Improvement Era*, May 1919.
Paulsen, David L. "Joseph Smith Challenges the Theological World." *BYU Studies Quarterly*, Vol. 44, no. 4, art. 16 (2005).
Phelps, W. W. *Joseph Smith's Last Dream.* Reprint. 1992.
Pooley, Emil. "A Hopi Prophecy Fulfilled." In *No More Strangers, vol. 1*, Hartman Rector Jr. and Connie Rector, eds. 1971.
Pope, Margaret McConkie. *This Chosen Generation: Armed with the Gifts of God.* 1994.
Porter, Larry C. and Susan Easton Black. *The Prophet Joseph: Essays on the Life and Mission of Joseph Smith.* 1988.
Pratt, Parley P. *Autobiography of Parley P. Pratt.* Scot Facer Proctor and Maurine Jensen Proctor, eds. 1985.
———. "Beware of Imposters." Letter from Amherst, Ohio, 26 November 1830. *The Telegraph*, reprinted in *The Reflector* (Palmyra, NY), 14 February 1831.
———. *Key to the Science of Theology.* 1874.
Pusey, Merlo J. *Builders of the Kingdom: George A. Smith, John Henry Smith, and George Albert Smith.* 1981.
Rector, Hartman, Jr., and Connie Rector. *No More Strangers.* 1990.
Reynolds, George and Janne M. Sjodahl. *Commentary on the Book of Mormon*, ed. Philip C. Reynolds. 7 vols. 1955.
Richards, Franklin D. In *Collected Discourses, 1886–1898.* Brian H. Stuy, comp. 1987–1992. 5 vols.
———. *Millennial Star*, vol. 55, no. 27 (July 3, 1893).
Richardson, Donald W. *The Revelation of Jesus Christ: An Interpretation.* 1939.
Robinson, Stephen E. *Believing Christ: The Parable of the Bicycle and Other Good News.* 1992.
Romney, Marion G. "Prayer and Revelation." *Ensign*, May 1978.
Romney, Miles. Miles Romney Report, ca. 1854–1856, [1]–[2]. Historian's Office, JS History Documents, ca. 1839–1860, Church History Library, Salt Lake City, UT.
Rudd, Glen L. "Memories of Matthew Cowley: Man of Faith, Apostle to the Pacific." In *Pioneers in the Pacific: Memory, History, and Cultural Identity among the Latter-day Saints.* Grant Underwood, ed. 2005.
Ryken, Leland. *How to Read the Bible as Literature.* 1984.
Scott, Richard G. "CES Satellite Training Broadcast," 4 August 2004.
———. "Finding Happiness." BYU devotional, 19 August 1997. Available at https://speeches.byu.edu.
———. "How to Obtain Revelation and Inspiration for your Personal Life." *Ensign*, May 2012.

WORKS CITED

———. "To Learn and to Teach More Effectively." BYU devotional, 21 August 2007. Available at https://speeches.byu.edu.

———. *21 Principles: Divine Truths to Help You Live by the Spirit*. 2013.

Shipps, Jan. "Joseph Smith and the Making of a Global Religion." *BYU Studies Quarterly*, Vol. 44, no. 4, art. 23 (2005).

Sill, Sterling W. "Father's Day." In *Understanding Death*, Brent A. Barlow, ed. 1979.

Simpson, Robert L. "The Lord Is Mindful of His Own." BYU devotional, April 4, 1962. In *BYU Speeches of the Year*. 1963.

Smith, George Albert. "Your Good Name." *Improvement Era*, March 1947.

Smith, Joseph F. *Gospel Doctrine: Selections from the Sermons and Writings of Joseph F. Smith, Sixth President of The Church of Jesus Christ of Latter-day Saints*. 1939.

Smith, Joseph F., Anthon H. Lund, and Charles W. Penrose. "A Warning Voice." *Improvement Era*, September 1913.

Smith, Joseph Fielding. *Life of Joseph F. Smith*. 1938.

Smith, Joseph, Jr. *Teachings of Presidents of the Church: Joseph Smith*. 2007.

Smith, Lucy Mack. *Lucy's Book: A Critical Edition of Lucy Mack Smith's Family Memoir*. Lavina Fielding Anderson, ed. 2001.

———. *The Revised and Enhanced History of Joseph Smith by His Mother*. Scot Facer Proctor and Maurine Jensen Proctor, eds. 1996.

Snow, Eliza R. *Biography and Family Record of Lorenzo Snow: One of the Twelve Apostles of the Church of Jesus Christ of Latter-day Saints*. 1884.

Steele, C. Frank. "A Delightsome People." *Improvement Era*, March 1932.

Swinton, Heidi S. *Pioneer Spirit: Modern-day Stories of Courage and Conviction*. 1996.

Talmage, James E. *Articles of Faith*. 1958.

Tate, Lucile C. *Boyd K. Packer: A Watchman on the Tower*. 1995.

———. *LeGrand Richards: Beloved Apostle*. 1982.

Tyler, Daniel. *A Concise History of the Mormon Battalion in the Mexican War 1846–47*. 1881.

Udall, Louise Lee. "Jacob Hamblin: Story of his later years." *Improvement Era*, October 1951.

Van Orden, Bruce A. "Founding a city, fighting fevers." *Church News*, Aug. 17, 1996.

Vogel, Dan. *Early Mormon Documents*. Vol. 1. 1996.

Weaver, Sarah Jane. "Expectations: Today's Youth Will Rise to Them." *Church News*, August 6, 2004.

Whitney, Orson F. *The Life of Heber C. Kimball*. 2001.

———. *Through Memory's Halls: The Life Story of Orson F. Whitney as Told by Himself*. 1930.

Woodruff, Wilford. In *Collected Discourses, 1886–1898*. Brian H. Stuy, comp. 1987–1992. 5 vols.

———. *The Discourses of Wilford Woodruff: Fourth President of The Church of Jesus Christ of Latter-day Saints*. G. Homer Durham, ed. 1998.

———. *Wilford Woodruff's Journal: 1833–1898*. 9 vols. Scott G. Kinney, ed. 1983–85.

Worthen, Kevin J. "BYU: A Unique Kind of Education." Brigham Young University Conference, August 28, 2017. Available at speeches.byu.edu.

Young, Brigham. *The Complete Discourses of Brigham Young*. Richard S. Van Wagoner, ed. 2009. 5 vols.

———. Diary of Brigham Young, 1837–1845. MS, Church Historical Department, Salt Lake City, UT.

APPENDIX

Dreams Listed by Dreamer

The table below lists the dreams in this book alphabetically (either by the name of the dreamer or the person who related that dream).

DREAMER, TITLE, PAGE

Amussen, Barbara Smith [related by Ezra Taft Benson], "Sleep Until the Eventide," 232
Ashton, Marvin J. [related by], "I Just Hoped It Wouldn't Come Too Soon," 175
Ballantyne, Richard, "A Dreadful Flood of Water," 122
Ballard, Melvin J. [related by Bryant S. Hinckley], "An Assurance that All Would Be Well," 197
Ballard, Melvin J., "I Shall Never Forget That Smile," 61
Ballard, Melvin J., "Nuggets of Tarnished Gold," 254
Barker, Ronald C. [related by], "Go Back to Sleep," 255
Barton, Peggy Petersen [related by], "My Eight-Year-Old Dreamed of My Call," 176
Batey, Carol, "A Photograph Was Handed to Me," 108
Bednar, David A. [related by], "God Knows Who I Am," 197
Bennion, Samuel O. [related by], "I Have Seen You in a Dream," 79
Benson, Ezra Taft [related by Sheri Dew], "A Choice People with a Major Role," 109
Benson, Ezra Taft, "I Felt the Warmth of His Embrace," 198
Boehme, Peter, "Bishop of Beenleigh Ward," 177
Bowen, Hubert E., "Write a Letter," 110
Brimhall, George, "Snow-White Birds," 143
Cannon, George Q., "Take Hold of That Rope," 145
Card, Charles [related by Heber S. Allen], "A Hive of Bees," 256
Christensen, Joe J. [related by], "What the Lord Wants Me to Do," 79
Christofferson, D. Todd [related by], "My Heart Changed," 146
Clark, Mary Stevenson, "He Took Me in His Arms," 62
Clarke, J. Richard [related by], "You Have Done It unto Me," 62
Cook, Carl B., "I Have the Same Privilege," 179
Cook, Gene R., "A Home with Fruit Trees," 256
Covey, Steven R. [related by], "Helping Grandfather Find Two Names," 111
Cowley, M. F., "Write Home for Money," 147
Cowley, Matthew [related by Glen L. Rudd], "I Wonder If I Ever Had a Patriarchal Blessing," 199
Cox, Martha Cragun, "A Heavy Chain about Her Neck," 200

APPENDIX

Daybell, William, "Every Detail Was Fulfilled to the Letter," 259
Domiciano, Liriel [related by], "You Are Worthy," 63
Dunn, Emile C., "I'd Better Do as I'm Prompted," 81
Dyer, Alvin R. [related by], "I Have Been Expecting You," 82
Estill, Brother and Sister Benjamin [related by James W. LeSueur], "On the Twentieth of March," 82
Eyre, Linda and Richard [related by], "She Prayed He Would Never Look Away," 65
Eyring, Heinrich [related by Henry B. Eyring], "He Was Told to Be Baptized," 83
Eyring, Henry B., "I Saw a Piece of Paper with a Name," 112
Eyring, Henry B. [related by], "Never Too Late or Too Hard," 202
Eyring, Henry B., "We Have Been Looking for You," 180
Featherstone, Vaughn J. [related by], "Messengers Will Come from Far, Far Away," 84
Flake, William, "I Want to Know If I Done Right," 150
Fonoimoana, Opapo [related by Carl Fonoimoana], "He Saw Two Foreign Missionaries," 85
Gates, Crawford, "Music in the Night," 260
Grant, Heber J., "I Would Not Struggle for the Child," 203
Grant, Heber J. [related by], "My Dear Friend Lost Nothing," 233
Grover, Thomas, "Return to Nauvoo," 151
Hale, Grace Mays, "Two Young Men in My Dream," 86
Hamblin, Jacob ("Jake") [related by Louise Lee Udall], "Go Home, You Are Needed There," 125
Hamblin, Jacob, "True Love at First Sight," 151
Hammond, (Brother) [related by Hugh Nibley], "Get Going and Join the Saints," 181
Hardy, David L., "I Can't Go to Work with You Today," 126
Harris, Lucy [related by Lucy Mack Smith], "Behold, Here Are the Plates," 153
Harris, Philip A. [related by Chad S. Hawkins], "A Temple in Kona," 112
Hartshorn, Leon [related by], "A Lesson My Father Could Understand," 70
Heidenreich, John F., "Do You Believe What You Are Reading?" 88
Hinckley, Alonzo A. [related by Bryant S. Hinckley], "Was This Not a Beautiful Dream?" 204
Holland, Jeffrey R., "A Five-Year-Old Driving the Car," 155
Hunter, Milton R. [related by], "The Teapot," 158
Hunter, Milton R., "We Have Come to Bring You the True Gospel," 89
Jenn [related by Ann M. Dibb], "You Planted a Seed," 90
Johnson, Joseph W. B., "What Could I Do?" 113
Jones, Dan [related by], "I Saw Myself Driven from Carthage," 55
Kimball, Heber C., "A Duty to Perform," 182
Kimball, Heber C., "I Have Felt Contented about You," 206
Kimball, Heber C., "I Wanted to Cross," 159
Kimball, Heber C., "A Jet-Black Panther," 127
Kimball, Heber C., "Keep Aboard the Ship," 160
Kimball, Heber C., "A Rod to Guide the Ship," 205
Kimball, Heber C. [related by Orson F. Whitney], "You Are Wanted at Preston," 91
Kimball, Heber C., "You Shall Now Have Strength," 160
Kimball, J. Golden, "The Devil Appeared to Me," 248
Kimball, Solomon F. [related by W. J. Kohlberg], "I Saw You in a Dream Three Days Ago," 92
Kimball, Spencer W., "Father, I'm So Glad to See You," 207
Kimball, Spencer W., "I Must Have His Acceptance," 183
Kimball, Spencer W. [related by Edward L. and Andrew E. Kimball Jr.], "The Man Seemed Pleased but Did Not Speak," 114
Kingsford, Elizabeth Horrocks Jackson, "Deliverance Is at Hand," 208
Laney, Isaac C., "Johnston's Army," 128
Laney, Isaac C., "Snake Bites and Bullets," 128
Lee, Harold B. [related by L. Brent Goates], "Mother Can Still Be with You," 209
Lee, Harold B., "My First Choices Were Wrong," 185

APPENDIX

Dreams Listed by Dreamer

The table below lists the dreams in this book alphabetically (either by the name of the dreamer or the person who related that dream).

DREAMER, TITLE, PAGE

Amussen, Barbara Smith [related by Ezra Taft Benson], "Sleep Until the Eventide," 232
Ashton, Marvin J. [related by], "I Just Hoped It Wouldn't Come Too Soon," 175
Ballantyne, Richard, "A Dreadful Flood of Water," 122
Ballard, Melvin J. [related by Bryant S. Hinckley], "An Assurance that All Would Be Well," 197
Ballard, Melvin J., "I Shall Never Forget That Smile," 61
Ballard, Melvin J., "Nuggets of Tarnished Gold," 254
Barker, Ronald C. [related by], "Go Back to Sleep," 255
Barton, Peggy Petersen [related by], "My Eight-Year-Old Dreamed of My Call," 176
Batey, Carol, "A Photograph Was Handed to Me," 108
Bednar, David A. [related by], "God Knows Who I Am," 197
Bennion, Samuel O. [related by], "I Have Seen You in a Dream," 79
Benson, Ezra Taft [related by Sheri Dew], "A Choice People with a Major Role," 109
Benson, Ezra Taft, "I Felt the Warmth of His Embrace," 198
Boehme, Peter, "Bishop of Beenleigh Ward," 177
Bowen, Hubert E., "Write a Letter," 110
Brimhall, George, "Snow-White Birds," 143
Cannon, George Q., "Take Hold of That Rope," 145
Card, Charles [related by Heber S. Allen], "A Hive of Bees," 256
Christensen, Joe J. [related by], "What the Lord Wants Me to Do," 79
Christofferson, D. Todd [related by], "My Heart Changed," 146
Clark, Mary Stevenson, "He Took Me in His Arms," 62
Clarke, J. Richard [related by], "You Have Done It unto Me," 62
Cook, Carl B., "I Have the Same Privilege," 179
Cook, Gene R., "A Home with Fruit Trees," 256
Covey, Steven R. [related by], "Helping Grandfather Find Two Names," 111
Cowley, M. F., "Write Home for Money," 147
Cowley, Matthew [related by Glen L. Rudd], "I Wonder If I Ever Had a Patriarchal Blessing," 199
Cox, Martha Cragun, "A Heavy Chain about Her Neck," 200

APPENDIX

Daybell, William, "Every Detail Was Fulfilled to the Letter," 259
Domiciano, Liriel [related by], "You Are Worthy," 63
Dunn, Emile C., "I'd Better Do as I'm Prompted," 81
Dyer, Alvin R. [related by], "I Have Been Expecting You," 82
Estill, Brother and Sister Benjamin [related by James W. LeSueur], "On the Twentieth of March," 82
Eyre, Linda and Richard [related by], "She Prayed He Would Never Look Away," 65
Eyring, Heinrich [related by Henry B. Eyring], "He Was Told to Be Baptized," 83
Eyring, Henry B., "I Saw a Piece of Paper with a Name," 112
Eyring, Henry B. [related by], "Never Too Late or Too Hard," 202
Eyring, Henry B., "We Have Been Looking for You," 180
Featherstone, Vaughn J. [related by], "Messengers Will Come from Far, Far Away," 84
Flake, William, "I Want to Know If I Done Right," 150
Fonoimoana, Opapo [related by Carl Fonoimoana], "He Saw Two Foreign Missionaries," 85
Gates, Crawford, "Music in the Night," 260
Grant, Heber J., "I Would Not Struggle for the Child," 203
Grant, Heber J. [related by], "My Dear Friend Lost Nothing," 233
Grover, Thomas, "Return to Nauvoo," 151
Hale, Grace Mays, "Two Young Men in My Dream," 86
Hamblin, Jacob ("Jake") [related by Louise Lee Udall], "Go Home, You Are Needed There," 125
Hamblin, Jacob, "True Love at First Sight," 151
Hammond, (Brother) [related by Hugh Nibley], "Get Going and Join the Saints," 181
Hardy, David L., "I Can't Go to Work with You Today," 126
Harris, Lucy [related by Lucy Mack Smith], "Behold, Here Are the Plates," 153
Harris, Philip A. [related by Chad S. Hawkins], "A Temple in Kona," 112
Hartshorn, Leon [related by], "A Lesson My Father Could Understand," 70
Heidenreich, John F., "Do You Believe What You Are Reading?" 88
Hinckley, Alonzo A. [related by Bryant S. Hinckley], "Was This Not a Beautiful Dream?" 204
Holland, Jeffrey R., "A Five-Year-Old Driving the Car," 155
Hunter, Milton R. [related by], "The Teapot," 158
Hunter, Milton R., "We Have Come to Bring You the True Gospel," 89
Jenn [related by Ann M. Dibb], "You Planted a Seed," 90
Johnson, Joseph W. B., "What Could I Do?" 113
Jones, Dan [related by], "I Saw Myself Driven from Carthage," 55
Kimball, Heber C., "A Duty to Perform," 182
Kimball, Heber C., "I Have Felt Contented about You," 206
Kimball, Heber C., "I Wanted to Cross," 159
Kimball, Heber C., "A Jet-Black Panther," 127
Kimball, Heber C., "Keep Aboard the Ship," 160
Kimball, Heber C., "A Rod to Guide the Ship," 205
Kimball, Heber C. [related by Orson F. Whitney], "You Are Wanted at Preston," 91
Kimball, Heber C., "You Shall Now Have Strength," 160
Kimball, J. Golden, "The Devil Appeared to Me," 248
Kimball, Solomon F. [related by W. J. Kohlberg], "I Saw You in a Dream Three Days Ago," 92
Kimball, Spencer W., "Father, I'm So Glad to See You," 207
Kimball, Spencer W., "I Must Have His Acceptance," 183
Kimball, Spencer W. [related by Edward L. and Andrew E. Kimball Jr.], "The Man Seemed Pleased but Did Not Speak," 114
Kingsford, Elizabeth Horrocks Jackson, "Deliverance Is at Hand," 208
Laney, Isaac C., "Johnston's Army," 128
Laney, Isaac C., "Snake Bites and Bullets," 128
Lee, Harold B. [related by L. Brent Goates], "Mother Can Still Be with You," 209
Lee, Harold B., "My First Choices Were Wrong," 185

APPENDIX

Lee, Harold B. [related by], "Plain Warning Signs along the Way," 130
Lee, Harold B. [related by], "Walking Out of the Fog," 210
LeSueur, James, "Take That Narrow Path," 261
Lund, Charles N., "Approved of the Lord," 65
Madeline, "A Light Shining in Darkness," 93
Magleby, Jim, "A Giant Puzzle," 262
McCarthy, John, "The Lord Favored Him with a Dream," 131
McConkie, Oscar, "A Man Came into the Room," 234
McKay, David O., "The City Eternal," 66
McKay, David O., "His Family Were Preparing a Happy Reunion," 235
McKay, David O. [related by], "I See You Have Received Your Sight," 211
Merrill, Marriner W. [related by Heber J. Grant], "What Does That Light Mean?" 213
Mich, Daniel, "This Man Has the Truth," 95
Miller, George, "You Ought Not to Have Left Me," 236
Miller, Mr., "I'm Going to Utah to Save My Parents," 95
Moyle, James H., "Tobacco Barns on the Tar River," 96
Mrs. P———. [related by Wreno Bowers], "They Are Heavy Tears," 213
Murphy, Castle H., "You Will Be Hearing from Me Very Soon," 186
Napela, Jonathon H., "You Must Feed Him," 97
Neibaur, Alexander [related by Hyrum L. Andrus], "He Saw the Book of Mormon," 98
Nelson, Andrew C. [related by Spencer J. Condie], "I Received My Commission to Preach the Gospel," 237
Oaks, Dallin H. [related by], "Exactly What He Had Seen," 99
Obinna, Anthony [related by E. Dale LeBaron], "Years of Waiting in Nigeria," 99
Packer, Boyd K., "A Dream Fraught with Darkness," 215
Packer, Boyd K., "Sister Spafford Is in Trouble," 215
Packer, Boyd K., "Ted Will Not Be with Us Much Longer," 239
Peck, Electa [related by Andrew Jenson], "It Will Be a Miracle," 216
Petersen, Mark E., "I Have Known for Weeks," 187
Pooley, Emil, "I Know Now That It Is True," 115
Pratt, Parley P., "A Battle in Jackson County," 131
Pratt, Parley P., "My Family Had Predicted My Arrival," 133
Pratt, Parley P., "A Promise of Deliverance," 217
Pratt, Parley P., "When Did I Ever Reveal Anything?" 263
Renouard, John [related by Kevin J Worthen], "Build a Drill," 161
Richards, Franklin D., "How Do You Do It?" 162
Richards, George F., "I Must Love My Enemies," 164
Richards, George F., "I Was Ordained an Apostle," 189
Richards, George F., "Make Every Sacrifice Necessary," 68
Richards, George F. [related by Spencer W. Kimball], "The Same Sense of Love," 67
Richards, LeGrand, "His Words Had Thrilled Me," 189
Richards, LeGrand [related by Lucile C. Tate], "It Was a Most Wonderful Thing," 68
Richards, LeGrand [related by], "I Will Share This Mission with You," 100
Richards, LeGrand, "Not Everyone Can Keep Books," 190
Richards, LeGrand [related by], "You Have the Gospel for Me," 101
Roberts, B. H., "An Honorable Release," 190
Roberts, B. H., "I Want You to Baptize Me," 264
Rowberry, John, "Your Turn Next," 240
Scott, Richard G., "Those Relationships Are Enduring," 165
Sheets, Edwin S. [related by William A. Morton], "Wanted on the Other Side," 241
Shreeve, Thomas A., "A Look of Baffled Rage," 249
Simpson, Robert L., "You Are Going to Need This Language," 101
Sloan, William R. [related by], "He Saw a Light Emanating from the Book," 167
Smith, George Albert [related by Merlo J. Pusey], "The Load Was Now His to Carry," 116

APPENDIX

Smith, George Albert, "What Have You Done with My Name?" 219
Smith, Joseph F. [related by Susan Arrington Madsen], "A Great Work Yet to Do," 220
Smith, Joseph F., "I Am Clean," 221
Smith, Joseph Jr., "My Old Farm in Kirtland," 58
Smith, Joseph Jr. [related by W. W. Phelps], "One of Joseph Smith's Last Dreams," 56
Smith, Joseph Jr. [related by Miles Romney], "Riding Up Mulholland Street," 54
Smith, Joseph Jr. [related by Miles Romney], "Two Snakes Locked Fast Together," 53
Smith, Joseph Sr. [related by Lucy Mack Smith], "A Fruit So Delicious," 48
Smith, Joseph Sr. [related by Lucy Mack Smith], "I Was Now Made Quite Whole," 50
Smith, Joseph Sr. [related by Lucy Mack Smith], "Traveling in an Open, Barren Field," 47
Smith, Lucy Mack, "Yielding to the Gospel," 51
Smith, Samuel H. [related by Lucy Mack Smith], "Warned of God to Come Immediately," 59
Smoot, Reed, "I Had a Chance to Thank Her," 223
Snow, Frank, "I've Seen That House Before," 134
Snow, Lorenzo, "He Is Worthy; Let Him Be Clothed," 224
Snow, Lorenzo, "A Mob at a School House," 135
Snow, Lorenzo, "The Smallness of My Prize," 266
Standing, Joseph, "Sudden Clouds of Intense Blackness," 136
Taylor, John, "We Are Here for a Short Time Only," 225
Terry, Nathan, "He Heard the Report of a Gun," 138
Trejo, Meliton G., "A Group of People Called Saints," 102
Tuttle, Theodore [related by Lucile D. Tate], "I Already Know," 193
Tyler, Daniel, "A House Filled with the Glory of God," 71
Walker, Elizabeth Staheli, "Do Not Bury Your Testimony in the Ground," 168
Wells, Rulon S., "Will You Ever Doubt Again?" 73
Whitney, Horace [related by Heber J. Grant], "Working with the Wayward Boys and Girls," 242
Whitney, Orson F., "I Was Asleep at My Post," 73
Wirthlin, Joseph L. [related by], "Go to the Little Chapel," 103
Wong, Patrick [related by], "Grandma, Why Are You So Unhappy?" 117
Wood, Edward J. [related by], "Have You the Authority to Say No?" 226
Woodard, Jabez, "Sacrifice and Obedience Bring Forth Honor and Immortality," 75
Woodruff, Wilford, "An Aged Man with a Beaver Hat," 243
Woodruff, Wilford, "An Indian Chief Came into the Temple," 118
Woodruff, Wilford, "Keep No One Out," 169
Woodruff, Wilford, "Let All Come into the Temple Who Seek," 118
Woodruff, Wilford, "A Log Cabin Full of Serpents," 139
Woodruff, Wilford, "Sarah Emma Died," 244
Woodruff, Wilford, "They All Appeared to Be in a Hurry," 244
Woodruff, Wilford, "To Teach Us a Principle," 245
Woodruff, Wilford, "A Temple of Granite," 267
Woodruff, Wilford, "Uncle Ozem Woodruff," 268
Woodruff, Wilford [related by Marion G. Romney], "Get the Spirit of the Lord and Keep It," 228
Wright, Steven B. [related by M. Russell Ballard], "I Saw Two Elders Dressed in White," 119
Yellow Face [related by C. Frank Steele], "Five Keys," 104
Young, Brigham [related by Dean C. Jessee], "All This I Saw in the Night Vision," 228
Young, Brigham, "Cut Off the Dead Branches," 170
Young, Brigham, "Don't Be in a Hurry," 171
Young, Brigham, "An Ensign to the Nations," 170
Young, Brigham [related by Ronald K. Esplin], "Keep the Spirit of the Lord," 229
Young, Brigham, "They Are All Good in Their Places," 171
Young, John, "Saw the Devil with a Looking Glass," 252
Young, John, "Take One More Step," 173